IN SEARCH OF
THE FRENCH REVOLUTION

IN SEARCH OF THE FRENCH REVOLUTION
Journeys through France

JOHN HAYCRAFT

SECKER & WARBURG
LONDON

First published in Great Britain in 1989
by Martin Secker & Warburg Limited
Michelin House, 81 Fulham Road, London SW3 6RB
Copyright © 1989 by John Haycraft

British Library Cataloguing in Publication Data

Haycraft, John
Search for the French Revolution.
  1. French Revolution, 1789–1799
  I. Title
944'.04

ISBN 0 436 19758 8

Typeset in 11/13pt Linotron Plantin by
Hewer Text Composition Services, Edinburgh
Printed and bound in Great Britain by
Butler & Tanner Ltd, Frome

To Anne-Marie *and* Jean Fargheon

'Fear creates what is feared.'
INGMAR BERGMAN, *The Magic Lantern*

ACKNOWLEDGEMENTS

I would like to thank the following who are not mentioned in the text for their help and advice:

M. Gérard Auglade; Lizzie Buchan; M. Giles Chouraque; Tony Duff; M. Yves Floch; Prof. François Furet; Mme Monique Hamel; Richard & Claudine Haycraft; M. Henri Hours; Prof. Maurice Hutt; M. François Macé de Lépinay; Jeff Mohamed; Prof. Claude Petit-Frère; M. Christophe Jacques; Mme Anne Kempf; M. Maximilien; M. Mouilleseaux; Joe Peeler; Jean Peto; John Sidgwick; M. Alain Taillade.

CONTENTS

List of Maps   *page* xv
List of Illustrations   xvii
Preface   xxi

[I] Reform Through Rioting
[1] Opening at Versailles   3
    Notre-Dame de Versailles – Cathedral of St Louis
[2] Versailles: the Château and Its Magician   11
    Château – Gardens
[3] Versailles: Conflict in the States-General   21
    Menus Plaisirs – Jeu de Paume
[4] Paris: Days of Disturbance   34
    Ancient Paris – Palais Royal – Place Louis XV
    (Concorde) – Garde Meuble – Champ de Mars –
    Invalides
[5] Paris: Symbolic Victory   46
    Bastille – Hôtel de Ville
[6] Surrender in Paris (Anarchy in France)   59
    Hôtel de Ville – Mâcon – Versailles
[7] Traffic between Paris and Versailles   67
    Hôtel de Ville – Château – Sèvres – Menus Plaisirs –
    Château – Tuileries

[II] Destruction of an Uneasy Peace
[8] Paris: Achievement   81
    Tuileries – Champ de Mars
[9] The Beginnings of Schism   91
    Chartres – Cluny
[10] Fiasco at Varennes   100
    Tuileries – Bondy – Chaintrix – Châlons – Pont
    Sommevesle – Ste Menehould – Clermont – Varennes

Contents

[11] Paris: the End of Constitutional Monarchy   117
    Tuileries – Manège – Cours de Commerce –
    Cordeliers – Jacobins – Tuileries

[12] Murder in Paris   130
    Place Vendôme – Abbaye St Germain – Carmes

[13] Decisive Skirmish   140
    Verdun – Argonne – Valmy

[14] Royal Death in Paris   144
    Temple – Chapelle Expiatoire – Place de la
    Révolution (Concorde)

[15] Paris: Struggle in the Convention   154
    Tuileries

[III] Counter-Revolution

[16] The Vendée: a Heroic Saga   161
    St Florent le Vieil – Durbelière – Saumur – Angers –
    Nantes – Cholet

[17] North of the Loire: the End of the Saga   178
    Laval – Granville – Le Mans – Savenay – Bois
    Chevalier – Vezins – Chanzeaux – Clisson –
    Puy du Fou

[18] Destruction in Lyons   192
    Place Bellecour – Hôtel de Ville – Place des
    Terreaux – Brotteaux

[19] British and Royalists in Toulon   205
    Cours Lafayette – Tour Grosse – Malbousquet –
    Château de Montauban – La Seyne – Battery of
    'Hommes Sans Peur' – Fort Balaguier – Fort
    L'Eguillette – Fort Napoléon – The Arsenal

[IV] Autocracy Through Vehemence

[20] Danton's Roots   221
    Arcis-sur-Aube – Troyes

[21] Danton's Death   227
    Tuileries – Notre-Dame de Paris – Luxembourg
    Palace – Conciergerie – Palais de Justice – Place de
    la Révolution (Concorde)

[22] Robespierre   244
    Arras – Versailles – Paris – Rue de Saintonge – St
    Honoré – Restaurant 'Le Robespierre'

Contents

[23] The Terror   255
    *Champ de Mars – Place de la Révolution – Place de
    la Nation – Picpus – Hôtel de Ville – Place de la
    Révolution*

[V] Retrospect

[24] Origins and Consequences   271
    Ermenonville – Park – Lake

Bibliography   279
Index   283

LIST OF MAPS

Frontispiece   *page* xxiv
Route of procession at Versailles.   8
Versailles in 1989.   22
Plan of States-General   24
Paris before 1793.   35
The Bastille before the Revolution.   47
The Bastille imposed on present-day street plan.   51
Early morning of 6 October, Versailles.   73
The Palace of the Tuileries 1790.   84
Area occupied by the National Assembly, with the 'new'
    Rue de Rivoli and Rue Castiglione imposed.   87
The route from Paris to Varennes.   103
Varennes 1791.   109
St Germain – Revolutionary centre.   119
The Jacobin Club off the Rue St Honoré.   124
The Abbey of St Germain des Prés.   134
The area of the Temple today.   145
The Temple 1792.   146
Map of La Vendée Militaire.   162
Journey of the Vendéan Army to Granville.   179
Lyons at the time of the Revolution.   195
Toulon and neighbourhood during the siege of 1793.   213
Paris 1793–4.   228
The Conciergerie 1793–4.   234
The Queen's cell.   238
The Revolutionary Tribunal in the Palais de Justice.   241
Robespierre's lodging 1791–4.   250
Route to Picpus today.   260

LIST OF ILLUSTRATIONS

Between pp. 24 and 25

1. Louis XVI. Callet, *Musée de Versailles*
2. The head of the 'tyrant' held up as a warning. *Bibliothèque Nationale*
3. Marie Antoinette at Versailles. Vigée LeBrun, *Musée de Versailles*
4. The ex-Queen going for execution in the Place de la Révolution. David, *Carnavalet*
5. The Church of Notre Dame, Versailles, today.
6. The Cathedral of St Louis, Versailles.
7. View from the King's bedroom at Versailles. Monnet, *Musée de Versailles*
8. The Salle de Mars.
9. The gardens at Versailles.
10. The Entertainments Room.
11. Opening of the States General at Versailles. *Bibliothèque Nationale*
12. Site of the States General today.
13. The Tennis Court. David, *Bibliothèque Nationale*
14. The Awakening of the Third Estate. *Carnavalet*

Between pp. 88 and 89

15. Playing card showing the Duke of Orléans as King of Spades. *Bibliothèque Nationale*
16. The gardens of the Palais Royal, today.
17. A lady being whipped for spitting on the portrait of Necker. *Bibliothèque Nationale*
18. The Place Louis XV, before the Revolution. *Carnavalet*
19. The first armed clash of the Revolution. Lallemand, *Carnavalet*
20. The mob attacking the Invalides. Lallemand, *Carnavalet*
21. Attack on the Bastille. Cholat, *Musée Renan-Sheffer*

22. Discovery of the skeleton of the Man in the Iron Mask in the Bastille. *Carnavalet*
23. The destruction of the Bastille. Robert, *Carnavalet*
24. The Queen's staircase at the Palais.
25. The Marble Courtyard at the Palais.
26. Confrontation between the mob and the royal family at Versailles. *Bibliothèque Nationale*
27. Louis XVI helping in preparations for the Feast of the Federation. *Bibliothèque Nationale*
28. The Feast of the Federation, dancing at the Bastille. *Bibliothèque Nationale*
29. The Feast of the Federation at the Champ de Mars. *Bibliothèque Nationale*
30. Satire on nationalization of Church lands. *Bibliothèque Nationale*
31. Satire on the Clergy abandoning orders. *Bibliothèque Nationale*
32. Cluny, showing the outline of the destroyed Abbey. Editions Combier.

Between pp. 152 and 153

33. Sauce's house, Varennes.
34. Room in Sauce's house occupied by the royal family.
35. Varennes.
36. Varennes today.
37. The Jacobin Club. *Bibliothèque Nationale*
38. Louis XVI during the invasion of the Tuileries. *Bibliothèque Nationale*
39. The attack on the Tuileries. *Bibliothèque Nationale*
40. The escape-route of the royal family, Tuileries gardens.
41. The royal family in the Assembly. *Bibliothèque Nationale*
42. The Temple tower. *Bibliothèque Nationale*
43. Two English satires: 'A Limited Monarchy' and 'An Unlimited Democracy'. *Bibliothèque Nationale*
44. The Abbaye prison. *Carnavalet*
45. The guillotining of Louis XVI. *Bibliothèque Nationale*
46. 'King Louis XVII'. Vien, *Carnavalet*

Between pp. 216 and 217

47. Château of Durbelière.
48. Statue of La Rochejaquelein. Photograph by Brita Haycraft.

49. Château of Clisson. Images de France.
50. Château of Saumur. Editions Greff.
51. Rebel hiding-place. *Archives Talladier*
52. Signalling windmills.
53. Drownings in the Loire. *Bibliothèque Nationale*
54. The bombardment of Lyons. *Bibliothèque Nationale*
55. Evacuation of Toulon. *National Maritime Museum, Greenwich*
56. Explosion of the powder ship, Toulon. *National Maritime Museum, Greenwich*
57. Danton's house. Photo Combier, Mâcon.
58. Danton going to the guillotine. Willie fils, *Carnavalet*
59. Corridor in St Lazare prison. Robert, *Carnavalet*
60. Marie-Antoinette going to the tumbril. *Caisse Nationale des Monuments*
61. The courtyard of the Duplay house.
62. A prisoner being battered and burnt. *Bibliothèque Nationale*
63. Waiting for the guillotine. Demachy, *Carnavalet*
64. Robespierre guillotining the whole of France. *Bibliothèque Nationale*
65. Blind man's buff à la Robespierre. *Bibliothèque Nationale*
66. A Section Committee. *Bibliothèque Nationale*
67. Stalls on the Pont du Change. *Carnavalet*
68. Rousseau's first tomb, Ermenonville. Moreau le Jeune.

PREFACE

It is often revealing to work out why something is fascinating. Recently, I tried to fathom why the French Revolution has stirred my interest and imagination for so long.

It started, I realized, when I was taken to Paris with my family when I was a child, in the black winter of 1938, just before the War. My mother had always talked a lot about history, and she took us to Versailles, the Palais Royal, the Carnavalet Museum and the Place de la Bastille. During this time of crisis, with Hitler beyond the frontier and Stalin behind him, both threatening to sweep our world away, it was easy to imagine mobs swelling and growling in the streets, the sans-culotte committees searching out suspects and the tireless guillotine.

Inevitably, my schoolboy imagination, bred on adventure stories and magazines, was stirred by all the great dramas of this brief five years, which were almost as full of extraordinary events and characters as the plays of Shakespeare. It is probably only the continuing rift between Left and Right which has inhibited the profusion of plays, great novels and films which the Revolution deserves.*

Back in England, I read the romantic novels of Orczy and Weyman, and Dickens's *Tale of Two Cities*. Still later, I studied the Revolution as a special subject at Oxford. Then, at Yale, I researched the effect of the American War of Independence on the political ideas of French officers who fought on the side of the insurgents.

I began to realize that the French Revolution fascinated me not

---

* The French film, *La Marseillaise*, directed and financed by the Popular Front in 1936, was criticized by its extreme left wing because it depicted Louis XVI, quite rightly, as jovial and sympathetic when they felt that according to their 'version' he should have been a monster. The Revolution is still dogged by propaganda, and the only outstanding play remains that based on the clash between Robespierre and Danton, probably because both were revolutionaries and the pivot was the human conflict between cerebral detachment (Robespierre) and impulsive passion (Danton).

only because of its drama but also because, like the Reformation, it split a world in two, and that this division still exists. As a postwar adult, I felt a burning sympathy for the oppressed, the poor, those colonized or under dictatorships. The fight against the Nazis had contained much of the basic clash between autocracy and systems where people could express their aspirations freely, which was at the root of the French Revolution.

Before going to University, I had served as a young conscript officer in India in the last year of the Raj, and often asked myself what I was doing there as an instrument of a colonial régime. And yet, I was also fascinated by 'the other side': I was impressed by the ruined monuments of Mogul power and the last realities of an Empire which the British had carved out over two hundred years. There were certain similarities here with the world of the Ancien Régime, with its leisured attitudes, beauty and culture.

After a year researching at Yale in the New World, I yearned for the Old. So I went to Toledo in Spain to write a novel while I supported myself giving English classes. In those days before mass tourism, living there was like going back centuries in time, with the old street cries, mules stepping gingerly up narrow, cobbled lanes, the spire of the cathedral glinting over the medieval houses as it did in the paintings of El Greco.

I disliked the Franco régime, with its hypocrisy, its ignorant, oppressive bureaucrats, its snuffing of talent and fresh ideas. But the fascination lay in living as an observer under what was, in many ways, an eighteenth-century régime. Over the town stood the battered ruins of the Alcazar, a relic of the Civil War of 1936–9, which in its ferocity, dogmatism and conflict between the masses and an élite, most reflects the traumas of the French Revolution in modern times.

Then, married, I went with my wife, Brita, to Cordoba in the south, where we were the only foreigners in town. There we started a school of English for adults which enabled us to get to know a large number of people and to learn the ways they thought. Yet, although we were immersed in everyday Spanish life, the division of sympathies continued. We were intrigued by living in the past, in a city where the mayor was rather like the local duke, where a few prominent families influenced everything in town. And yet we were conscious of the poverty and the suppression of any unorthodox opinion. The climax to this paradox came when, just as I was to be given the local honour of 'hijo predilecto' ('favourite son') for what we had achieved with our school, I published a book, *Babel in Spain*, on our life in Cordoba under the Franco régime, and was expelled.

I have gone into these details to illustrate how, living in old conservative régimes, I was torn by the contradictory pull of fervour for ideas of individual freedom and yet awareness that its achievement meant sweeping away much of the old beauty, contemplation and traditional unity. In Spain, it was also a question of religion, although I am not a Catholic: stirrings of nostalgia for a world where Christian values were an integral part of a way of life, however often they were abused, however restrictive they may have been. This in opposition to attitudes where happiness – a by-product of other things if ever there was one – is the supreme aim, to be acquired mainly by material benefits.

Perhaps these attitudes have much in them that is English: the belief in organic change and development rather than in extremes and dogmatism, and yet impatience for change. So, I am critical and yet sympathetic of the two extremes of Jacobin and counter-revolutionary, and it is perhaps my inability to find a reconciliation between their points of view which creates my restless interest in the Revolution, rather like electricity flowing between positive and negative terminals.

This book, then, is an exploration, a pulling together of my divided sympathies. As history is always frustrating because you are not actually there, I have tried to come closer by telling the story through places. At least the stones and many of the buildings where the events actually took place can be seen today. Even if some have been destroyed, the relics still help to evoke past happenings. In the search for these places, it has also been revealing to meet people who have been brought up in their shadow.

John Haycraft
Blackheath

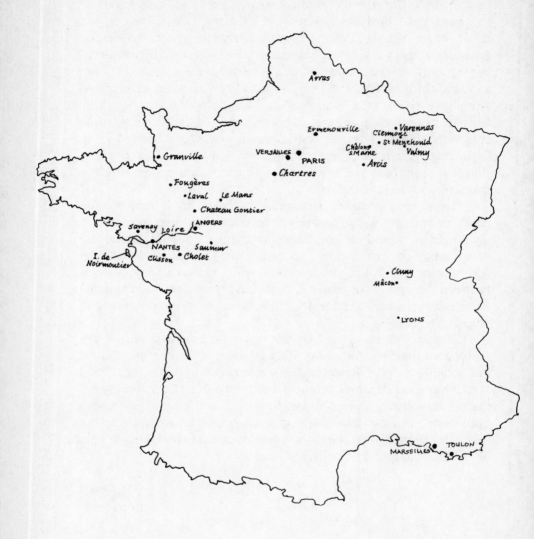

I

Reform Through Rioting

[1]

OPENING AT VERSAILLES

The great only appear great because we are on our knees . . . Let us get up!

ANTOINE TOURNON

Versailles haunts me. I have been there over twenty times on the sleek train which takes twenty-five minutes from the Gare St Lazare in Paris. It passes by the river Seine, and then enters an area where other royal pleasure castles once stood before they were destroyed by revolution: St Cloud, Meudon, Marly-le-Roi. Also nearby is Louveciennes, where Louis XV's mistress, Mme Du Barry, lived after the King's death in 1774.

Versailles is now a dormitory town for Paris. Yet the extraordinary thing about it is the way it has been preserved almost as it was two hundred years ago. Now it has a much larger population than the thirty thousand it then had, and has sprouted modern suburbs. But still it has its magic: the long, tree-lined avenues of white, terraced, eighteenth-century houses, with shutters and blue-tiled roofs in which attic windows are set. Still it has its great château, its broad, green park with the Trianon pavilions which served as a royal escape from the pomp and routine of the Court.

The best time to stroll around the town is early on a Sunday morning, when no alien cars block the straight streets and most people are in bed. As you walk along the empty pavement, you can imagine carriages with the pert clop of hoofs and the brown horse dung in the streets, the sedan chairs, the gentlemen with cloak and cane and powdered wig, out with their ladies; the valets, porters and tradesmen threading their way through, with little bows and the doffing of hats.

I find Versailles both disagreeable and admirable. It still evokes all that I most dislike in France: the snobbishness, the pretension, the exclusivity, the seeing of life in supercilious categories of

3

fashionable good and bad, which you still often find, although fortunately more rarely. With it, paradoxically, goes all that I most enjoy: the refinement of taste, the harmony of most buildings and of town planning, the tradition of delicious cooking, developed in an age of luxury in châteaux all over the country, the discrimination and search for formal beauty and excellence, which the wealth and leisure of the Ancien Régime has left as an inheritance.

Even today, many of the values and assumptions of the eighteenth century persist. When we lived in Paris for a year in 1970–71, I remember the French teacher at our school who was disliked by others because she had the aristocratic particle 'de' in front of her name. Older people had a courtly formality, and the young, whatever their extremes, a hierarchical outward respect for those of their parents' generation. Bureaucrats and the police still talked as if they represented a ruling class and were not simply the paid servants of the taxpayer. Dinner parties were lively forums of wit and yet had the individual remoteness of people who strove to make conversation an art. De Gaulle had just died, De Gaulle whose presence and personality, if not his power, were those of a *Grand Monarque* who had just stepped out of the Apollo throne room at Versailles.

It is appropriate that the drama of the Revolution should have started in a town which, for a hundred and twenty years, had enshrined the formality and rigidity, the ceremony and the strength of autocracy in France. Apart from previous rumblings the beginning of the Revolution was marked by a procession to celebrate the opening of the States-General, the old representative body of France. Like the English Parliament, it had medieval origins, but the Hundred Years War, the Wars of Religion and the autocracy of Versailles had prevented it from gaining control of government as had its English equivalent. The last time it had been summoned was as long ago as 1614.

Three Estates were represented in this one body: the Clergy, the Nobility and the Third Estate, or Commoners. The King, Louis XVI, called it together because French participation in the American War of Independence, followed by a policy of large loans,* had bankrupted the monarchy. Louis wanted to solve his crisis by taxing both Nobility and Clergy. These two Estates in turn

---

* In 1788, 49% of the national income was spent on the interest of loans.

4

saw the States-General as an opportunity to wrest more control from the monarchy as had their aristocratic brothers over the Channel. They were also determined to maintain their privileges and resist taxation as they had already done in separate, previous Assemblies in 1787–78.

In conflict with Nobility and Clergy, the Third Estate, which represented a bourgeoisie grown stronger and more prosperous over the previous century, hoped to obtain a constitution in which it had some control of government and a role in public affairs, now blocked by the aristocracy. Already, by the time this opening of the States-General took place, France had been inflamed by riots provoked by the aristocracy, and what were called *cahiers de doléance*: statements from each electoral district of the reforms they would like to see. All these *cahiers* were monarchist in spirit: many praised the King for his good will and initiative in summoning the Estates. But asking subjects to comment on what they felt was wrong with France raised hopes which would not easily be appeased.

The procession which opened the States-General is significant because it was to be the last great pageant of feudal pomp and ceremony of the Old Régime, and because it held many portents of the upheaval that was to follow.

It began on Monday, 4 May 1789, outside Notre-Dame, a huge domed church built by Louis XIV in the seventeenth century, which still stands almost in the centre of old Versailles.

From the steps of Notre-Dame, you look out today on the same straight street, now called after Hoche, a Revolutionary general. Gazing at shops selling pâtisserie, a restaurant protruding onto the pavement, and an office of 'Manpower', the employment agency, I tried to visualize the scene in 1789. As I watched the women carrying shopping bags, a figure in white overalls stretched her arms across a window of one of the tall buildings nearby, like a phantom being tortured, as she cleaned the glass.

Two hundred years ago, at half past ten in the morning, an immense coach preceded by gorgeously uniformed cavalry drew up near where I was standing. From it stepped Louis XVI, Most Christian King of France and Navarre, a heavy man, in his thirties, thick-necked with incipient double chin. His face was broad and fleshy, with an aquiline nose and greenish-grey eyes. He wore cloth of gold, and the famous Pitt diamond in his hat. As he descended, he stared short-sightedly about him. Handkerchiefs fluttered and arms waved. 'Long live the King!' shouted the onlookers, and the cry spread to the spectators thronging the streets. Louis was well loved for his gentleness, his bonhomie and his spirit of reform, which had already eliminated some of the more outrageous practices of the Old Régime such as torture, serfdom on royal lands, and the ban on public worship for Protestants.

Another immense coach approached. From it emerged Marie-Antoinette, Queen of France. She was in her early thirties, pretty, dressed in silver tissue, with pearls and flowers in her hair. The crowd watched her silently.

To the sound of fifes, drums and trumpets, King and Queen entered Notre-Dame. The King went to a throne at the far end of the church. The Queen sat on his left, while the royal family were ranged on benches, covered in blue velvet, embroidered with the golden lilies of France. In what is still a great, cavernous church, pale with its ochred walls, its sparse decoration and simple Romanesque arches, the deputies of the new States-General passed before the throne, each carrying a candle. First, they bowed to the King and then to the Queen. Then they filed out slowly through the open doors into the street.

Outside, beribboned masters of ceremonies fussed here and there like colourful cockatoos, first marshalling the five hundred and fifty deputies of the Third Estate, or Commoners, who, dressed in black, looked like a parade of undertakers. In colourful contrast, behind them came the nobility, wearing white-plumed hats and gold-trimmed capes. Unlike the drab deputies of the Third Estate, they swaggered with the panache of centuries of power and privilege. 'What mean these gold mantled Chivalry figures walking there in velvet cloaks in high plumed hats of a feudal cut?' asks Carlyle. And answers: 'Reeds shaken in the wind.'

The procession began to stretch up the street, reaching the little square where now stands the black metal statue of General Hoche. Even hanging on to chimney pots on the roofs, the tumultuous crowd ignored the nobility, whom they disliked for their arrogance and privileges. Deliberately, they only acclaimed the Third Estate.

Behind, came the last element in the States-General, the Clergy. First, the cardinals in scarlet vestments, then the bishops in red and purple robes. Immediately behind them marched the King's musicians, striking up with fifes and drums, trumpets and hautboys. At the request of the higher clergy, these musicians had formed a deliberate barrier between the aristocratic princes of the Church and the humble, liberal-minded priests.

Then came the Archbishop of Paris, carrying the Holy Sacrament under a baldachin. He was followed, as a final climax, by the King, the Queen and the Princes of the royal family. However, as the Princes assembled, something unusual happened amidst the rigid formality of this procession. White plumes could suddenly be seen amidst the black three-cornered hats of the Third Estate. It was the King's cousin, the Duke of Orléans, who had joined the Third Estate instead of taking his place with the Princes. The crowd noticed this and cheered him. Publicly, the Duke was showing that underneath this show of unity, the royal family was divided and that his sympathies lay not with the King or nobility, but with the Third Estate. Hurriedly, a master of ceremonies was despatched to bring him back. From the schism among the rulers which this incident illustrated was to grow much of the turbulence and licence in the early stages of the Revolution.

Slowly, the procession of almost twelve hundred people emerged from the end of the street into the great Place d'Armes in front of the château, where now the tourist buses park. Tapestries were hung on frames between masts on which flapped *oriflammes*, the ancient banners of Royal France. The deputies walked over the sand spread to avoid mud, like a long file of insects of the same species but decorated by Nature according to their different roles of workers, drones, and royals.

On, past the end of the three avenues which come together at this point, past the large symmetrically arranged stables, on the roof of which the little Dauphin, the heir to the throne, was watching. Racked with the disease which made one hip higher than the other, he was to die exactly a month later, leaving his younger brother as the new Dauphin.

Then down the hill, with the crowd cheering the Third Estate and the King, but shouting occasional insults at the Queen. She was detested because she came from Austria – one of France's traditional enemies – because she was extravagant, because it was rumoured that her children were not the King's; because she had recently been deceived by an adventuress and a naïve Cardinal who ordered a diamond necklace, worth more than a million sterling, in her name. This was without her knowledge, but how could one ever be sure? The incident stimulated a flood of obscene satirical

7

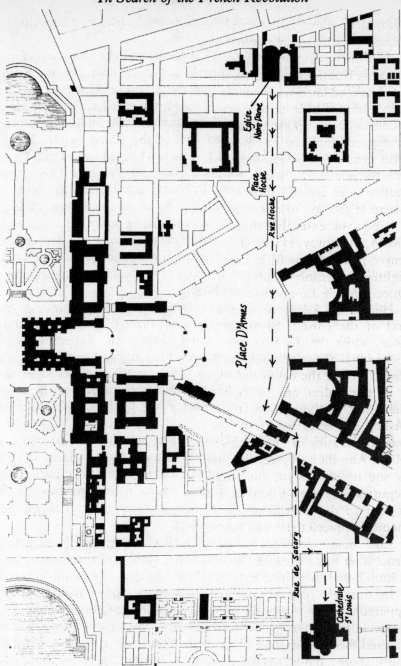

Route of procession at Versailles.

pamphlets which had served further to rouse the people against those who ruled them from Versailles.

A witness of the procession, Miot de Melito, described the Queen's reactions to the crowd's insulting coldness: 'The Queen, her forehead lined with worry, and her lips pressed tightly together, vainly tried to hide her uneasiness.' At one stage, it was thought she would collapse, and the whole ceremony be stopped. However, she continued down the narrow Rue de Satory, which now is crammed with market stalls on Saturdays. Then the procession turned left into the main street which leads from the part of the château where orange trees are still grown in pots, and into the Place St Louis, where at the end of the square stands the Cathedral of Versailles.

When you enter this church, you are struck by the greyness, the gloom, the grimy, even arches and undistinguished windows whose frosty panes admit little light. In slight compensation, this large eighteenth-century church has glass lamps given by Louis XV's Queen, Marie Leszczynska of Poland, hanging from the roof.

Here a Te Deum was sung. The King and Queen sat at the end of the church by the altar, which is fronted by a marble floor, while the deputies crowded benches and chairs. You have to imagine them not only sitting but also strolling about in the casual way of the eighteenth century.

In the pulpit on the right, at the top of the curved steps, there was further provocation. From under a wooden crest, the Bishop of Nancy leant out and delivered a sermon attacking the wasteful luxury of those close to the King. Again, one can see Marie-Antoinette's face, the lips pressed together yet more tightly as she listened, with the smiles and subdued comments of the deputies opposite. When she and the King returned to the palace at four in the afternoon, she was so furious that she broke the diamond bracelet she was wearing.

Like many decisions of the Court at the time, holding this procession was a mistake. By emphasizing the differences in dress, it humiliated the Third Estate, and exposed the Queen to insult.

In this last pageant of the Old Régime, many tensions were apparent. Some who were to play a major role in the Revolution marched in its ranks: neat Robespierre; Mirabeau, with his pock-marked face and mane of hair; Talleyrand, with his limp, among the bishops; Bailly, who within two months would be mayor of Paris; Dr Guillotin, whose name would go to the most notorious mechanism of the Revolution; La Fayette, with his thin, protruding face and receding powdered hair, nodding in answer to the cheers he received. He had already made his name fighting beside George Washington in America.

This then was one of those embryos of history. With the knowledge of the past which we now have, it is possible to see in the mind's eye, not only the procession wending through the streets, which today are largely unchanged, but also the crowd of spectators that would soon become a mob; the deputies who would first create a constitutional monarchy and then a republican autocracy; the nobles and the clergy, many of whom would be dispersed to the four winds of exile, or to a violent death.

[2]

VERSAILLES: THE CHÂTEAU AND
ITS MAGICIANS

'The following morning I came to see the Château by myself. He has
seen nothing, that has not seen the pomp of Versailles.'
CHATEAUBRIAND, *Memoirs From Beyond the Tomb*.

On the right of the deputies as they crossed the Place d'Armes was
the symbol of much that they were about to destroy and change.
The cobbled courtyards of the immense château rose gently up a
slope to the original small hunting lodge of Louis XIII which is
still the core of the palace.

Constructed of red brick and stone, the château is set in straight
lines with only three storeys, so it impresses not because it towers
over you, but because of its mass and complexity: its columned
pavilions and balconies, its statues and forested chimneys, its lines
of tall windows. With roofs seen beyond other roofs, buildings
glimpsed behind other buildings, passages and streets between
solid façades, it seems almost a town in itself.

And yet as you look at it from the Place d'Armes through which
the procession passed, you realize that it is a harmonious whole,
with the wings and columned pavilions balancing each other. You
realize that you are looking at the centre of it all, with courtyards
narrowing until they reach the small Marble Courtyard, which is
overlooked by the shrine of the King's bedroom beyond the central
balcony. From this centre the other buildings spread out like the
rays of the Sun King, which is what its founder, Louis XIV, liked
to be called.

For more than a hundred and twenty years, Versailles had
been the model of the royal palace, generating imitations all over
Europe from Sans Souci in Prussia to Chatsworth in England. It
was designed as a royal country house which was also the seat of
government, and the two functions were blended. Thus, one part

of the Ministry of Foreign Affairs looked out on an orangery and a lake called the Eau des Suisses, with the great trees of the park beyond.

Because it was the centre of a splendid Court, Versailles attracted a nobility which had often been tumultuous. It gathered them in inoffensive idleness, ensnaring them in a ritual focused on the glory of the monarch. The château served also as a display of all that was most tasteful in France: the furniture, carpets and tapestries, the porcelain and silverware, paintings and sculpture, or for that matter, fashion and cuisine, music and drama. Much has been said about the extravagance and luxury of Versailles, but if Court and monarch spent six per cent of national income, they also encouraged manufacture and design which made France richer.

In the state rooms, on the northern side, there are two principal themes. First, the evocation of Rome in its imperial majesty, so common to autocrats from Charlemagne to Mussolini. Second, the glorification of the monarchy. In almost every room, there are paintings, tapestries or bas-reliefs representing 'Louis XIV trampling on his enemies', or 'Fame spreading the King's Glory to the Four Parts of the World'. The figure of France is also represented, but sitting obediently at the King's side, and always bearing the royal lilies on robes and shield.

These state rooms were like over-decorated theatre sets, laid with carpets, mainly of French design. The ceilings were covered with great allegorical paintings, framed with bronze. From the walls, often encrusted with marble and bronze traceries, hung tapestries and paintings, with statues set in niches. The furniture varied with each king, and the styles of Louis XIV, XV and XVI marked design all over Europe.

The northern part of the central building was the King's domain, starting with the War Drawing Room, following through six other great halls. The southern part was the Queen's, starting with the Peace Drawing Room and going through to her bedroom and her cabinet, and to the Hall of the Guards. Linking the two was – and is – the Hall of Mirrors, vast and long, with tall windows looking onto the gardens on one side and giving access on the other to the King's bedroom and Council chamber, the central nerve of government.

To the south of this central part stretched the apartments of the Princes of the royal family. To the north, a long corridor leads to the Chapel and to the incomparable Entertainments Room, built in 1770, which the Duke of Croy described as 'one of the most beautiful rooms ever seen in Europe'. Now it has been restored to what it was, with mirrors set behind its boxes to reflect the light of chandeliers, with blue-cushioned seats, fabric of floss silk and Utrecht velvet, and delicately carved arabesques and female figures.

In the midst of this formal splendour, though, King and Queen could find refuge in smaller, more intimate apartments. Imperceptible doors can just be seen, cut in the gilded wood, which lead to the boudoirs and inner cabinets: the room where Marie-Antoinette rested at midday, the bedroom where Louis XV had slept on a camp bed because he said the State bedroom was too cold – when, in truth, it was easier from there to get to his mistress's apartment, above.

In these small rooms the intimate suppers were held, and Marie-Antoinette gathered with her friends to discuss the latest trends in fashion. Corridors and staircases were bored through walls and under the floors. Part of one still remains which ran under the floor of the Hall of Mirrors and connected the King's bedroom with that of the Queen.

Meanwhile, in the state rooms outside, courtiers strolled in silk and satin finery. In the Hall of Mirrors they waited for the royal family to pass through on their way to and from Mass. Ambassadors from Venice or Turkey, from Persia or Seringapatam in India, were received, new courtiers were presented, the birthday of a member of the royal family celebrated, or the King washed the feet of thirteen poor men on Maundy Thursday. Three times a week, from seven till ten in the evening, there were what were called Apartment Days, with refreshments, gaming and dancing.

In the Apollo Drawing Room stood the throne. The three eye-bolts which suspended the dais are still there. Here, balls were held and the King would sit on the steps, watching his courtiers perform the minuet or the gavotte.

Through the windows of the Hall of Mirrors can be seen the gardens, still much as they were, with straight parallel avenues leading down to the great stretch of water known as the Grand Canal. Copses encircling intimate groves blend stateliness with suggestions of dalliance.

These gardens were the scenes of fêtes, of water pageants,

of magnificent firework displays. You have to imagine them at night with the terraces illuminated with tall glittering arches, while the fountains sent up great jets of silver water. Men in their three-cornered hats and women with wide skirts crowded everywhere, while landaus topped with little parasols, even at night, were pulled through the mass of people by lackeys with powdered hair. While Versailles was alive and inhabited, the rest of France seemed hypnotized by this pomp and display – whatever misery it lived through, however many military disasters it suffered.

The King was its centre. Anointed at his coronation at Reims, he was God's representative by Divine Right, and the whole country belonged to him as, today, a freeholder owns his property. His government was one of rights rather than obligations, his role confined to defending and enlarging his kingdom, ensuring internal tranquillity, and dispensing justice – although there were also feudal courts, presided over by local nobles. Road building was carried out by peasants working for a few days a.year as a feudal obligation. What we would call Welfare was looked after by the Church with its hospitals, schools, and homes for old people and orphans. Government, then, was not regarded as responsible for the entire running of the country.

In eighteenth-century France, in any case, the fact that many provinces had different charters with the Crown worked against real unity. So did the separate jurisdiction of the nobility and the slowness of communications: it took three days to get from Paris to Lyons by stage-coach. Six out of about twenty-five million subjects communicated in languages other than French and loyalty was stronger to the province or the district than it was to the nation which was synonymous with the King.

More than half the aristocracy who surrounded the King at Versailles represented dynasties dating back to the Middle Ages, or before. I remember a student in one of my classes in Paris who was descended from the ancient family of Polignac, and who told me that the origin of his name came from the guardians of the Well of Apollo in Roman times. In France, the aristocracy increased continually in numbers as all sons inherited their father's title, unlike primogeniture.in England, and at the Revolution they are estimated to have numbered 400,000. Unlike the English, again, they were not allowed to enter commerce. Essentially a military caste, they gave service whenever there was a war, as in medieval

14

times. They, therefore, paid few taxes, and defended their privileges with arrogance. Some even laid claim to an innate superiority which they justified with Boulainvilliers's absurd theory that nobles descended from the virile, conquering Franks while the mass of the population originated from feeble, subdued Gauls.

For the Court nobility, Versailles was a battleground where personal favours were obtained by making a request at the King's *Lever* or *Coucher*, as the sovereign's ceremonies of getting up or going to bed were called, or by using the influence of a Prince of the Blood, the Queen, or even the powerful royal valets. Calonne, the Director of Finances, complained that a minister at Court was like a tree swarming with caterpillars who devoured every leaf. The palace, therefore, was threaded with intrigue, and the malice of those who had been slighted poisoned everything. Most of the charges which were to be levelled at Marie-Antoinette before the Revolutionary Tribunal originated in rumours which had been circulated at Court.

It was the nobles who anticipated the Revolution, not in 1789 but two years earlier, with riots and disorders aimed at sharing power with the Crown. Already they had increased their privileges. Louis XIV had felt better served by middle-class ministers, but by 1780 all were noble, except for Necker, the Swiss financier. The rank of officer in the army and navy was restricted to those with at least two generations of nobility on either side. Those feudal dues which had lapsed were revived. By 1789, all bishops were noble, however irreligious they might have been. When it was proposed to promote Loménie de Brienne, a noble prelate, to the Archbishopric of Paris, Louis XVI protested: 'But surely he needs at least to believe in God!'

The King was supposed to be bountiful. He was also expected to be a stud who bred sons to ensure the succession. Royal amours and illegitimate children were a respected sign of virility.

Elaborate ritual based on daily, royal activities enshrined the concept of the King as the august, semi-divine father of his people, acting out his family role with splendour. On waking, he was handed his clothes by the highest nobles in the land, who also chatted with him while he defecated on his *chaise percée*. King and Queen dined publicly in the Room of the *Grand Déjeuner*, which can still be seen in the Queen's apartments. Their food was brought in great dishes through underground corridors from kitchens a quarter of a mile away. When the procession of laden lackeys passed, there was the cry 'The King's Meat!', and men took off their hats while ladies curtsied.

Commoners, in France two hundred years ago, could speak to the King only on their knees. This was significant at the beginning of the Revolution because it made it difficult for the King to consult and manoeuvre individually, or with small groups, as he should have done with the deputies of the Third Estate.

Nevertheless, anyone could go to the palace so long as women were well dressed and men wore a hat and a sword, which could be hired at stalls near the palace gates. Prostitutes solicited in the candle-lit corridors at night. Parisians flocked to the festivities: at the wedding of Louis and Marie-Antoinette, over two hundred thousand people attended the fireworks, the races of illuminated boats on the Great Canal, and the distribution of food and wine in the gardens. Even having children was a public event: when Marie-Antoinette gave birth to her first child, her bedroom was so crowded that she almost suffocated, and Louis XVI had to wrench open a window to let in air.

The small population of the towns and the feeling that the King belonged to everyone encouraged familiarity. The fish-wives of Paris, who later shouted abuse at those going to the guillotine, could see the Queen when they wanted: when Marie-Antoinette had no children for eight years they sent a delegation which bantered obscenely with her, telling her to get her legs open and do her duty.

Four thousand people lived at Versailles in shabbiness and splendour, surrounded by etiquette, intrigue, pretentious snobbishness, and yet a kind of chaotic informality.

Only three kings spanned the years of Versailles's splendour: all of them were named Louis – XIV, XV and XVI. The first had made his palace a shrine to monarchical absolutism. The second maintained his predecessor's form of government. The third, Louis XVI, was quite unlike his forebears. If the King was expected to be a warrior and, like Louis XIV and Louis XV, be present at battles, Louis XVI was a failure. Despite France's participation in the American War of Independence, he hardly reviewed his troops, and during his absolute rule of fifteen years, he only once visited the Invalides, which were equivalent to the Chelsea Pensioners in London – although he did rebuild the navy.

As a person, he was awkward, lacking in confidence, and short-sighted. He lost both mother and father before he was twelve, and felt overshadowed by an elder brother who died about the same time. As a result, he was easily swayed by anything which compensated for lack of affection and might make him popular with his people.

To add to his own uncertainty, he was anything but virile. He is thought to have had a disorder of the foreskin which prevented him fathering a child until, according to his brother-in-law, Joseph II, he had an operation seven years after his marriage.* This virtual impotence and childlessness meant that his high-spirited, adolescent young queen, Marie-Antoinette, flung herself into a round of dissipation and extravagance which ruined her reputation. It also gave Louis a sense of guilt which made it difficult for him to refuse her anything.

Louis's great passion was hunting, which separated the couple still further. As a boy, he shot pigeons from the roof of the palace and, when older, he returned so exhausted from days in the forest that the malicious said he was always tippling.

Born and brought up in Versailles, he became king at nineteen, and he and Marie-Antoinette wept at the news. His kingdom he rarely visited: Cherbourg was the only distant place he had been to before 1789. Otherwise, he only set out on the annual round of palaces: the summer stay at Compiègne, the autumn procession to Fontainebleau; or the state visits to Paris. Royal tours were too expensive with all the panoply of retainers, hospitality, and appropriate presents.

Versailles made Louis powerless in other ways. He was so trammelled by etiquette that he had little time for anything else. 'If I were King of France, I would appoint a representative,' said Frederick of Prussia, alluding to the endless ceremonies which took up most of the King's day. Much had to be delegated to people who had acquired their positions through courtliness and intrigue rather than ability. Hierarchy obstructed everything at every level. Thus, when Louis's father decided to take up the violin, he had to have an instructor he didn't like, who was senior to the person he preferred.

Louis XIV and Louis XV had been sufficiently dominating and

---

* Many historians say there is insufficient evidence for this. However, it is certain that Louis did not consummate his marriage until years after his wedding.

17

decisive to keep their extraordinary system functioning. They also had fewer financial problems, created by the inflation of the last half of the eighteenth century.

Fattening and sluggish, Louis XVI had only good will and benevolence to offer in his attempts to solve the crisis of 1789. He resisted when it was unwise to do so, and gave way too easily when his initiatives failed. Carlyle described him as 'like clay on a potter's wheel: perhaps the most pitiable and pardonable of all clay figures'.

Louis was hard-working, well educated, particularly in geography and history, and was also sincerely religious – in fact, there has recently been talk of having him beatified as a martyr of Catholicism. He regarded himself as 'the father of his people', and hesitated to shed the blood of his 'children'.

It is, unfortunately, the nature of power and politics that it is the strong and ruthless who usually succeed. The historian Lavisse wrote: 'The fall of the monarchy was the absence of a king.' Whatever the other causes of the Revolution, this was undoubtedly an important factor. In an autocracy, the weakness and indecisiveness of the monarch is crucial, as it was with Henry VI of England before and during the Wars of the Roses, with Tsar Nicholas II of Russia in 1917, and as it had been previously in France when Charles VI's madness helped to create the divisions and intrigues which led to English domination during the Hundred Years War.

In France, Louis XVI has been spared much criticism and blame: a French friend of mine explained it in terms of the guilt French people still feel about his being guillotined during the Revolution – 'A lot of the blame has been put on his predecessor, Louis XV who, in most ways, was a better ruler.' Another friend, a naval officer, told me: 'Louis XVI was intelligent and highly educated. He just couldn't cope with the turbulence and selfishness of us, the French – which still continues!'

The end of Versailles came unexpectedly and suddenly. As late as 1786, Arthur Young, an English traveller in France, wrote how loyal the French seemed to their King. One person he met even reproached him for belonging to the nation which had executed Charles I.

The real contrast at Versailles was the splendour of this temple to monarchy and the violence and rapidity of its destruction. 'Look after my poor Versailles,' said Louis to the Governor when he left for Paris, never to return. Yet, within four years, all the furniture, carpets and paintings were being auctioned, mainly to wealthy English aristocrats, and in 1797 a German commented sadly when he visited it: 'The silence of the tomb reigned. My footsteps echoed between the solitary walls.'

When I first went there, as a boy on a winter's afternoon before the War, it was still an empty mausoleum, with bare unfurnished rooms, few visitors and only the occasional guardian lolling against faded gilt tracery. Now, the generosity of many people is slowly filling it again with furnishings recovered from all over the world. The ground floor of the main building, with over fifty rooms, which once contained the apartments of the Dauphin and the King's aunts has been restored with carpets, furniture, curtains and even shelves filled with the kind of books there might once have been. Marie-Antoinette's bed is where it was, with fluffy ostrich feathers above the canopy, the Savonnerie carpet on the floor, and alcove hangings which are modelled on those of the last summer furnishing before the Revolution. Paintings all over the palace have been restored and the gilt tracery on the walls re-touched. In the gardens, fêtes with fireworks and Son et Lumière are held during the summer, and if you are lucky you can get tickets to a Pergolesi or Mozart opera in the Entertainments Room. Indeed Versailles is most evocative at night, under the light of new electric candles which give off the same glow as did those of wax, two hundred years ago.

Part of the reason for this restoration is mass tourism, which in the last few decades has flooded everywhere. Part of it is genuine interest in a château which for over a century dominated France and Europe. In the computer age, the events it witnessed seem sufficiently far away to rouse nostalgia. It is no longer a threatening, controversial monument to autocracy, but an evocation of tasteful attitudes, and of romantic, martyred people strutting on their formal stage. As Christopher Isherwood wrote in *Lions and Shadows*: 'To me, the modern age began with the French Revolution. Before that, everyone wore fancy dress.'

Now visitors from all over the world flock in to stare at Lebrun's paintings on the ceilings, to enter the private apartments of Marie-Antoinette and of Louis XVI. They gape as, two hundred years ago, those who had hired a sword must have stared. The state rooms are as crowded as they were then. The difference is that there are no bejewelled courtiers doffing their hats to each other, no ladies tiptoeing along with the little footsteps that were fashionable at the time; no King and Queen savouring their dinner in the Drawing Room of the *Grand Déjeuner*. Otherwise, the setting is gradually becoming much the same.

[3]

VERSAILLES: CONFLICT IN THE STATES-GENERAL

'No matter how useful you are,' they said. 'No matter how able you
are, you can go so far and no further. Honours are not for the likes
of you.'

From the pamphlet, *What is the Third Estate?*,
published by ABBÉ SIÉYÈS in 1778.

When my wife, Brita, and I asked friends who lived in Versailles
where the site of the States-General was, some hazarded that it was
in the château itself. M. LeMoines, the Director of the Museum of
Versailles, looked vaguely embarrassed for some reason when we
asked him, and told us briefly that the building had been in the
town, but it had been destroyed.

I was surprised. I remembered the impressive prints of the first
session, with the King tiny on his throne at the end of the vast
hall, with the nobles and clergy ranged opposite each other, and the
Third Estate in serried black ranks at the back. Doric pillars lined
the sides, and behind them, spectators peered at Necker, the finance
minister, as he delivered his opening speech – which lasted three
hours. Like so much at Versailles, the scene seemed like theatre,
with the masters of ceremonies showing their stockinged calves
below multi-coloured breeches, the deputies sitting on stools of blue
velvet fringed with golden tassels. Every surface was decorated. The
royal arms above were surrounded by moon-shaped plaques, with
the lilies of France on curtains and hangings. The flat ceiling was
painted with circles and wraiths, while great ovals of white taffeta
let in the light above, and behind the throne.

Although M. LeMoines's word was not to be doubted, it seemed
extraordinary that all this had disappeared. The hall seemed so
solid, and as a monument to the birth of modern France, surely
no government could have allowed it to be pulled down.

21

We went to the Tourist Office to make further enquiries. This is lodged in what used to be Mme de Pompadour's house, a large building set against the northern wing of the château. There, we saw Mme Carcy, the lady in charge, who also looked slightly embarrassed when we asked about the hall of the States-General.

'You mustn't expect anything,' she said, hesitantly. 'You see it does not really exist. In fact it never really existed.'

'How do you mean?' we both asked at once.

'Well, there are some original buildings. But the actual hall was put up only a few years before the Revolution for an Assembly of Notables. Then it was taken down after the meetings of the States.'

'But why?'

'It was never a real building. It was temporary, like a vast marquee.'

'You mean all that great hall was made of canvas and plaster?'

'Well, other things as well – '

'And the Revolution started in what was virtually a tent?'

'Putting up splendid temporary structures was normal at this time,' said Mme Carcy. 'Don't forget that the cathedral at Reims was decked out with classical pillars and balconies for Louis XVI's coronation in 1775. Ceremony was theatre: it had its stage sets.'

'So what is there to see?'

'Well, there are still the old buildings of the Menus Plaisirs where the Assembly Hall was erected, and the remains of the hall where the nobles and clergy met separately.'

She took out a piece of paper and drew on it with a pencil. 'Here, look:

'The entrance from the Avenue de Paris is here. I've marked it A. The building where the nobles and the clergy met separately, is B. Then C is the staircase between the two courtyards, up which came the King, clergy, and nobles. The throne stood here, D. Then the actual hall where the Estates met is this large space marked E. The Third Estate entered from F in what is now the Rue des Etats-Généraux. What remains is not very impressive I'm afraid.'

'What goes on there now?' I asked.

'It's the offices of the Versailles municipality, the Maintenance Services. They are responsible for all the parks and gardens.'*

---

* This was in 1986. Now the whole site has been evacuated in preparation for a Museum of the Revolution.

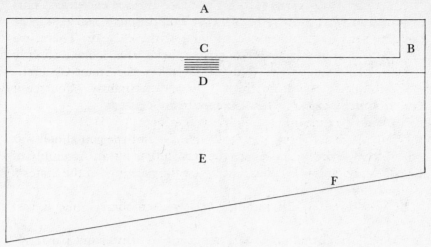

Plan of States-General.

'And what was there before the Revolution?'

'It was the offices and storehouse for all the entertainments of the Court. That's why it was called Menus Plaisirs – lesser pleasures.'

'What kind of pleasures?'

'Oh – there were stages and theatre sets, the billiard balls and cues, the spare games of dominoes and tric-trac – '

'All the things used in the palace on rainy days?'

'Exactly.'

We thanked Mme Carcy and got up to go.

'I haven't told you where it is – ' she said.

'Nor you have.'

She took a map of Versailles. 'You go over the Place d'Armes, and then to the Avenue de Paris, opposite. Past the town hall and it's about a hundred metres further on, to your right. The original painted board is still above the entrance.'

We thanked her once again and went out into the sunlight.

As we walked, I counted seventeen Japanese tourists* in two minutes and wondered what they thought of the great château on our right. Probably they were amazed at the solidity of everything, after their light wooden palaces and shrines in Tokyo, Nara and

---

* I discovered later that there were so many Japanese visiting Versailles because one of their most popular cartoon books represents the life of Marie-Antoinette.

23

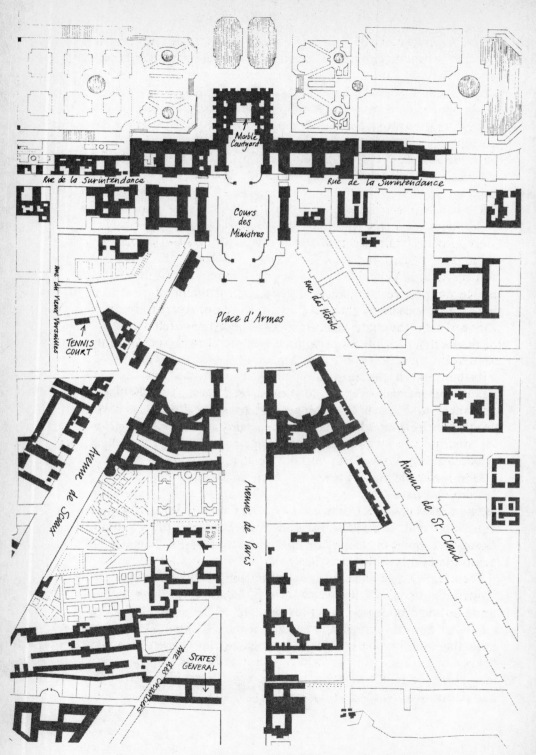

Versailles in 1989.

1. Louis XVI as a plump,
beloved young king of twenty-seven.
Callet, *Musée de Versailles*

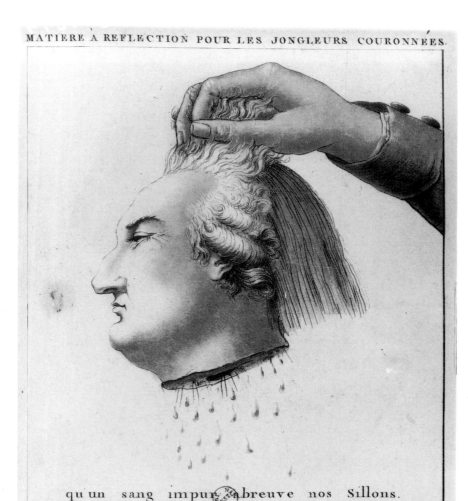

qu'un sang impur abreuve nos Sillons.

Lundi 21 Janvier 1793 à 10 heures un quart du matin sur la place de la revolution, ci devant appelé Louis XV. Le Tiran est tombé sous le glaive des Loix. ce grand acte de justice a consterné l'Aristocratie anéanti la superstition Royale, et créé la république. Il imprime — un grand caractère à la convention nationale et la rend digne de la confiance des français.

ce fut en vain qu'une faction audacieuse et des — Orateurs insidieux épuisèrent toutes les resources de la calomnie, du charlatanisme et de la chicane, le — courage des republicains triompha : la majorité de la convention demeura inebranlable dans ses — principes, et le génie de l'intrigue ceda au génie de la Liberté et a l'Ascendant de la vertu.

Extrait de la 3.e Lettres de Maximilien Robespierre — à ses commetans.

A Paris chez Villeneuve Graveur rue Zacharie St Severin Maison du passage N.º2.

2. A dozen years later, the head of the 'tyrant'
held up as a warning to 'royal tricksters'.
Bibliothèque Nationale

3. Marie-Antoinette in the luxury of Versailles
with her three children.
Vigée Le Brun, *Musée de Versailles*.

4. Six years later the ex-Queen, her hair shorn
for the guillotine, goes to execution in what is
now the Place de la Concorde. She was thirty-
seven. David, *Carnavalet*.

5. The Church of Notre Dame, Versailles, today. It was down this street, lined with spectators, that the procession of Deputies started out. Author's photograph.

6. The Cathedral of St Louis, Versailles, where the procession ended. The King and Queen sat in front of the altar and heard a sermon from the pulpit on the right, denouncing the spendthrift Court. Author's photograph.

7. View from the King's bedroom at Versailles. Later the States-General was a few hundred yards on the right of the Avenue which stretches into the distance. Monnet, *Musée de Versailles*

8. The 'Salle de Mars' exemplifies the everyday luxury of the King's Court at Versailles. Note how every inch of wall and ceiling is decorated.

9. In the Versailles gardens, the broad walks and ponds
contrast with intimate copses concealing statues and small temples.

10. In this lavish theatre was celebrated the last 'Feast of the Bodyguards'.
This precipitated the march of the women from Paris, which ended
the century-long royal residence at Versailles. (See p. 67)

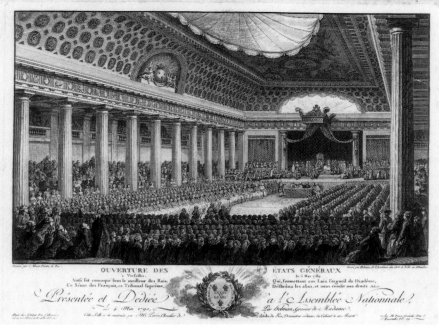

OUVERTURE DES ÉTATS GÉNÉRAUX

Présentée et Dediée à l'Assemblée Nationale.

11. The opening of the States-General at Versailles. Twelve hundred Deputies heard the opening speeches. In fact, this magnificence was temporary plinth and plaster, later dismantled. *Bibliothèque Nationale*

12. The site of the States-General today. The hall covered the whole area. The throne was in front of the building opposite. (See p. 28) Author's photograph.

13. The Tennis Court, which still exists. Here the Deputies swore an oath
never to separate until a constitution was created.
(See p. 28–9) David, *Bibliothèque Nationale*

14. The Awakening of the Third Estate. Symbolizes the nation
at last breaking its chains. Nobles and Clergy
are prostrated. *Carnavalet*

Le tems passé n'est plus.

Kyoto. Of all foreigners, it is surely the Italians who feel most at home in Versailles, because so much is an extension and adaptation of what they had already created, long before, in Italy.

In Versailles, we were staying with a cousin of Brita's. The house was in one of the parallel streets off the Boulevard de la Reine, still called after the saints' names of Louis XV's daughters: Ste Adélaïde, Ste Sophie, Ste Victoire. No one seems to know who then inhabited the three downstairs rooms and four upstairs, with the old shutters and black and white tiled floor, the dainty brass door handles and ample attic where, presumably, the servants lived. Probably, the house had belonged to an official of the administration at Court. Or, perhaps, to a country nobleman who preferred having his own house to being crammed into one of the tiny attic rooms at the top of the palace where most courtiers lived.

Surprisingly, Versailles was a radical town at the beginning of the Revolution, reacting against what made it memorable, stirred by visiting Parisians to eliminate what it lived on. Apart from those who worked at the château, the inhabitants must have felt deep envy for the luxury and splendour of the Court, and resentment at being excluded.

In the sunlight, we walked into the Place d'Armes and down to the Avenue de Paris, which divides the two great stables where the horses and coaches were kept. Now, these buildings lodge government offices, the archives, and a reading room where you can summon theses on eighteenth-century music, or the annual accounts of the château on old, white paper.

As we walked over the round cobbles, we discussed whether the Revolution was inevitable. If not, the château would still be inhabited as a royal residence, like Buckingham Palace today. After all, I argued, the real crisis of the monarchy was its bankruptcy. Without it, survival was possible. Certainly, the régime was incapable of facing the events which followed, but without the financial effects of French participation in the American War of Independence, the régime could perhaps have meandered on for years. At the time, no one thought it would collapse.

Louis was in favour of reforms, and these might well have come gradually, as in England. At least, Louis could have paid his soldiery to keep order, and would not have had to cope with the weakness and shattering of his prestige which the financial crisis produced. The reforming doctrines of Rousseau and the Encyclopedists might well have seeped through the body politic, changing it from inside, instead of erupting into the tumultuous slogans of the Revolution.

After all, the people were no poorer, I said, than they had been for centuries, and certainly no worse off than the industrial proletariat of Britain in the nineteenth century. When one thinks of all the misery that has existed in the world without ever producing an upheaval, or to be more specific of that terrible winter of 1709, eighty years earlier in France, when peasants froze in the fields, crops were decimated, and thousands died of starvation, one comes to realize that revolutions rarely occur if authority does not crumble.

What of inevitable historical tendencies? argued Brita. They are over-estimated, I said. It is too easy to regard them as inevitable simply because they have come to fruition. The real question is how they express themselves in the circumstances which hedge them, or the compromises which can dilute them. After all, after the War, many of us believed the whole world would be Communist within a few years, but it isn't.

Talking, disagreeing, arguing, trying to resolve a question which could never really be resolved because the events had happened, we entered the Avenue de Paris, broad enough to be a motorway, lined with trees, sloping gently up to a hill in the distance. On our left were the modern blocks of the police barracks, and on our right an uneven mixture of buildings of different epochs. Two hundred years ago, the Avenue was the main route to Paris, filled with galloping messengers, and the coaches of noblemen, going to and from their town houses in the capital.

Beyond Louis XIV's stables, we passed a riding school in the same seventeenth-century style. But it had been built later: instead of the habitual crossed 'L's, representing Louis, the letter 'N' for Napoleon was engraved in the crumbling stone. The motivation behind 'Kilroy was here' once extended to the highest in the land, although with emperors and kings it tended to be 'Kilroy built this'.

We passed the nineteenth-century town hall, and came to a row of shabby eighteenth-century buildings. At the end was an entrance, and above it a wooden board inscribed in faded paint: 'Menus Plaisirs du Roy'.

We had arrived. Our steps quickened as we entered a shabby courtyard, with men hurrying from one side to the other in shirt sleeves. Scanning Mme Carcy's map and looking around, we understood why she had warned us not to be disappointed. On our left was a long building, and it was easy to see that it had once formed the wing of the entrance courtyard of imposing offices, fallen into disrepair. Sheds of rusty corrugated iron clustered in front of the long building before us, which was intersected by a steep staircase.

We entered the building on our left. Here, according to Mme Carcy's rough map, the Nobles and Clergy had their separate Assembly Halls in 1789. Stubbornly, backed by the King, they had refused to join the Third Estate because they would have been outvoted. A few months before the Revolution, Louis had decreed the doubling of the deputies of the Third Estate. This was done under pressure and, as so often, he had not thought out the consequences. As a result, there was a fatal deadlock which lasted no less than five weeks because the Third Estate refused to verify their credentials unless they could take advantage of their numbers and meet in one Assembly. During this time, the King took no initiative while the Third Estate gained confidence, got to know each other and had time to work out their tactics.

These five weeks were crucial. The King still had respect and authority. He could almost certainly have compelled the nobles and clergy to join the Third Estate in one united Assembly. In this way he would have gained the support of the Third Estate and compelled the other two orders to accept equality of taxation, which would have solved his immediate problems. Then he could have submitted his own moderate plans for reform from a position of strength. At least he would have kept the initiative and the support of his people.

Inside the building where the Nobles and Clergy had held their own separate assemblies during these first weeks, we wandered round surreptitiously. The sunlight shone through the windows, and wooden stairs divided two floors of offices, their partitions now painted battleship grey. Behind smooth doors, the clerks of the Maintenance Services of Versailles seemed to be working silently. The only traces of what the building had once been were wooden arches sunk in the ceilings on the upper floor.

Presumably, all this had once been open, so that both groups could be accommodated. As the halls contained the leading figures in the realm, they must have been luxuriously furnished, with little cabinets for officials and private consultation.

We returned to the courtyard. Broad, dusty steps faced us. This was the straight staircase up which King, Nobles and Clergy had entered to take their seats.

At the top, to our amazement, we were confronted suddenly with a car park. Scattered among the Peugeots and Citroëns were little white prefabs, on which was printed 'Espaces Vertes', indicating their use for the administration of parks and gardens.

As we stood just behind where the throne had been, I felt moved and bewildered. Out in the open, the space seemed small. Yet here, where now lay the bric-à-brac of improvised twentieth-century organization, over a thousand people had been assembled. Here modern France had been born.

Measuring by eye, I traced where the Third Estate had sat. To begin with, they had been uncertain and subdued. However, as the weeks went by, they grew impatient. On 10 June, they openly defied the King and invited the other two Orders to join them. On 17 June they went further and declared themselves the National Assembly responsible to the people of France. Those of the other two orders who refused to join them would be excluded. Slowly, the Court reacted to this usurpation and announced a royal session on 22 June, later postponed to the 23rd.

However, then began a series of tactless mistakes on the part of the Court which provoked the Third Estate unnecessarily. To prepare for the royal session the hall of the States-General was closed without the deputies being told. When they arrived outside the doors on the morning of 20 June, the entrance was barred by soldiers. In the rain, the five hundred deputies clustered together in what is now the Rue des Etats-Généraux, protesting bitterly. Were they not the National Assembly, the representatives of the people of France?

Some deputies suggested holding their session under the balcony of the King's bedroom. Dr Guillotin, however, proposed having it in the royal tennis court near the château. Accompanied by over a thousand cheering onlookers, they walked up what is now the Rue Edouard Lefebvre and then along the Avenue des Sceaux. Then they turned left up the narrow street where the Jeu de Paume, or tennis court, still stands.

Today, the tennis court is as it was then, with bare walls topped by windows which let in the light. An armchair was brought in for the President, Bailly, who refused it; everyone stood.

At one end is now a reproduction of David's painting of the scene: Bailly stands on a bench in the foreground, improbably with his back to most of the deputies, who stretch out their arms towards him, vowing never to separate 'until the Constitution of this realm has been established on solid foundations'. All signed their name, except one deputy from Languedoc who, later, was declared mad. It must have seemed a historic drama to the participants, but also a moment in which the proximity of the King's troops induced fear and perhaps increased defiance. At the end of the session, all the deputies and the crowd outside shouted 'Long live the King!' It was almost as if they were insuring themselves against future charges of *lèse-majesté* or high treason.

When we visited the tennis court, it was being redecorated. There was a smell of paint, and pots stood on a trestle table. The workmen were having a break and stood round, drinking from tins of Fanta. The walls were brown and the names of all the deputies of the National Assembly and their constituencies stood out in gold letters. To one side was an enormous whitish statue of Bailly, the President, with wide, empty eyeballs, giving what would now be deemed a fascist salute. 'The tennis court has hardly been played in since,' said our official guide. 'It is somehow too sacred for a mere game.'

To the deputies' claim to a share of sovereignty, the King hardly reacted. He was saving his spleen for the royal session. On the following day his brother, the Comte d'Artois, announced that he wished to play tennis in the court. Here the deputies deferred, which showed that they did not want an open clash, and met in the Cathedral of St Louis where they had sung a Te Deum at the opening of the States. There, a hundred and fifty of the lower clergy joined them, which further encouraged the deputies.

On 23 June the royal session opened with the usual pomp. King, Court, Clergy and Nobility were admitted first, up the stairs, now dusty, which we had climbed. Meanwhile the Third Estate waited in the rain. They were admitted last, entering, bedraggled in their wet clothes, two by two, to take their seats in front of the King and the two other Orders in all their finery.

The King stood once more before his throne. In a nervous voice, he made it clear that he was unwilling to abandon the privileges of his nobles. Naturally, he accepted equality of taxation, which from his point of view was why the States-General had been assembled. However, the nobility were still to continue their monopoly of ministerial posts and as officers in the army and navy. The bourgeoisie would still have no outlet for their talents, or their ambitions.

29

On the crucial question of voting together, the King was more equivocal. He conceded that the Estates could do so on a limited number of occasions, but these were not to include discussion of the rights of the aristocracy and Church. Where he did meet public demand was in upholding the liberty of the individual and, dangerously, freedom of the press, which was already a source of endless libellous allegations and false rumours.*

'If you abandon me in this great enterprise, I alone will work for the good of my people and alone will consider myself their representative,' the King threatened.

The deputies were silent.

The King ordered them to leave the hall and meet again in their separate Orders the following day.

He then committed another tactical error which etiquette made inevitable. He should have waited while the deputies filed out, and then departed himself. However, following procedure, he left with the Nobility and most of the Clergy. Thus the Third Estate remained in possession of the hall.

As can be imagined, the deputies of the Third Estate were furious and resentful, both because of their humiliation at the beginning of the session and the way the King had conceded little of what they wanted. Their defiance in the last few days had emboldened them and consolidated their belief that, as representatives of the people, they and not the Clergy and Nobility were truly the nation. As Louis went out, no one except a few nobles raised the once habitual cry of 'Long live the King!'

The indignation exploded in front of the young master of ceremonies, the Marquis de Deux Brézé, who now reminded the deputies that the King had ordered them to leave the hall.

'It is not for the National Assembly to receive orders,' snapped Bailly, the President, in reply.

Mirabeau rose: 'Go and tell those who sent you,' he roared with his great voice, 'that we are here by the will of the people and we will not leave except by the force of bayonets.' It was the first time the King had been expressly disobeyed.

When news of the Assembly's defiance was brought to Louis, he did not know how to react. He could have ordered his troops to

---

* The flood began when the calling of the States-General was decreed in 1788, and there are no fewer than 2,500 pamphlets from this period in the Bibliothèque Nationale.

eject the deputies, but that would be to make martyrs of them. For him, the day had been a disaster. His speech had been received in ominous silence. On his return from the Assembly to the château, the people who lined the route had watched him sullenly, with none of the usual acclamations. His minister, Necker, who in the Council had argued for greater concessions to the Third Estate, had been conspicuous by his absence. Louis had no alternative but to yield, or to clear the hall with his troops, which he knew would provoke riots all over France. '*Foutre!*' he is reported to have said, with a shrug of the shoulders. 'Let them stay.'

The deadlock continued. From all over France, Louis summoned regiments of mercenary soldiers, who were more obedient to their paymaster than French troops, already infected by revolutionary ideas. Whether he did this in preparation of a counter-revolution or, as he told the National Assembly, to keep order is open to interpretation. Certainly, rumour had it that 40,000 people were coming from Paris to kill the nobles and burn the château. In Versailles itself, the streets were suddenly crowded with demonstrators who tried to force the railings which stand between the Place d'Armes and the château. The French Guards were ordered to fire. But they refused, and eleven of them were arrested and taken to the Abbaye prison in Paris, from which they were later released by a mob.

In Paris, itself, Arthur Young, the English traveller, wrote: 'The ferment . . . is beyond conception; 10,000 people have been this day in the Palais Royal . . . The constant meetings there are carried to a degree of licentiousness and fury of liberty that is scarcely credible.' Hunger added to fear and desperation: the price of bread reached its highest level of the century. One in ten of country people had been reduced to begging by a slump which had hit the cottage industries, and many vagrants flocked into Paris and Versailles. As Ferrières, a noble deputy, wrote about the royal government: 'They have had the folly to link the general interest of twenty million people to the particular interests of six hundred representatives.'

Meanwhile, in Versailles, the royal refusal to allow joint sessions of the Orders was ignored. Soon after the royal session, a hundred and forty-seven liberal nobles joined the Third Estate and those who had previously gone over to them from the Clergy. Only a reactionary rump remained in what are now the offices of the Maintenance Services of Versailles.

As his troops had not yet arrived, the King yielded again to necessity. One can see him in the ornate Council Room at Versailles writing two urgent letters to the Duke of Luxembourg, the President of the noble deputies. In them, he now implored the duke to persuade his colleagues to join the Third Estate, in contradiction to his pronouncements only a few days earlier, and by the end of June the three orders were united in one Assembly.

At the beginning of July, Louis's troops began to pour into Paris and its neighbourhood. Five thousand were stationed in the capital on the Champ de Mars, which today is where the Eiffel Tower stands, just by the river Seine. The Champ is slightly narrower than it was then because new buildings have encroached. However, it is still a long, open, grassy stretch, leading up to the Ecole Militaire, a graceful array of eighteenth-century buildings with colonnades, tall windows and rounded roofs, erected by Louis XV. Here, Bonaparte had recently been trained as an officer.

Two hundred years ago, the Champ de Mars was a vast parade ground. Where tourists flock and schoolchildren now arrange themselves in groups to be photographed, stood the tents of the royal army. Regimental flags with their crosses and lilies fluttered above them. What today is smooth grass was muddied by the tramp of soldiers' boots and the churning of horses' hoofs. Bugles sounded, and the smoke from field kitchens rose into the air. Then, as now, there was the babble of many tongues apart from French: Swiss dialects, Hungarian, Flemish, German. Then the different languages were those of foreign mercenaries; today they are those of tourists on their way to and from visiting the Eiffel Tower.

The effects of the Court's fear at Versailles increased fear in Paris, like an echo resounding from one rock-face to another and back again, but, unlike an echo, growing stronger and stronger. The French were accustomed to severe repression from their kings. In the past, the royal government had bowed to an outbreak, only to take revenge later when their troops were ready. Such had happened at Lyons with a strike of silk-workers, when demands had been agreed to, only to be revoked six months later when a royal army invested the town and hanged the ringleaders.

On 11 July, Louis felt strong enough to dismiss Necker, who was the idol of the people because he had shown his disapproval of the royal edicts by not attending the royal session of 23 June. Known as it was that the King was greatly influenced by his Austrian Queen and the reactionary princes at Court, the rallying of troops seemed the beginning of a counter-revolution in which all the concessions Louis had made would be revoked.

In what had once been the Menus Plaisirs, we stood amidst the cars and prefabs, trying incongruously to invoke these events. At one side, we noticed an old timbered building, standing where the Doric columns and spectators galleries had been. Inside were two floors, lined with metal shelves on which stood large cardboard boxes: the building was now a warehouse. On the first floor, between two shelves, we noticed what looked like a proclamation on the wall. Black letters were blurred on a white background. The first lines were decipherable: 'Here, in 1789,' they ran, 'the first meetings of the States-General were held . . .' The only other clear letters were of a date, 1916.

'Where does this come from?' we asked the workman who accompanied us.

'It was done by soldiers in the First World War.'

On another wall was a vegetable-like figure with stalk eyes and walrus moustache. It resembled Hindenburg, the German Commander-in-Chief. Beside him was the caricature of a thin figure with cap and receding chin leaning back at an angle. He resembled Little Willie, as he was called, the Kaiser's son. Next to him were scrawled the words: '*Con aux Princes.*'

We stared for a moment. Here in another epoch when the country was also in danger, when the people of France were likewise roused against an enemy, was the same expression of defiance, of hatred.

'*Con aux Princes.*' On the site of the old States-General, the words could have been written about the royal princes up in the château who also seemed to be plotting the invasion of Paris and the downfall of the National Assembly. It was a dramatic coincidence.

[4]

PARIS: DAYS OF DISTURBANCE

'I had hoped to serve your majesty at sea and instead I seem to have
forfeited the favour of my father-in-law, the future of my children,
the happiness of my wife and my own reputation.'

Letter from the DUKE OF CHARTRES to Louis XVI
after the battle of Ushant in 1778, where he was accused of cowardice.

At Versailles, the beginning of the Revolution had resembled a chess
game. Stage by stage, the Assembly had defied the King without a
clash of force. Monarchists almost to a man, they had no intention
of achieving a violent revolution but aimed at recognition of their
political importance as elected representatives of 'the Nation'. As
such, they were determined to create a constitution which would
give them a voice in the government of the kingdom.

Now, with the dismissal of Necker and the approach of the royal
troops, a full blown counter-revolution seemed to be under way. All
the deputies could do was protest, but in Paris there was a violent
reaction.

Paris in 1789 was by far the largest city in France, with 600,000
inhabitants, compared to the next biggest, Lyons, with only 100,000.
Despite this, Paris was in an unusual position: it was a capital and yet
not the seat of either government or King. Throughout its history,
it had always been turbulent and independent-minded. During the
Hundred Years War, it had expelled Charles VII to Bourges. In the
Wars of Religion, in the sixteenth century, the Protestant Henry IV
had only captured it by becoming a Catholic. It was the Civil War
of the Fronde, in the next century, that had compelled the young
Louis XIV and his minister, Mazarin, to flee from Paris. This had
decided Louis XIV to remove his capital to Versailles and create his
royal absolutism. Even as late as 1753, a revolt had made Louis XV
build a road round Paris, known as the *Route de la Révolte*, so he
could avoid the city on his way from Versailles to Fontainebleau.

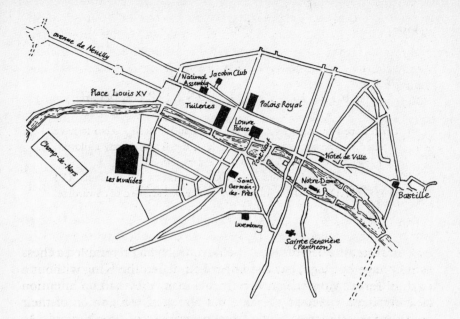

Paris before 1793 showing the Tuileries. *Bibliothèque Nationale.*

And yet much that the tourist admires today dates from the splendid city which Paris became before the Revolution, with its royal palaces in the Louvre and Tuileries, with its spacious squares of Louis XV (Concorde) and Vendôme, with its noble houses along the Rue de l'Université, south of the river. Close to the Bastille, other quarters like the Marais still contain splendid palaces and the superb seventeenth-century Place des Vosges (formerly Place Royale).

You can get a sense of how much remains if you stand on the Pont Neuf and look down the river. The view is the same as in eighteenth-century paintings, with the half-mile stretch of the Louvre on your right and the Mint and the Hôtel des Quatre Nations on your left. If you then turn round, there is the Place Dauphine immediately behind you, with its red and white brick houses, the line of its façades expanding from the narrow entrance into the forecourt of the Palais de Justice, where once stood the medieval palace of the Kings of France.

The glory of London is its parks; that of Paris is still the remaining buildings and perspectives created by its absolute monarchs: the view of Concorde from the other side of the river with its colon- naded buildings and balconies by Gabriel, while the intersecting Rue Royale reveals the columns of the Madeleine; the Place des Victoires; the Luxembourg Palace; the Tuileries gardens – all have changed little.

Before the Revolution, there were a hundred and forty monas- teries and convents with their gardens, cloisters, churches and quiet walks. Even today, there are more gardens than meet the eye, rather like an Andalusian town with hidden patios. A friend of mine who climbed a church tower overlooking the district of St Germain told me that at least half the area still consists of patches of green, which a passer-by wandering its labyrinthine streets would never guess.

The great changes were brought about by Haussmann, the Prefect of Paris under Napoleon III. Between 1853 and 1870, he pushed long boulevards like St Michel, Sébastopol and St Germain through ancient medieval housing, broadened the narrow, winding streets on the Ile de la Cité, and rebuilt the quarter near the Opéra. Since the nineteenth century, the external appearance has been further transformed as in most cities by huge plate-glass windows, street lighting and above all the demands of cars, multiplying like the sands of the sea, for broader streets, parking, and ugly embedded garages.

Although it is estimated that over a third of Paris had been built or rebuilt in the quarter of a century before the Revolution, the poorer quarters were still medieval. Streets were muddy and unpaved, with a ditch running down the centre for the rain. Pavements were not generally introduced until after the Revolution, in 1805. At night, the city was lit by oil lamps suspended from cords over the streets, with reflectors which gave a glare but shed little light. Rubbish was collected irregularly by passing carts, and water was obtained from neighbouring wells or fed to pumps and fountains by two primitive steam pumps near the river, one of which gave its name to the Samaritaine emporium. The mud of the streets exhaled an odour of piss, horses and rotten vegetables, and of everything which had been ground in for years, including the blood of cattle often slaughtered outside butchers' shops. Other small shops huddled between the entrances of houses. Or goods were sold by hawkers whose cry added to the clamour, or who laid out their wares on the ground. The scene must have been somewhat like parts of Naples today, with the same noise, liveliness, colour and disorder.

It has been estimated that 5,000 of the population were noble and 10,000 were clerics. There were perhaps 100,000 rich bourgeoisie who owned a large proportion of the real estate. About 300,000 workers lived not so much in particular areas as all over the city. They were not workers in a modern, industrial sense: few were employed in big concerns or factories. Most were shopkeepers, journeymen, artisans. One in three were in the building trade and a sixth were domestics. Some were apprentices living cheek by jowl with their employers in the same house, eating at the same table. Many others were unemployed, or immigrants, seasonal or otherwise. Indeed, it has been calculated that as many as 87% were born outside Paris.

Life for the majority was as rough as in any big city of the time. In July 1789, as many as two thirds of the population were in want, needing relief. Medicine was primitive, life expectancy low. Pain was a commonplace. Barbers acted as surgeons, sawing off a leg, or arm, after the 'patient' had been sodden with brandy, tarring the stump to stop the blood-flow. A 'dentist' practised on the Pont Neuf. There, for a few sous, he extracted teeth in public with no palliative to pain, and held them up for all to see, rather like the executioner holding up heads, later, in the Place de la Révolution.

Despite the poverty and tumult, those with money lived well in comfortable rooms warmed by fires of wood, with domestics and cheap, good wine and food. The poor lived as they had for centuries. Never before, though, had the price of bread been so dear, so that it cost almost 40 per cent of their wages. Never before had their betters talked of the rights of the people. Never, since the Wars of the Fronde, a hundred and fifty years earlier, had they actually been encouraged to riot against the forces of order which had kept them brutally in check through innumerable previous disturbances.

I remember going to the Palais Royal in the rain as a small boy, just before the War, when France was shaken by rumours and threats from beyond the frontier. We took refuge in the arcades which surround the gardens.

'The Revolution started here,' my mother told us.

I looked out on the empty gravel walks, the lady without an umbrella hurrying for shelter. 'Here?' I questioned.

'It was the centre of revolt.'

'It looks so empty,' my brother protested.

'It is now. But then, these empty arcades were full of cafés and gaming houses. Journalists, soldiers, strollers discussed the latest events. Orators got up on chairs in front of the cafés. It was from here that the crowd who attacked the Bastille started off. The Duke of Orléans who owned all this made it into an island of revolt.'

'Why?'

As I remember it, we were told that the Duke of Orléans hated the King and Queen. He had wanted to be Lord High Admiral, like his father-in-law, but had been disgraced after the battle of Ushant against the English, when still Duke of Chartres. He had failed to follow orders and attack. Humiliated, accused of cowardice, despised by the Court, he did all he could to take his revenge. For us, he fitted neatly into place as the wicked relative, a kind of Richard III, plotting to seize the throne.

Today, the Palais Royal is still as sad and empty as it was when I first visited it. The long courtyard with its rows of trees, its fountains, seems like one of those ancient race courses in Rome or Istanbul, once the turbulent centres of Empire, but now the grazing ground of occasional tourists looking for a place to eat their sandwiches. The shops under the arcades sell mainly nostalgic objects: ancient coins, old books, antiques. If you go up any of the curving staircases to the apartments above, which once were used mainly by courtesans, you can see they have been taken over by the rich and respectable. Of the hundred restaurants, only two remain. The Café de Foy, one of the main centres of political disturbance, where Camille Desmoulins is supposed to have made the speech which led to the attack on the Bastille, is now a tourist agency, obscured by a long façade of tinted glass. When I asked the lady in charge if she knew what had happened on her premises, she confessed she didn't, and thanked me for telling her.

The arcaded gardens were built just before the Revolution, on the model of St Mark's in Venice, and the interlacing branches of its chestnut trees formed what was once called 'the most beautiful ballroom in Europe'. Shops included jewellers, florists, merchants of cloth and 'everything which the sumptuosity of princes adores'. The theatre, rebuilt after a fire, has become the Comédie Française, and there were also marionette shows, a bath-house with hot and cold showers, a wax works, a masonic club, concert halls, and a circus in the centre, where Mlle Lapierre, a giantess two metres twenty in height, and Paul Butterbrodt, who weighed 238 kilos, were on show.

Karamsin, an enthusiastic Russian, tells of the 'nymphes de joie' who lured him into their grottoes. Here Napoleon met the first woman he slept with, when he was eighteen. Naïvely, he asked her why she followed her profession. 'Monsieur,' she replied, with hauteur, 'one must after all do something.'

One of the aims of the Duke of Orléans was to make money out of his venture. Jokingly, the building was called the Palais Marchand, and when, one Sunday, the Duke went to Versailles, the King quipped maliciously that as his cousin was now a shopkeeper, Sunday was, presumably, the only day he could get off.

How valid, though, was the picture I had been given of the Duke's conspiracy when I first visited the Palais Royal? Inevitably, it was melodramatic and simple and, as I discovered later, the Duke's role is still uncertain, although some historians have seen the outbreak of the Revolution as a great masonic conspiracy, and the Duke was Grand Master of the Grand Orient of France. He was what the French call an *anglomane*, and a frequent visitor to England. Like many of the liberal nobility, he was in favour of a constitutional monarchy with predominant aristocratic influence, as in Great Britain.

There is little proof, however, of his having used English gold to bribe royal troops and stir discontent, as is often alleged. For one thing, he was immensely wealthy himself.* Certainly, he showed his sympathy for new ideas from the beginning, as we have seen when he tried to join the Third Estate at the opening procession (p. 7). He was also one of the first nobles to go over to the Third Estate after the royal session of 23 June. To see him, though, in the sinister role which so many royalists have given him, of a treacherous royal prince always present in the shadows at every disturbance, seems exaggerated. He was too easygoing, weak and pleasure-loving to be a serious conspirator, or even, perhaps, to

---

* It is amazing how this is still part of historical folklore. On a recent visit to Mme Tussaud's, I heard a Frenchman in front of the wax figures of Louis XVI and Marie-Antoinette saying to his small son: 'There is Louis XVI, who was guillotined by the English.' When I protested, he insisted that it was English gold, distributed in revenge for Louis XVI's participation in the American War of Independence, which had started and maintained the Revolution. We argued for some time.

want to be King. Like so many of his class and background, he was probably content to make liberal noises, and be a figurehead enjoying popularity.

True, in the end the Duke did become a deputy in the Convention, under the pretentious name of Philippe Egalité, and voted for his cousin Louis XVI's death, which horrified even Jacobin colleagues. But by then he was caught up in events, like so many revolutionaries, and fear probably compelled him to participate rather than wait on the sidelines for his fate. In the early stages of the Revolution, his political sympathies and resentment against the King and Queen were probably manipulated by his secretary Laclos, author of *Les Liaisons Dangereuses*, who also had a grudge against the régime because his career as a brilliant artillery officer had been blocked by his lack of noble ancestors.

Whatever his underlying motivation, Orléans is significant because he headed what was known as the liberal nobility, those who believed that France should have a constitution rather than absolute monarchy. In their attitudes there was a great lack of realism. 'We walked on a carpet of flowers,' wrote the Marquis de Bombelles, 'without realizing there was a precipice underneath.' Their motivation was also to shake off the control of the Crown, imposed by Louis XIV more than a hundred years previously. As Orléans was a royal prince, and a possible alternative occupant of the throne, he led the split in the ruling class. In autocracy, division among the rulers is an inevitable step to Revolution.

The Palais Royal now became the centre of what Hardy, a chronicler and bookseller, called 'the extreme revolutionary party'. Because the Duke was of royal blood, rioters felt safe in the Palais Royal, where the police were not admitted. A gendarme pursuing a criminal into the gardens was chased, had an ear cut off, and was thrown into a fountain. Sentiment against the Court was so high that a lady of quality who spat on Necker's portrait had her skirts lifted and was beaten on her bare buttocks. More important, soldiers were given drink and money and told to cry 'Long Live the Third Estate!' On 30 June, a crowd directed from the Palais Royal released the eleven French Guards who had been imprisoned in the Abbaye for refusing to fire on the crowd in Versailles (p. 31). They were brought to the Palais Royal to be feasted and congratulated. Another group of eight artillerymen who had deserted from the Invalides were similarly treated.

When one considers that the beginning of the Revolution resembles the start of an avalanche which once begun cannot be stopped, and that it had previously been the royal army which had kept disorder in check, the importance of the Palais Royal as a centre of revolt becomes clear. In his pamphlet, *Discours de la lanterne aux Parisiens*, written some months later, Camille Desmoulins trumpets forth:

It is the Palais Royal which for six months inundated France with all the brochures that have made of everyone, even of the soldier, a philosopher. It is at the Palais Royal that the patriots, mingling joyously with the cavalrymen, the Dragoons, the Horse Guards, the Swiss Guards and the cannoneers, embracing them, intoxicating them, and lavishing gold on them to drink the health of the nation, won over the whole army.

Arthur Young, the English traveller, also gives a specific and dramatic description of the atmosphere at this time:

. . . the cafés at the Palais Royal present even more singular events; not only are the interiors full, but there is also a crowd of listeners at the doors and windows who gape open-mouthed at speakers who climb on chairs and tables, and have each their own audience. It is difficult to imagine the ardour with which they are listened to, nor the thunder of applause which greets any expression of boldness and violence against the government which oversteps normal bounds. I am amazed that the ministry allows such nests of sedition at such centres of revolt.

On 12 July, when news of Necker's dismissal reached Paris, revolutionary fervour approached breaking point. More and more people gathered under the chestnut trees and around the cafés. A shop near the Temple which sold plaster figures was ransacked, and busts of the Duke of Orléans and of Necker, which was covered with black crêpe to mourn his dismissal, were carried at the head of a procession of some six thousand people. Slowly, they moved to the Place Vendôme, and from there, to the Rue Royale, and through to the Place Louis XV (Concorde).

Apart from the obelisk in the centre, the Place has changed very little. An eighteenth-century oil painting in the Musée Carnavalet shows it in the early sunlight at dawn. Two men are fishing on the bank opposite, where the bridge had not yet been built,* and give it the contrast of a great city square, on the fringe of the countryside. In the middle is the large statue of Louis XV, solitary in the crisp dawn, while behind are the palatial buildings of Jacques-Ange Gabriel. Round the square, eight little pavilions, now replaced by statues of French cities, used to conceal staircases which descended to patches of grass and flowers. These were only filled up, in 1852, because they were used by prostitutes in a more outwardly respectable era. To the left, outside the painting I have described, the Champs Elysées stretched up through woods to the open space where now stands the Arch of Triumph. To the right, the Gardens of the Tuileries extended on the other side of an old moat spanned by a swivel bridge dividing two ramps. These still remain today as ancient relics of the fortifications of Paris.

As they filed into the square, the crowd was confronted by four hundred horsemen of the Royal Allemand, a German mercenary regiment, who were drawn up at the side.

Suddenly, the cavalry charged, striking with the flats of their swords.

The crowd fled into the Tuileries Gardens. The cavalry pursued them, and were pelted from the top of the ramps with stones, chairs and even glasses from the tables of the open-air cafés. However, the crowd was too dense and the cavalry withdrew while the two rearing stone horses by Coysevox, which have been at either side of the entrance for almost three hundred years, looked down on the tumult.

Rumours immediately spread through Paris: the threatened massacre had begun. In fact, this was untrue, like so many mainsprings of the Revolution: one man had been dragged to the statue of Louis XV and had been pierced by a sabre; an old man had been hit by the flat of a sword. However, whether these two victims died or not is unknown.

In any case, a momentous event had occurred. The Parisians now had reason to believe that the royal attack had started. Hearing this, the French Guards, a crack regiment who normally mounted guard at Versailles, now marched from their barracks in the Rue Chaussée d'Antin and fired on the Royal Allemand, who retreated over the river to the Champ de Mars. The dissolution of the army, which

* This was built in 1787 and called after Louis XVI.

42

was to play a much more significant role than the antics of the mob, had begun in earnest.

At the Hôtel de Ville, an alternative emergency government was set up by the electors who had chosen the deputies in Versailles. A militia of 48,000 bourgeois guards was decreed to keep order and defend Paris. But how were they to be armed?

Throughout the next day, 13 July, arms were sought everywhere. Armourers' shops were ransacked, while further rumours inflamed Paris. In the Palais Royal and elsewhere, it was reported that fifteen thousand troops were advancing up the Rue St Antoine. The Royal Allemand were fighting again at the Place du Trône – since renamed the Place de la Nation. Another regiment was advancing south from St Denis.

All these rumours were false. At Versailles, the King's new cabinet seems to have had no definite plans, as usual. 'All I need is a hundred million livres and a hundred thousand troops,' said Breteuil, the new Keeper of the Seals. He had neither.

In Paris, a mob invaded the Garde Meuble, which still stands on the right of the Rue Royale as you look across Concorde from the river. It has since become the Ministry of Marine, and a naval officer, Captain Guillaume, who is in charge of cultural affairs, showed me the way the mob had taken.

Initially, we were delayed in the courtyard while a medal was presented. An admiral stood in front. Trumpets blew. An officer stepped forward. The admiral applied the medal. The trumpets blew again, and the parade was dismissed. It was a contrast to that day on 13 July 1789 when people swarmed over the courtyard, rushed up the stairs, shouted, threatened, called for arms.

'What was the Garde Meuble?' I asked as we ascended the eighteenth-century staircase.

'It was the royal warehouse for furniture, valuables and anything used to decorate the royal châteaux. The Crown Jewels were here, too. Anybody could come and see the collection between Quasimodo and St Martin's day. There were also some old weapons: halberds, a suit of armour belonging to Henry IV, a silver cannon presented to King Louis XIV by the King of Siam. It was these arms, useless as they were, which the mob wanted.'

'They must have been desperate.'

'They were. The Ancien Régime was ruthless in suppressing riots. Or had been up till then.'

We entered what Napoleon had turned into a dining room with polished table and upholstered chairs. 'The arms were here. Real museum pieces they were, ranged round the walls.'

I imagined the halberds being snatched up, the armour discarded, the silver cannon being trundled to the stairs.

'The Crown Jewels were here.' We went through a room which was resplendent with gilt and mirrors. 'The Jewels were exhibited in a tall case by the window.' Captain Guillaume showed me a drawing of the ornamented stand. 'The most valuable diamonds in the royal collection were on show: the Blue, the Regent, the Sannsy.'

'And they weren't touched?'

'No. People were still afraid of authority. They could justify taking the arms to defend themselves, but stealing the diamonds would have been a crime, almost *lèse-majesté*.'

Throughout that day of 13 July the search for arms went on, but with little success. A certain amount of gunpowder was distributed at the Town Hall. The Arsenal and the monastery of St Lazare were ransacked but no arms were found.

At six o'clock on the morning of 14 July, an enormous crowd gathered on the esplanade of the Invalides, the immense building constructed by Louis XIV to house veterans and war wounded, an example followed in London with the Chelsea Pensioners. Then, as now, the Invalides was protected by a gate and a shallow moat, nine feet deep, surrounding the terrace. Beyond was the broad façade, four storeys high, with an arch at the entrance and the figure of Louis XIV on horseback above. Behind this were courtyards, and a great dome which could be seen from almost anywhere in Paris. It crowned the ornate church in which Napoleon's tomb now lies. Below, in the cellars, thirty thousand muskets were stored.

The Governor, M. de Sombreuil, was a liberal-minded, hesitant gentleman. Later, so the story goes, his daughter saved him from slaughter by drinking the blood of a nobleman to prove that she and her father detested aristocrats. Now, he went to meet the crowd, and fatuously he opened the gate to explain that he could not let them in. Naturally, they pushed through, while others dropped into the moat and helped each other to climb onto the terrace. Here, cannon were ranged and old soldiers from the Invalides stood with burning brands at the touch-holes. However, not a shot was fired.

At the Champ de Mars, not four hundred yards away, the royal commander, Besenval, a Swiss general more renowned for his amours than his bellicosity, held a Council of War. He says in his unreliable memoirs that his colonels told him with tears in their eyes that their troops would not march against the people.

In the Invalides the crowd rushed over the terrace, through the great doors and into the arched courtyard. They distributed the muskets, or carried them to the Town Hall. But there was no powder. The only place where it was stored was the Bastille, to which it had been moved from the Arsenal, a few days earlier.

5

PARIS: SYMBOLIC VICTORY

'One could make a volume – a hundred volumes, rather – by collecting
the monstrous lies which during the Revolution and since, the people
of Paris have been made to swallow.'

G. LENOTRE

The Bastille was part of the old defensive walls of Paris, controlling
the eastern gate. Built in the late fourteenth century, it had eight
massive towers with two courtyards. Surrounding it was a deep
moat through which ran a stream which filled it up when dammed.
Shortly after the Bastille was built, it became the scene of battles
and skirmishes when France was riven by feuds between Armagnac,
Burgundians and the invading English. For a time, it had an English
commander, John Falstaff. In the wars of the Fronde, the guns at
the top of the towers were fired at the royalist army which was
pursuing the Frondeurs into Paris. As times grew more peaceful,
it became notorious as a prison, particularly for noble captives such
as Voltaire, Sade, Cardinal de Rohan, and the Man in the Iron Mask.
If they could afford it, prisoners lived in style, with domestics and
dinner parties for friends invited from outside. Below them, the
dungeons on the water level of the moat were left to rats and toads.

In 1784, there was a plan to pull the Bastille down and build
a square on its site, called Place Louis XVI, rather similar to the
present one. However, the cost was too high. It is intriguing,
though, to consider what would have happened had the scheme
been carried out. Probably the gunpowder would have been stored
in the nearby Arsenal, which could have been captured more easily,
and there would have been no great dramatic 'event'.

Brita and I had often been to the Place de la Bastille. I remember
taking part in a crowded popular dance there one night of 14 July,
some years after the War. A band played near the column in the
centre and the Place was full of whirling, exuberant people. It

46

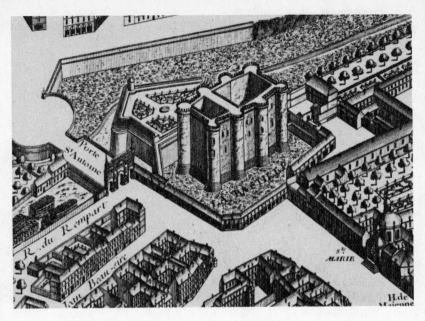

The Bastille before the Revolution. *Bibliothèque Nationale.*

was reminiscent of Victory Day in London in 1945 – as if we were celebrating a liberation that was as important. Briefly, we had also visited it with Americans, who at one stage we used to take round Europe on tours. Never, though, had we explored what remained of the Bastille, as we intended to do now. The first thing, we decided, was to ask people who lived and worked there.

The approach to the Bastille is noisy and rather formless. You go up the long and ancient Rue St Antoine from the end of the Rue de Rivoli, past small shops and cafés. Narrow streets on the left lead to the palaces in the Marais, and old and uncleaned buildings, like the Hôtel de Sully and the domed temple of Ste Marie, emerge like grey rocks beside a river of cars and hurrying pedestrians.

The first time you go up the Rue St Antoine, you know you are approaching where the Bastille once was. You remember, perhaps, that this was one of the most turbulent faubourgs in Paris. You notice the maps and prints of the Bastille in bookshops. You pass the Place Beaumarchais, with the statue of the creator of the satire on which *The Barber of Seville* and *Figaro* were based. Then, on the pavement and roadway, you suddenly notice the outline, marked in thin, red bricks, of the towers and walls. At the end of the street there is suddenly the openness of the Place, with a tall, bronze column in the middle which celebrates not the fall of the fortress but a later revolution in 1830.

Absurdly, I am always disappointed to find no Bastille. It is as if the Rue St Antoine were a neck without a head, or a signpost leading nowhere.

After some hesitation, Brita and I started our enquiries at the Banque de France, which stands on the corner of the Rue St Antoine and the Place de la Bastille. We were admitted with little clicks through security doors and confronted by long, low desks, diligent bank clerks, and a grave individual who asked if he could help.

'The Bastille,' I said. 'It was here. There is the outline of the towers on the pavement – '

'The Bastille,' he repeated ruminatively, as if trying to recall an acquaintance he remembered vaguely.

'Yes – you're right on top of where the Bastille was,' I insisted, 'there must be some remains in your cellars.'

'Ah, yes. There were, I think. Some stones, perhaps some prison cells. But we cemented it over years ago. It could have been dangerous. People might have come through to rob the bank from other buildings.'

I imagined robbers delving through the dank, crumbling walls of the dungeons. Or ghosts: clanking, medieval soldiers, or prisoners dragging ball and chain.

Outside again, we stood a little disconsolately. Returning down the Rue St Antoine, we passed another bank, the Société Générale, and noticed a plaque high on the wall, marking the original entrance to the outer courtyards of the Bastille. Here it was that people had gathered in little groups at about nine in the morning. For some reason, the Governor, De Launay, who had already been forewarned, had decided not to defend these outer courtyards. But he had pulled up the small drawbridge between the first and second courtyards, and also the main drawbridge of the fortress.

We went into the Société Générale and enquired, but the blonde lady we met was even vaguer. Yes, certainly the Bastille had been somewhere in the vicinity. She had noticed the outlines of red bricks on her way to and from work. But apart from the plaque on their wall, the Société Générale had nothing to do with the Bastille.

Further down the Rue St Antoine, we noticed an ancient house which had certainly witnessed the storming, two hundred years ago. However, the lady who answered the door thought we wanted to buy her house. She looked perplexed at mention of the Bastille, and told us she ran 'natural' excursions in the countryside for young people, and knew little of the Bastille and nothing of how old her house was.

We walked back towards the Place. 'I suppose it isn't surprising that they're not interested,' said Brita. 'Although they live and work here, the Bastille has nothing to do with their everyday existence.'

'Yes,' I agreed. 'However much its capture may have affected their present way of living.'

'Perhaps. But most people don't think like that. Inevitably, they take their environment for granted. They are whatever they are, and that's that. They're not even conscious of the reasons.'

Further frustration followed when we noticed a restaurant called 'The Carillons of the Bastille' – which naturally intrigued us. However, it was firmly locked, with its windows whitewashed. When we enquired of a newspaper seller, he told us that he had seen the carillons in the restaurant. They were two and a half metres high, and still chimed. He wasn't sure, though, where the proprietor had gone. He thought he had sold the restaurant and bought a 'self', somewhere nearby.

Without much hope, we looked around for a self-service restaurant and found one facing the Place. Here, to our delight, we were welcomed warmly by the owner, Jean-Louis Viguès, an exuberant man in his late thirties, who was a Bastille enthusiast. Yes, he owned the carillons. Huge they were, made of grey, ancient metal. Originally, they had been suspended in the inner courtyard of the fortress. Prisoners had liked their chimes, but after a few weeks, the monotonous repetitions every quarter of an hour had become intolerable, marking as they did the length of tedious time ahead.

Jean-Louis told us that when the Bastille was pulled down, the carillons were salvaged by an unknown individual and handed down from person to person. Early this century they were acquired by a doctor who left them on one night when he went to the hospital. In the apartment building where he lived they made such a reverberating noise that his neighbours had to call the police to switch them off. When the doctor died, he left them to a patient of his with poliomyelitis, who had to keep them in a warehouse where the storage fees were more than his small pension. So he sold them to a friend who thought it a good idea to exhibit them to the public, and sold them in turn to Jean-Louis Viguès for his restaurant, in 1979.

We began to talk about the Bastille. 'Of course, if you live here as I do and read a lot about it,' said Jean-Louis, 'you realize that the event was quite different from the way history presents it. It was much more personal. Many of those involved were simply attracted by curiosity. Others just enjoyed taking part in a riot. Most didn't think they had a hope of actually taking the Bastille. Others were just bystanders. Certainly, none can have been aware of the significance of what they were doing.'

He told us that some of the remaining stones could still be seen, piled on top of one another in a little garden near the river, at the end of the Boulevard Henri IV. Had we been down to the Métro? Some trains ran through the original dungeons. On the platform for Bobigny, you could still see stones from the outer escarpment.

We went down to the Bobigny platform. To one side, a triangle of smooth, well finished slabs of limestone, laid more than six hundred years ago, jutted from the wall. Nearby was a little exhibition. There was the replica of a naïve painting of the siege in 1789, painted by Claude Choat, who was sixty-six at the time. In it, bony men aimed their muskets at the parapets, while a defender fell into the moat, like a shot duck. Although the towers did not seem quite straight, the courtyard could be seen clearly, with people emerging from the entrance under a two-storey building which, presumably, had now been transformed into the Société Générale. To the left of the courtyard were the locked and shuttered shops which the Governor owned as a perquisite. Round the corner was the first drawbridge, and beyond it the second courtyard, with the Governor's house on the right and a stone bridge on the left, which spanned the moat. This led to the main drawbridge of the fortress, which was raised, leaving a gap above the moat. At the side of the stone bridge were the kitchen buildings, which the artist had distorted, but whose outline was still reasonably clear.

There was also a plan of the towers, sketched over the present street plan. So we decided to follow the events on the ground. By the plaque marking the original entrance, the Rue Jacques Coeur followed the approximate line of the first courtyard. Now, it too had shops at the side, among them a chemist's with the red cross outside, a furniture mart called Daisy Simon, and a window display of toys.

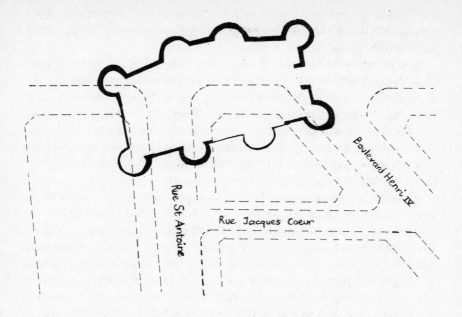

The Bastille, imposed on the present-day street plan. Le Nôtre, *Carnavalet.*

As we walked slowly along, I imagined the wall on the left, fringing the moat, and the towers sixty feet above, now replaced by a massive apartment block. The defenders, thirty-two Swiss and eighty old soldiers from the Invalides, had been ranged on the parapets, with the barrels of their muskets protruding, and the mouths of cannon gaping through the embrasures.

We rounded a sharp curve into a broad street, the present Boulevard Henri IV. We measured some twenty yards and came to where the small drawbridge had stood, raised under an archway, surmounted by the royal arms. This was the way the first delegation had come from the Town Hall at about ten in the morning. They were eminent citizens representing the committee of those who had elected the deputies of Paris to the Assembly, and who had now taken over the municipality.

They came to ask the Governor for arms and ammunition with which to defend themselves. The irony is that they should ask for these from a royal officer in order to defend themselves against the King's troops. It is an illustration of the way loyalties had been fragmented. Now, the real issue was whether to side with the invaders of Paris, or the defenders. It must have been rather like the beginning of the Civil War in Spain, where whole garrisons were uncertain of their allegiance.

With all the courtesy of his class, De Launay invited the delegation to lunch at his house, which was situated on the other side of what is now the Boulevard Henri IV. There, over an ample meal, De Launay explained that they were asking him to commit treason, that he was answerable for the Bastille with his head. However, he promised not to fire unless he was attacked, and gave orders to pull back the cannon from their embrasures. Then the delegation departed, to the imprecations of the groups standing in the first courtyard, who presumed the cannon had only been pulled back so that they could be loaded.

To reassure a second delegation which arrived shortly afterwards, De Launay took one of them up to the parapet to show him the unloaded cannon. The view from there must have been much the same as that from the top of the bronze column, today, except that the neighbouring streets were dotted with people carrying the muskets they had taken from the Invalides. To one side was the river, and on the other the arcaded Place Royale – now Place des Vosges. The great houses of the Marais could be seen amidst their courtyards and gardens, while the broad ribbon of the Rue St Antoine ran down to the bulk of the Town Hall.

When the second delegation left, something happened which ended all hope of peaceful negotiation. Two men, greatly daring, climbed over the roof of a perfume shop by the first drawbridge. Then they jumped into the second courtyard beyond. Unable to find the keys in the empty guardroom at the side, they chopped with axes at the chains. The drawbridge crashed down, killing a man standing nearby.

The crowd then surged into the second courtyard, which took up most of what is now the end of the Boulevard Henri IV where it joins the Place de la Bastille. From there, they rushed onto the stone bridge which spanned the twenty-five feet of the moat, and which started near what is now a traffic island, a few feet from the pavement.

Over at the Town Hall, another delegation was just setting off when they heard the boom of cannon and the rattle of musketry. What had happened was that De Launay had interpreted the lowering of the first drawbridge as an attack, and had opened fire. In the narrow courtyard, the crowd was an easy target, and many of them were killed or wounded. The reign of chaos had begun. The slaughter which would go on for twenty-six years, until 1815, had started.

Although it was they who had lowered the drawbridge, the besiegers took this as a deliberate trap. Cries of 'Traitor' and 'Death to De Launay' rang out. Some took refuge in the Governor's house where the amicable lunch had taken place. In the atmosphere of fury and panic, a girl was thought to be De Launay's daughter, and there was talk of burning her alive in sight of her father, but fortunately some neighbours identified her, and she was released.

Those with fire-arms sniped ineffectually up at the parapets, while others went into the street and returned with two carts laden with straw and manure. These they pushed through the courtyards under fire from the parapets.

As the straw was lit, a cloud of smoke shrouded everything. Shooting petered out and, coughing, the crowd advanced once more. However, they were powerless to bring the main drawbridge down.

Above them, the sky was cloudy, with the sun shining through from time to time, illuminating the turmoil. Although it was not hot for July (22°), the air was humid and oppressive with promise of rain and thunder.

Under cover of the smoke, the dead and wounded were dragged out to carts and home-made stretchers, and a series of pathetic processions wended their way to the Town Hall. Today, the Rue St Antoine leads into the Rue de Rivoli, which was built later in the nineteenth century. However, the way to the Town Hall follows an old Roman road and was much the same, going via the Rue François Miron.

In front of the Town Hall, on the Place de Grève, three companies of mutinous French Guards were drawn up. A sergeant on leave, called Hulin, besought them to join in the attack on the Bastille. Significantly, he said nothing about destroying a symbol of despotism but wept and asked them if they wanted to see the Parisians slaughtered like sheep, as if the tiny garrison in the Bastille were attacking Paris. The French Guards were persuaded and marched up to the Bastille, dragging four cannon behind them. At the same time, an officer called Elie joined the crowd round the Bastille with 400 more citizens. Now, instead of a poorly armed mob which had only killed one of the defenders on the battlements, there was not only military leadership but professional soldiers handling cannon.

Outside the Bastille, the French Guards set up their guns. Their shot, however, had no effect on massive walls and towers, thirty feet thick. So, under fire, they moved their cannon into the second courtyard and placed them opposite the main drawbridge.

This had a disastrous effect on the morale of the defenders. In the courtyard behind the main drawbridge in the Bastille, three cannon had been placed. Determined defenders would have lowered the drawbridge for a moment, and fired on the surging crowd and opposing cannon before raising it again. However, the Invalides, if not the Swiss, were fighting against their own people, and the risk was that this would ensure the massacre of the entire garrison, should the Bastille fall. Wasn't it better to capitulate before the raised drawbridge was shattered by the cannon of the French Guards? Officially, this would guarantee the defenders would be spared.

At this stage, De Launay seems to have gone mad. He is said to have rushed down to the powder room under the Tour de la Liberté, whose shape is still outlined on the Rue St Antoine. In his hand was a lighted brand. With it, he intended to blow up the garrison, the attackers, and much of the surrounding district. He was only stopped by two of his own soldiers, at the point of the bayonet.

Parleying began, and it is important in these days of modern warfare, where you rarely see your enemy, to realize how close the assailants and defenders were to one another. You can appreciate this if you glance up from the Rue Jacques Coeur, or the Boulevard Henri IV, and realize that the entire Bastille and its moat could be contained in little more than the one block of buildings and the street beyond. Even amidst the noise of musketry, to parley and to communicate was possible.

In order to obtain a cease-fire, De Launay sent a drummer and a man waving a white handkerchief up to the battlements. Firing ceased and they repeated their demand for a capitulation. But the crowd yelled up their refusal. De Launay then wrote a note, a copy of which still exists:

We, with twenty thousand pounds of gunpowder, will blow up the garrison and the whole district if you do not accept capitulation. Bastille, five o'clock in the evening, 14th July 1789, Launay.

This note was pushed through a hole in the raised drawbridge, and as firing had ceased, the crowd approached the end of the stone bridge. However, the gap over the moat was too wide, so several men went off to a carpenter's shop in the Rue des Tournelles and brought back a number of planks. The longest was weighted down by people sitting on the end, and a cobbler, Michel Bezier, stepped carefully along it. However, he fell into the moat and broke his elbow. Someone else, probably Elie, took his place and grasped the piece of paper.

However, the crowd definitely did not want a capitulation and the French Guards were about to fire their cannon into the drawbridge when suddenly it was lowered.

The Bastille had fallen. The incredible had happened. The crowd surged in, arrested the garrison, and released the seven prisoners, including a mad Irishman who thought he was God. The chaos was such that those outside, ignorant of the surrender, continued firing and some of the assailants who now appeared on the parapets were hit and wounded.

There were shouts for the execution of De Launay. However, when Elie had taken the paper from the drawbridge, he had promised the officer who handed it to him to spare the garrison. With the French Guards, he now protected the Governor, the Swiss and the Invalides.

As the victorious crowds made their way down the Rue St Antoine towards the Town Hall, the spectacle was extraordinary, with dancing, weeping, and cries for revenge.

De Launay in his blue coat was jostled, hit and wounded. When he came to the Town Hall, he seems to have gone crazy with fear. Rolling his eyes and grinding his teeth, he shouted: 'Kill me! Kill me!' Suddenly, he kicked an unemployed cook called Dénot in the backside. He was then bayoneted, hacked with swords, and shot with a pistol.

With his knife, Dénot cut off De Launay's head. Proudly, he paraded it on a pike round the streets and cafés for several days. At night, he even deposited it with the police in the Châtelet, and was given a receipt. This was the first street murder of the Revolution, the first killing of a royal officer. To judge it in any way, one should perhaps bring it closer to our times. A parallel would be the mobbing of a German Commander whose troops had shot civilians as these attacked his outpost in August 1944, just before the relief of Paris by the Allies. Sympathy would probably have been scant, as it was for De Launay.

The taking of the Bastille had many portents. Among them was the way the city of Paris had challenged and defeated the royal government, reviving a role it had played so often in its past.

The surrender showed the Ancien Régime's lack of confidence in suppressing revolt, certainly a contrast to later, reactionary régimes who learnt a lesson from the Revolution. De Launay of course was not a military man but, even so, surrender should have been unnecessary. As one of his Swiss officers, Deflue, told him just before capitulation, the garrison and actual structure of the Bastille were unharmed. De Launay, like so many royalist commanders, was a man uncertain of what he should do. Official confidence had been sapped by new political ideas and evidence of government weakness in the last few years. So nervous was he that he had even imagined the shadows of trees were enemies, during the nights preceding the assault.

Significant, too, was the way the Bastille could not have been taken without the mutinous French Guards, despite the courage of the crowd. During the five hours' battle, no royal troops had attempted to relieve the garrison, although they were only an hour's march away, across the river. No messages from Versailles came to the troops during the three days' period after the dismissal of Necker. However great the fury and determination of the Parisians, the whole event was a perfect example of the crumbling of the authority of the Crown, largely through its own inactivity.

In any case, if the troop movements round Paris really had represented a counter-revolution, what would the Court have done had they succeeded? To take a modern parallel, the situation resembled the extraordinary revolt of Colonel Tejero and the Civil Guards in favour of a Franco-style reactionary régime, in Madrid in 1981. If Tejero had succeeded, what policy could a restored Francoist régime have followed? Most of the population were against it. Similarly, what could Louis have achieved with his troops uncertain, his Treasury empty, and the population aflame with new ideas of Liberty and self-government? The calling of the States-General had roused too many hopes for repression to be possible, as did the period of democracy in Spain since Franco's death.

Inevitably, many myths sprang up. Perhaps most influential is that the Bastille was attacked because it was the symbol of centuries of oppression. More important, as we have seen, was the need for gunpowder to defend Paris against the royal troops.

Despite the anticipated liberation of scores of political captives, manacled and in rags, with the marks of misery and torture on them, only seven prisoners were released. Of these, no fewer than four were common criminals, two were mad, and only one, the Comte de Solage, had been imprisoned arbitrarily at the request of his family, but that not on a royal whim but because he had committed incest.

Propaganda dramatically exaggerated everything. Part of an old printing press in the fortress was exhibited as a wheel used to torture prisoners, and a piece of fifteenth-century armour was described as an iron corset used to keep prisoners in 'total immobility'. A contemporary print even showed the patriots bursting into a cell to find the skeleton of the Man in the Iron Mask, grinning up at them from a mattress on the floor.

Left empty, the Bastille was pulled down almost immediately by a builder called Palloy, who falsely claimed to have taken part in the assault. The parapets were crowded with a thousand workers, now armed only with crowbars, as they levered up the great stones, stuck together with lead instead of cement in the medieval fashion.

A year later, at the anniversary celebration, the remains were turned into an improvised dance hall. The bases of the towers stood, like enormous elephant feet, and were used to hold the seats of the spectators. The courtyards served as a dance floor with the bandstand in the middle, from which a pole stuck up, crowned with a Phrygian cap.

As Brita and I had satisfied our curiosity by tracing the events on the ground, we accepted an invitation from Jean-Louis to go up and see his collection of mementoes from the Bastille on the first floor above his restaurant. The room was long, with windows looking out on to the Place. A desk was covered with papers and historical magazines. Jean-Louis reached into a drawer and brought out blue and gold medallions, sculpted from the 'chains' which were supposed to have bound the prisoners.

'Obviously, the storming of the Bastille is of outstanding importance,' he said. 'But all the fuss surrounding it is exaggerated.' He showed us the special badges awarded to the 954 'Heroes of the Bastille' on which perhaps the later denomination of 'Heroes of the Soviet Union' was based. Ninety-eight had been killed, and the badges were given to their nearest relatives.

'If the besieged had just stayed put, only reacting against those who tried to hack or burn the drawbridge down, the crowd would probably have gone away, sooner or later,' he continued. 'The great mistake of the royalists was to provoke, and then not to have the mettle to resist intelligently. Louis XVI should have sent an official messenger to the Electors in the Town Hall saying he did not intend to attack but only to contain disorder, if that was really his intention. Historians of Right and Left argue differently about whether he really intended a counter-revolution. Probably, he didn't know himself. On July 14th, he went out hunting as usual and wrote "Rien" in his diary because he didn't manage to shoot anything.'

'But the fall of the Bastille finished him, didn't it?' asked Brita.

'In a sense. It was the beginning of the slide down.'

I went to the window and looked out at the Place. 'Where are we now, in relation to the Bastille?' I asked. 'Actually inside it?'

'That's right. We would probably be looking out on the larger courtyard. You know we, too, were stormed here the other day.'

'How d'you mean?'

'Well, there was a political meeting with 200,000 people, the Sunday before last. There were bands playing on the other side of the Place, where the new opera is being built, and the crowd near here couldn't see. So some people climbed up onto the glass overhang below these windows. I had to go out and fight them off. There was a real scuffle, with people shouting up abuse at me. The battle for the Bastille still goes on!'

It does, I thought. National days in most countries are tepid affairs. But in France, the celebration is international, marking the beginning of a struggle between autocracy and the people which has been going on for two centuries. 'It has its paradoxes, too,' I said aloud. 'In Algeria and Indo-China those who were struggling for independence ignored July 14th deliberately: they saw it not as the symbol of a fight for liberty but of the might of colonial France.'

'Yes,' said Jean-Louis, 'I was brought up in a colonial family in Morocco. Perhaps I am so interested in the storming of the Bastille, because, underneath everything, I wish it hadn't happened.'

[6]

SURRENDER IN PARIS
(ANARCHY IN FRANCE)

'The greatest revolution that we know of has been effected with comparatively speaking the loss of very few lives. From this moment we may consider France as a free country, the king as a very limited monarch, and the nobility reduced to a level with the rest of the nation.'

Letter from the DUKE OF DORSET,
the British Ambassador in Paris, July 1789.

In the evening of 14 July, the oppressive weather broke. Heavy rain fell on the empty courtyards and parapets of the Bastille. A hundred years later, in 1889, it also fell so heavily that the centenary celebrations had to be cancelled. 'If the weather on July 14th 1789 had been the same . . . it is likely that no one would have taken the Bastille,' commented a contemporary newspaper, appropriately named *Le Temps*.

After their triumph, the citizens of Paris retired to their taverns, cafés and houses to await the royal reaction. There was great uneasiness. Vengeance, surely, would come as it always had when riots had broken out. At least, the new militia, which was shortly to become the National Guard, now had enough arms and gunpowder to defend the city.

When, at Versailles, Louis was told of the events in Paris, he said he was pained. 'But it was impossible they were caused by the orders given to the troops,' he wrote to the States-General. Gradually, the significance of what had happened seeped through, and Louis decided to yield. It is difficult to know what was in his mind. Afterwards, when a virtual prisoner in the Tuileries, he said he should have gathered troops still loyal to him and retired to a garrison town far from Paris. It would have meant civil war, but in retrospect that would have been better for him than the gradual attrition of his authority and power which followed from the fall of the Bastille. Possibly, he was influenced by the fate of Charles I of England, who was always very much in his mind, and who had departed to raise his standard at Nottingham, only to be defeated and executed after a long civil war.

Probably, too, his surrender was due to fear, not for himself but for his family. His troops were unreliable, and would no longer be a barrier to a triumphant mob of Parisians, come to sack the château at Versailles. He ordered his unpopular brother, the Comte d'Artois, to leave the country. Marie-Antoinette's friends, the Polignacs and the Prince de Condé, also left with many other noblemen. The courtyard of the château was full of departing carriages. The emigration had begun. Soon, whole wings were deserted and silent.

On the following morning, Louis made his way on foot to the Assembly, down the Avenue de Paris through the crowds of spectators. He was received in expectant silence. 'The silence of the people is the lesson of kings,' Mirabeau had told the deputies.

Louis entered the great hall of the Estates. He announced to the deputies that he had ordered his troops to leave Paris, and asked the Assembly to help him restore order. 'I am at one with the Nation,' he declared.

A roar of approval went up from the deputies. They rose and, surrounded by an immense crowd, escorted him back to the Palace. A great mass of exuberant people swept up the Avenue into the Place d'Armes and the Marble Courtyard. Marie-Antoinette and the royal family were already on the balcony. The King joined them to rapturous cries of '*Vive le Roi!*' and even '*Vive la Reine!*'

This fervent demonstration shows how effective the King could have been had he led his people in giving them more representative institutions. Perhaps, as he stood on the balcony, he remembered the advice his minister Malesherbes had given him a few years back: 'Create the constitution of your country. Take your place in the world and do not be afraid of founding it on the rights of your people. In order to create great events one has to create them oneself.'

Two days afterwards, Louis set off for Paris. Uncertain whether he would be assassinated, he heard Mass in the early morning and appointed his brother, the Comte de Provence, Lieutenant-General of the kingdom.

He entered Paris with few acclamations. The cortège went up the Rue St Honoré and into the Place de Grève, where lithe, glistening fountains now flow. In those days, the Place was much smaller and sloped down to the quays on the river. Jefferson, the American Ambassador, who was an eye-witness, describes the procession: 'The King's carriage was in the centre, on each side of it [deputies of] the States General in two ranks, afoot, and at their head the Marquis of Lafayette as Commander-in-chief on horseback, and Bourgeois Guards before and behind.'

They stopped in front of the Town Hall, of which only a reconstruction remains as the original was burnt by the Commune in 1871. Inquisitively, I visited it one March afternoon. The double staircase in the centre has been rebuilt, rising in straight, opposite flights to the first floor. The magnificent Salle des Fêtes, with its chandeliers, its double row of white columns, its painted ceiling, is in the same place as the original. In the mayor's study there is a tapestry showing Louis XVI being received outside by the new mayor, Bailly, with a cluster of noblemen around him, and an arch of crossed swords under which he is about to climb the stairs.

Inside, the new mayor, Bailly, gave Louis a tricolour cockade which he put in his hat. It had the red and blue of the city of Paris, either side of the white of the Bourbons, and was to become the flag of France, apart from a period between the Restoration of 1814 and the Revolution of 1830, when the white, royalist, flag returned.

In the Town Hall, speeches of welcome were made, to which the King burbled a few unconnected sentences as he had prepared no reply. In conversation with Bailly, De Launay was mentioned. 'He deserved his fate!' said Louis. We still don't know what he meant. Was it that he blamed De Launay for firing on the people, or for surrendering?

Then Louis and the officials went onto the balcony, and Bailly delivered a conciliatory speech which he said came from the King. At this, the whole Place de Grève resounded with cheers. '*Vive le Roi!*' they cried and, alluding to the cockade, 'Well done! He now belongs to the Third Estate.' Tears welled up in many eyes. As Louis was escorted back to Versailles by the National Guard, he was cheered everywhere. As Jefferson also wrote: '. . . and thus concluded such an *amende honorable* as no sovereign ever made and no people ever received.'

Meanwhile, news of the fall of the Bastille and the royal surrender spread anarchy all over France. Many towns followed the example of Paris and formed new municipalities and their own National Guard, while the royal intendants fled. The local town halls were stormed and tax records dispersed. In Strasbourg, Arthur Young was surprised to see soldiers with the royal cockade still in their hats, and citizens 'so decently dressed' encouraging the mob.

In the countryside, the peasantry could not believe that the royal authority which had ruled them with an iron rod ever since the great peasant revolt of the Jacquerie in 1356 had suddenly crumbled. Ignorance and illiteracy swelled illusion: a print shows a crowd of rustics spearing a Montgolfier balloon which had come down near a village, in the belief that it was a monster. For them, the world outside was full of monsters. The nobles and the King's forces would surely soon return. As in Paris, before the fall of the Bastille, menacing falsehoods filled the air. Troops from over the frontiers, or 'brigands', intent on pillage, were coming. If the local nobleman was hated, his château must be attacked before he turned on the people. Peasants armed themselves and set off into the countryside. The dust they raised on the sun-baked tracks produced additional alarms, with the result that in other villages the inhabitants also sallied forth to burn local châteaux, search for food and destroy all records of feudal dues.

To get an idea of what had really happened, Brita and I searched high and low for a château which had been burnt during this time, which is known by the evocative name of 'La Grande Peur', the Great Fear. I wrote to associations of those who still owned noble houses, like the 'Maisons de France', but none of them had had their châteaux attacked during 'La Grande Peur'. I even wrote to the Duke of Edinburgh, as he belonged to an international royal family, to see if he had contacts who could help. But he had not.

Finally, I came across a description naming some châteaux which had been devastated in Lefebvre's book *La Grande Peur*, published before the War. These were in the Mâconnais, north of Lyons. Brita and I set off to find them, and in Mâcon were given the address of a Mlle Maurice, a local historian.

Mlle Maurice was a lady in her seventies but still slim and alert, living alone in the equivalent of a council flat. She belonged to what one might call the old revolutionary guard, free-thinking, anti-Catholic, pro-sansculotte, but gentle, generous and welcoming.

Her mother, she told us, married a free-thinker who refused to have a church ceremony. As a result, her grandmother vowed never to see the family again, and she herself had never met her and had been brought up with her parents' principles.

Together, we set out to visit the château of Cormatin, near Cluny, which had been attacked but saved from the peasants. It had originally been a medieval stronghold, converted into a civilized summer residence in the seventeenth century. A Renaissance courtyard opened onto a moat. Inside the house, the walls were covered with wood, extravagantly painted, and the bedrooms were still furnished to receive guests, as was then the custom.

One day in July 1789, a hundred and fifty peasants arrived to destroy the archives, but the crowd did not realize that all the feudal records were kept in a building a few miles away. The owner was an eccentric, ruthless soldier who had fought in the American War of Independence. He brought out wine for the peasants, and at the same time sent messengers to bring soldiers from the neighbouring village. When a few of these arrived, he threw gold coins into the courtyard. As the drunken peasants bent to pick them up, the soldiers attacked. They arrested some, while others fled. Later, many were tried, and six were hanged.

'It was a martyrdom,' said Mlle Maurice. 'The town bourgeoisie were terrified by this rising of what they called the "Fourth Estate". There is a place still called the "Croix des Brigands" where the ringleaders were hanged.'

We then drove to the site of the château of Senozan, ten kilometres from Mâcon, driving through the hilly green countryside, through little hamlets which under massed, grey clouds seemed as sad and miserable as they must have been during the Great Fear. 'Of course the peasants were cruelly exploited by the nobles and the priests,' said Mlle Maurice. When I agreed with her but also talked of the violence on both sides, she said: 'You can't make a revolution without violence.'

We arrived at the village of Senozan. Beyond it was a large, flat stretch of land on which the château and its dependencies had stood. It had been one of the most magnificent in the region, belonging to Talleyrand's family. The owner was away when the peasants arrived, and the blaze was so bright that it was visible from Mâcon.

Now, the site is full of placards announcing the sale of the land

for a new housing development. All that was left of the original
estate was a chapel which was locked, and the low buildings of an
orangery which we went to look at. Peering through an archway,
we met an old man with a beret. We asked him about the château
and the fire.

'The château? It was enormous.'

'Did your family live here then?'

'We have worked in the orangery for generations. In fact my
great-great-grandmother took part in the burning of the château
when she was a child of twelve.'

At Versailles, the National Assembly found themselves in the same
situation as that in which they had placed the King. All over
France, they were being challenged by anarchy and the peasant
rising. How could they ensure their authority, the safety of their
property and that of their bourgeois constituents? Still wary of
counter-revolution, they were reluctant to use the royal mercenary
army.

Like the King, they yielded, and feudal rights were abolished
on the euphoric night of 4 August. A painting shows the Clergy on
one side of the great hall of the Assembly, in their dark robes, with
the Nobles beside them in rich, coloured coats. A nobleman stands,
forswearing his feudal rights, while the Third Estate applaud, with
their backs to the Presidium. Everyone seems to be talking to their
neighbour, or those behind them.

By early morning, the atmosphere was almost one of hysteria with
Nobles giving up their feudal rights, the Clergy renouncing their
tithes, the cities their special privileges, and even the distinction
between masters and journeymen being abolished.

'What a nation! What glory!' cried a deputy from Bar-le-Duc.
'What an honour to be French!'

Meanwhile, the Queen was giving a ball in her apartments, and
the next day the King was to write to the Archbishop of Arles that he
would never consent to any reduction in the privileges of his nobles
and his clergy. After all his concessions, he was still not prepared
to range himself with the Third Estate. His reactionary advisers,
including the Queen, were still clustered around him. His years in
the gilded hierarchies of Versailles made it impossible for him to
accept the right of the representatives of the people to participate
in the running of the State.

During the following weeks, the Assembly tried to bring order to their emotional renunciations. Feudal servitude of any kind had been abolished but dues were to continue until redeemed by the peasantry, which of course most were too poor to do. A Declaration of the Rights of Man and the Citizen was also decreed, following the American model. These rights challenged the sovereignty of the monarch. 'No body of men,' runs the second clause, 'no individual can exercise authority which does not issue expressly from the will of the Nation.'

On 13 August, the deputies went to the château to present the decrees abolishing feudalism. They were met by the ubiquitous Master of Ceremonies and led up to the Hall of Mirrors, where stools had been arranged for them in front of a dais under which sat Louis XVI. The President, Le Chapelier, congratulated the King on his new title of 'Restorer of French Liberty', which the Assembly had conferred on him, and then virtually ordered him to sign the Abolition of Feudalism.

The scene is one of the few still evoked by the Hall of Mirrors. Twelve hundred deputies were seated in this long, stately gallery, reflected in the mirrors on one side. Through the tall windows, on the other, the formal gardens stretched out in the sunlight.

The Marquis de Ferrières, a liberal-minded noble deputy, describes it with aristocratic nostalgia:

The ceremony was beautiful . . . But the sentiments of the majority were sad . . . the clergy lose everything; many of the great lords are ruined; there is no rank any more, no pensions, no special arrangements . . . I couldn't refrain from a feeling of sadness at seeing our President, Le Chapelier, a lawyer from Rennes, giving orders to Louis XVI, commanding him to approve the decrees which deprived him of his most precious prerogatives, and to thank God that he was no longer King;* and that in this gallery where Louis XIV, his great-great-grandfather, displayed his fastidious luxury and all his power. Vanity and emptiness of all human things.

To us, it seems ridiculous that an individual should expect to rule an entire nation without the participation of a representative

---

* Presumably de Ferrières means king in the ancient sense of absolute monarch.

assembly. It has only occurred in our day with repugnant dictator-ships. But to enter the minds of the time, one must remember the whole superstition of power, the time-honoured beliefs in Divine Right and inherent aristocratic superiority, which had evolved over nine hundred years. In only two months, this ancient system had vanished. Loyalties and assumptions were shattered as suddenly as the canvas of a drum staved in by a violent blow. The shreds remained around the gaping hole.

His reservations made Louis equivocate about appending his signature to the decrees. He printed them but did not 'promulgate' them, leaving the sheets in his printing house instead of distributing them.

Meanwhile, Paris was still in ferment. The harvest of 1789 had been good but the corn was still not entirely threshed, and the dis-turbances had interrupted transport to the capital. No new loans had been raised by the Assembly, taxes were collected with difficulty, and there was hardly enough money in the Royal Treasury to pay the troops.

Still fearful of attack, the King made the same mistake as two months earlier. He summoned the Flemish regiment of a thousand men from Douai to Versailles to protect the town. This time, he was responding to an appeal from the municipality of Versailles, endorsed by the National Assembly itself.

However this made no difference to excited rumour. Gorsas, the extremist editor of *Le Courier de Versailles*, reported the arrival of the regiment in inflammatory terms. The Palais Royal took up allegations of counter-revolution, once again. To those who wanted a constitutional monarchy, the revolution seemed only half-achieved. Enclosed in his palace, the King could still obstruct the measures passed by the Assembly. Residence at Versailles still gave the Court a certain independence and a symbolic continuity with the ancient, absolute monarchy. It seemed essential to bring the monarch to Paris, where he would be under the control of the people, and where Louis and his Queen would find it more difficult to plot a counter-revolution in secret corridors.

TRAFFIC BETWEEN PARIS
AND VERSAILLES

'My friends, I shall come to Paris with my wife and children; I
entrust my most precious possessions to the love of my good and
faithful subjects.'
LOUIS XVI, to the mob in the Marble Courtyard at Versailles.

On 1 October the King's bodyguards, all from noble families, gave
a banquet in the exquisite Entertainments Room, at the north end of
the Palace, in order to welcome the officers of the Flemish regiment.
The specially designed floor was raised to the same level as the stage,
and a large U-shaped table was laid with all the lavishness of silver,
floral arrangements and the splendid plates and glasses which the
Palace could provide. Round the table sat two hundred officers,
joking, talking, becoming bawdier and more exuberant as the meal
progressed and the supplies of wine grew lower.

This was the last time this beautiful Entertainments Room was
to be used. Within a few years, all its tapestries, mirrors, carvings
and chandeliers had been sold. It would become an appropriately
drab and devastated meeting place for the earnest sansculottes of
Versailles.

Now, as the dessert was served, the King and Queen entered the
Royal Box. The King was fresh from the hunt, and wore riding
boots, and the Queen was carrying the little Dauphin in her arms.
At sight of them, a roar of acclamation went up and the officers
toasted them, enthusiastically. The regimental band struck up a
nostalgic royalist song, which referred to Richard Coeur de Lion,
imprisoned in Austria on his return from a Crusade:

O Richard, O my King,
The universe is abandoning thee . . .

The words were taken up in chorus by everyone.

'I was enchanted with Thursday!' repeated Marie-Antoinette rhapsodically on following days. Now the officers accompanied her to her apartments, and then went outside, under the balcony in the Marble Courtyard, shouting, dancing, and calling for the King to appear.

Outside, beyond the railings of the Place d'Armes, a vast crowd gathered to watch these antics, observing and commenting, like a sullen army which surveys an enemy before attacking.

The rumour soon spread by way of *Le Courier de Versailles* that the tricolour cockade had been trampled underfoot, during this 'orgy'.

'That could not have happened!' said Marie-Antoinette later, before the Revolutionary Tribunal. 'After all, the King himself wore the cockade.'

In Paris, in the Palais Royal, speakers called for the King to be brought to the capital, where he would be with his people, and away from reactionary advisers.

On the morning of Sunday 5 October, a woman borrowed a drum from one of the National Guards in Paris. Beating it, she walked slowly through the market of Les Halles. Other women followed as if she were the Pied Piper of Hamelin. The procession went to the Town Hall, and then along the quays, carrying swords, pikes and even broom handles, and dragging two cannon behind them. Soon, a crowd of six or seven thousand, mainly women, had assembled in the Place Louis XV. Like so many surges of the Revolution, it is difficult to say whether this was a spontaneous movement or not. Afterwards, the royalists accused the Duke of Orléans of master-minding it, but there is no direct evidence for this.

From here, the twelve-mile march to Versailles began in the rain.

Today, the best approach is by motorway. You can also go the way the women marched, via Sèvres. Now, there is a new high bridge, beside a skyscraper, which has replaced the old one across the Seine. In the eighteenth century, the bridge had been deliberately made of wood so that it could be burnt as a defence against this kind of invasion, which had occurred, and been rebuffed, before.* However, in the confusion at Versailles, the order had not been given.

* In 1775, a crowd of 8,000, furious at the price of bread, invaded the palace. Louis spoke to them from a balcony and was shouted down. The mob was dispersed by the Prince de Poix at the head of the royal bodyguard, who promised them bread at a cheaper price. This was not fulfilled.

The route they took via Viroflay is still there. Modern villas have replaced the wretched villages where the women hammered on the doors of bakers' shops, demanding bread. Then as now, the narrow road begins to widen after a few miles, advancing between plane trees. As it approaches Versailles, it expands into the beginning of the Avenue de Paris. You stand on a slope, and, there, below you, is the château of Versailles, half a mile away, with its roofs and chimney stacks, its columns and railed courtyards, like a castle of sleepy giants suddenly revealed.

To imagine Versailles on those two fatal days, you have to see it with heavy rain dripping from the eaves, streaming between the cobbles, turning unpaved surfaces to mud. You have to be there in the middle of an autumn afternoon, with dusk descending, and imagine newly lit candles glimmering through the château windows and in the houses along the Avenue de Paris.

The mob of women was expected. Couriers had warned of their coming. Through the windows of the King's bedroom, the moving mass was just visible in the wispy rain at the top of the long slope which leads down to the château. The excited crowd pushed through a wooden barrier which stood across the Avenue de Paris. They advanced up to the Menus Plaisirs, while ahead of them the soldiers of the Flanders regiment stood erect under the rain in the Place d'Armes, like toy soldiers with their muskets and white trousers. With them were Royal Bodyguards, Dragoons on horse-back, contingents of Swiss, and the Versailles National Guard.

It was a clever manoeuvre, deliberate or accidental, to get women to form this march of protest. Women were more indignant about the lack of bread for their families. Most of them did not work, and therefore did not lose a day's wage. There was also another advantage: when the Captain of Bodyguards, the Duc de Guiche, asked the King whether he should attack, Louis answered: 'Come, come! Against women? You must be joking!'

The Assembly was not particularly glad to see this unkempt crowd. It agreed to admit only fifteen of them. However, other women crept in and even sat among the deputies. The Assembly agreed that twelve should go to the château, see the King, and get him to authorize supplies of bread for Paris. At the same time, taking advantage of the situation, Dr Guillotin and Mounier, the President, were sent to persuade Louis to sign the August Decrees.

The delegation set off through the rain. Already, the Place d'Armes was crowded with women, cajoling, and flirting with the soldiers. After much jostling, five were admitted into the inner courtyard. In their drenched clothes, they climbed the stairs to the state rooms, which were full of courtiers, dressed in their plumage, with silk stockings and velvet coats. For the women, it must have seemed like fairyland after that steady downpour. Somewhere, amidst the gold and ormolu, behind the polished doors, the magician was hidden, while his supercilious and mincing minions flocked around them.

The delegation was admitted to the Council Room. The King stood by a table with a green cloth, surrounded by his ministers. He seemed moved by the description of the famine in Paris, and promised to give orders for the provisioning of the capital. One of the women fainted, overcome by excitement. She was lifted up and given wine out of 'a great gold goblet', and when she thanked the King, he took her in his arms and kissed her on both cheeks.

However, when the women got outside they were assailed and insulted by their fellows. They had obviously been corrupted, or why should they praise the King so fulsomely? Where, anyway, was Louis's signature on the order? The woman who had been kissed was almost hung up by her garters to a neighbouring lamp-post. 'Without the help of several of the royal guards and other honest people, who saved me,' she said later at the official enquiry, 'I would have lost my life.' She and the women returned to the château. The King received them again, and signed the order.

When they got back to the Menus Plaisirs, it was in chaos. A nineteenth-century historian, J. A. Le Roi, comments that it was more like a theatre than the hall of deputies of the nation. 'All the tribunes and most of the benches of the deputies had been invaded by women from Les Halles and men in rags,' he writes. 'There were shouts, interruptions. The words of the parliamentary speakers were scarcely audible.'

The King's orders to provide bread for Paris were, however, listened to. Then the women went round embracing the deputies, including a bishop who was acting as President. Shouts rang out demanding the lowering of the price of all foodstuffs. Cries of '*Vive la Nation!*' resounded.

Those women who had seen the King departed for Paris to pass on the royal order.

Mounier, the President, who had remained in the château, finally got the King to yield once more, and sign the August Decrees. For the first but not the last time, the Assembly had been invaded by the people. But at least it had served a purpose in extracting a royal assent for decrees which laid the foundations of equality and the representation of the people.

Meanwhile, fifteen thousand National Guards had set out from Paris at six that evening. Now, at midnight, the light of flaming torches and the tramp of marching feet announced the arrival of this army at the end of the Avenue de Paris. They halted outside the Menus Plaisirs, and La Fayette went in to explain his presence in Versailles. Then he rode to the château to reassure the King that the National Guard were there to protect him, and they took the place of all the regular soldiers outside the palace, while the Body Guards remained on duty within. At four in the morning, La Fayette went to the Hôtel de Noailles and threw himself on a bed.

By five, everyone seemed asleep. The women slumbered in the churches which had witnessed the splendour of that opening procession, only five months previously. Great bonfires were lit in the outer courtyards, and round these slumped other women and vagrants.

Suddenly, at five thirty, a group pushed open an unlocked gate, opposite the small Cour des Princes on one side of the main façade. In her bedroom, next to the Hall of Mirrors, Marie-Antoinette woke and asked her lady in waiting, Madame Thibault, what was happening. 'Oh, it is only some of those women looking for a place to sleep!' came the reply.

Below, a furniture maker called L'Héritier tried to climb a pillar beneath the balcony overlooking the Marble Courtyard. A shot rang out from a window and he fell to the ground, breaking his skull. In fury, the mob smashed through the gates leading to the Queen's staircase, killing a bodyguard who tried to resist. He was dragged into the courtyard and decapitated with an axe by a rag merchant who came to be known as Coupe-tête Jourdan. Another wounded bodyguard followed, and was also decapitated. Their heads, dripping with blood, were impaled on pikes. Inside the château, the mob rushed up the Queen's Staircase.

The Queen's Staircase has not changed since that fatal night. It still gives a sense of excessive decoration. There is the contrast in colour between the pale steps and rich marble balustrade. On the

71

walls, hardly an inch is left uncovered. There is gilt and sculpture, a *trompe-l'oeil* painting of flowers and figures. Turtle doves sit below a crown of roses, which symbolizes the femininity and majesty of the Queens of France.

Versailles must have been the most sociable place on earth. Not only was it crowded with courtiers, valets, spectators and guards, but its walls and ceilings also abound with human and allegorical figures: heroes and monsters, cherubs and gods, devils and warriors. It must have been difficult ever to feel alone, except in the hidden apartments and dingy attic rooms at the top of the building, where so many of its inhabitants lived.

The early morning of 6 October brought in a new mass of humanity. You have to imagine this staircase where, today, even great clusters of tourists seem small, now filled with howling women and men disguised as women, running up beneath the faint light of the chandeliers, their pikes, swords and axes clanging on the marble as they passed.

At the top stood a solitary bodyguard, Miromandre de Sainte Marie. 'You love your King,' he shouted. 'Yet you come to disturb him in his palace!' The mob flung themselves on him, pulling him by his hair and cartridge belt. Somehow he managed to escape and took refuge in the Salle des Gardes. This hall has changed considerably: its ceiling has been raised and its walls are covered with paintings of Napoleon's Coronation and of other events in the Emperor's life.

Here, where the King's Maundy Thursday ceremony took place, the Body Guards now found refuge. Outside, the mob battered at the white doors, decorated with gold tracery. A panel was smashed, and, inside, the Body Guards piled furniture against it. The mob then broke into the adjoining room, taking the defenders in the flank. While they were fighting, Miromandre opened the door leading to Marie-Antoinette's antechambers, and shouted to the frightened ladies in waiting: 'Save the Queen!'

In the room where Miromandre stood, there is a representation in the corner panel above the door of two courtiers with full Louis XIV wigs, standing shoulder to shoulder, with blue skies above. Beside them, though, is a writhing turmoil of dark limbs, and a demonic face, which seems to represent humans dragged down, or rising up, from Hell. So it must have been that night.

While the struggle went on, Marie-Antoinette was woken behind

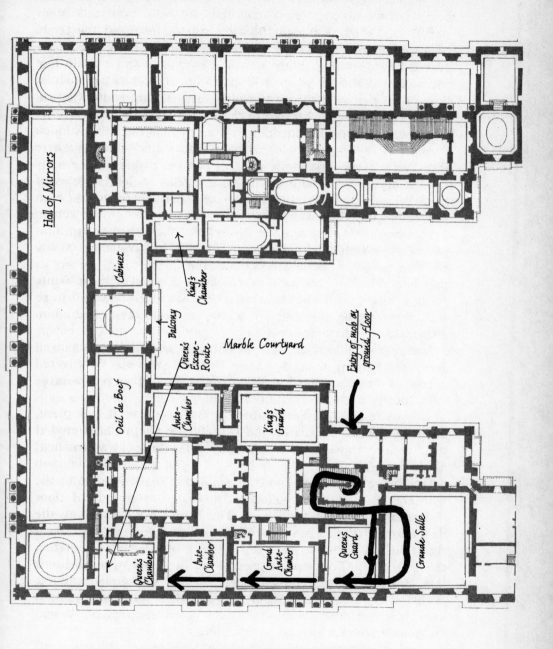

Hall of Mirrors

Cabinet

Ocil de Boef

Balcony

King's Chamber

Queen's Escape-Route

Marble Courtyard

Entry of mob on ground floor

Ante-Chamber

King's Guard

Queen's Chamber

Ante-Chamber

Grand Ante-Chamber

Queen's Guard

Grande Salle

The early morning of 6 October, at Versailles.

the gilded balustrade under the great ostrich feathers in her bed-room, where nineteen royal children had been born and three queens had died. Through the antechambers sounded the crash of breaking wood and cries of 'Death to the Austrian she-wolf!' Her ladies-in-waiting threw a mantle over her, and pushed her through a little door which still exists on the left of her bed. It opens on a narrow passageway which leads straight to the Oeil de Boeuf, the main antechamber to the King's apartments.

You can still see this corridor with permission from the Admin-istrator. Now it is lit by electric light, but you have to imagine it then, with Marie-Antoinette and her women rushing along with candles or oil lamps, with the shouts and noise of fighting echoing from behind. At the end of the passage, the women paused: the interconnecting door was locked.

Standing there, one can feel their panic. Were they going to be pulled out roughly, like clucking chickens, to have their throats cut near the embroidered stools beside the Queen's bed? Or would they be stabbed and hacked to pieces where they stood, by assassins coming through in the semi-darkness? There seemed no escape from this narrow tunnel. Fortunately, a footman heard their cries. After a moment, the door was opened.

Meanwhile, the King had woken and seen the mob in the courtyard surging through to the Queen's Staircase. Pulling on a pair of breeches, he hurried along a parallel secret passage, later mostly destroyed by Louis-Philippe during his restoration of the palace in 1840. Seeing that the Queen was no longer there, Louis questioned the guards who were clustered before her rumpled bed, and returned by the same way that Marie-Antoinette had taken.

One by one, the royal family assembled in the King's bedroom. The Dauphin and Marie-Thérèse, his sister, were fetched from their rooms on the ground floor. The King's brother, the Comte de Provence, with his sallow Piedmontese wife, and Mesdames Adélaïde and Victoire, the King's elderly spinster aunts, all clus-tered together. They must have had the unattractive plainness of their Spanish Bourbon cousins, painted in a family portrait a few years earlier by Goya, except that they were dishevelled with mantles over their nightwear, with none of the immaculate splendour and arrogant ugliness which Goya reproduced.

Marie-Antoinette stood to one side, holding her children, half tearful after her shock, while the four-year-old Dauphin played with his sister's hair and complained that he was hungry.

Meanwhile, the château had been cleared by the Paris National Guard under the command of Captain Gondran, once a French Guard. The mob had reached the last room before the King's apartments when Gondran and his troops arrived. The Body Guards inside were surprised at the sudden silence. Opening the doors, they embraced their rescuers who, according to Carlyle, told them they had come to their assistance because the Body Guards had saved the French Guards at the battle of Fontenoy, some forty years earlier. Such are the links of History, even in the anarchic turmoil of a Revolution.

Outside, the courtyards were crowded. There were shouts for the King who, after a while, went on the balcony and stood with La Fayette as he tried to calm everyone.

Someone came to the Queen and told her that the crowd were now calling for her. Madame de Staël, who was there, describes the scene:

> The Queen then appeared . . . her hair was untidy, her face pale but dignified . . . as all the courtyard was full of men who had firearms in their hands . . . one could see in the Queen's expression what she was afraid of. Nevertheless, she advanced without hesitation, with her two children who served as safeguard.
>
> The crowd seemed softened at seeing the Queen as a mother and political fury was quenched at this sight; those who the night before had perhaps wanted to assassinate her shouted her name to the clouds.

Then came reconciliation with the Body Guards, who were detested for the banquet they had given to the Flanders regiment, and their reputed trampling of the national cockade. A few came onto the balcony and swore the oath to 'Nation, Law and the King'. Some put on the hats of the National Guard and threw their cartridge belts into the crowd who, after previous attempts to kill them, now shouted: 'Long live the Body Guards!'

However, there was one concession which the invading mob had still not extracted. The repeated cry went up: 'The King to Paris!'

Louis called a rapid Council of Ministers in the room where

for more than a century decisions had been made on wars and new buildings, peace treaties and pageants, taxation and help for the starving. After a few minutes, the last decision ever to be taken there was made. La Fayette came out on the balcony and announced that the royal family would go to Paris.

Could Louis have avoided this decision, which stripped him of his home, much of the splendour and prestige of the French monarchy, and, most important of all, made him a prisoner in his own capital? Certainly, a move to Paris was necessary if a new constitutional monarchy was to be formed, as buildings are important symbols. But the way this decision was extracted from him after an attempt to assassinate his wife implied he was a supine puppet whose strings could be moved by violence and assault, a lesson his subjects learnt only too fast.

At this stage, Louis had no alternative. Among the National Guard who, apart from a handful of Body Guards, were his only defence, were many old soldiers of the French Guards who had mutinied in Paris, and who were largely responsible for taking the Bastille. They had forced a reluctant La Fayette to follow the women because they hoped to be re-employed to guard the palace as they had done before the Revolution. If the King stayed at Versailles without giving them a guarantee of this, they had nothing to gain. And the King had not had time to transmit a decision of this sort, even if he had thought of it, or wished it. So, as before, there was virtually no one to defend Louis and his family if he made the unpopular decision to stay at Versailles.

In fact, most of Louis's decisions during the Revolution were inevitable because he failed to anticipate events. As a result, he was driven into corners where all he could do was yield.

Hurriedly, now, preparations began. The Queen left many things behind but took 'a chest of diamonds'. At one o'clock, the royal family descended the winding staircase which has recently been removed but which once climbed up from near the office where tourists now buy entrance tickets. Thus the royal family avoided the sight of blood on the Queen's Staircase.

They were never to see Versailles again. An Englishman, Sir John Dean, describes the state of the château thirteen years later:

Who, without emotion, could look at these broken windows, now boarded up, these doors falling from their hinges, the grass covering the cobbles in the courtyards? All the royal emblems have been scratched out, various cornices are pitted with musket fire, and over all these things, there is a sense of approaching ruin. The apartments are full of filthy individuals who wander to left and right as if they were in their own homes. Rain comes through in various places so that, if the necessary measures are not taken, everything will soon be completely destroyed.

The last, bizarre journey to Paris took six hours through mud trampled the day before by thousands of feet. First came the women who had arrived the previous afternoon; then carts full of corn, which had been taken from the markets of Versailles; then the National Guard and the royal coach. Finally came the carriages of the ministers and of a hundred deputies, all surrounded by dancing, exuberant women, with men discharging their fire-arms as a sign of rejoicing, even over the King's coach. Marie-Antoinette had feared that the heads of slain Body Guards would be carried on pikes beside them. But those bearing them had already hastened triumphantly to Paris, and been arrested for their pains, which shows that some sense of order and discipline remained, in spite of everything.

The royal family's destination was the Tuileries, a Renaissance palace stretching between the present Gardens and the courtyards of the Louvre. It has now disappeared, burnt by the Commune in 1871. Then, it had a central pavilion and two on either side, breaking up the long three-storey façade.

Many today think the main entrance of this palace was through the gardens. In fact it was by way of the courtyards on the other side, like most châteaux, based presumably on medieval fortified farmhouses with a courtyard in front and fields behind. Now, if it still existed, the Tuileries would form the western side of the vast rectangle of the Louvre. Then, the courtyards of the palace and a jumble of houses, mansions and small streets filled the whole quadrangle where the Pyramid now stands, and reached over the present Rue de Rivoli.

Unoccupied by the Court for more than sixty years, the Tuileries had been given over to 'grace and favour' residents. As a result, it had become a rabbit warren of partitions and little rooms, protruding onto staircases, where families and individuals had marked out their domains.

77

When news of the royal arrival reached Paris in the early afternoon, immediate notice was served on all these inhabitants. As happens when smoke is blown down rabbit holes, innumerable hidden beings now scuttled from their burrows. The neighbouring streets were suddenly crowded with overladen carts trundling to relatives' homes, or hastily found lodgings. Within five hours, the palace was empty. Sometimes the efficiency of the Ancien Régime surprises, at least in matters of procedures affecting the royal family, as does the smoothness of State weddings and funerals in Britain today.

It was almost eight o'clock before the tired and hungry royal family crossed Paris by way of the Hôtel de Ville, where they were welcomed. The Tuileries had been sparsely and hurriedly furnished, but it was ready to receive them. In the next few days, all the extraordinary apparatus of the monarchy was fitted into this château, built by Catherine de Medici two hundred years previously. Houses and hotels in the vicinity were rented, or taken over to accommodate the Masters of Ceremonies, the Falconers, the Grooms of the Bedchamber, Cup Bearers and Officers of the Roast, who, no longer hidden in the warrens of Versailles, amazed the Parisians with their numbers and the quaintness of their titles.

Paris had recaptured its King, and made him sign the Abolition of Feudalism and the Declaration of the Rights of Man. Once again, it was not the Assembly that had achieved this but a mob of ragged, hungry furies.

Because he had yielded, the King was popular again. But this was yet another step in the loss of that dignity which made him King, another surrender to a threatening mob, another confession of a lack of will and firmness.

II

Destruction of an Uneasy Peace

[8]

PARIS: ACHIEVEMENT

'It is my belief, gentlemen, that it is essential in a great empire such as ours for men placed by fate in a position of dependence to understand the just limits of natural liberty rather than hope for an extension of those limits.'

MALOUET, a monarchist deputy of the Assembly.

In revolutions, there is usually a halcyon period when freedom seems won at last, when a brave new society is about to begin. It is a period of exuberance before real problems arise. So it was in Russia after the Civil War of 1918–20. So it was in newly emancipated colonies after 1945. So it was in France after the King had been brought to Paris.

The nearest I have come to witnessing this period of release was in Algeria in 1963, after independence from the French. I went out to start a school of English and found the buildings of the city repainted as a symbol of the freshness of a new start. Slogans, including '*Vive l'Enseignement!*', were on the walls, and taxi drivers refused to accept my fares because I was an educationalist come to help them.

This Algerian experience gave me at least a feeling of what it must have been like in France during the eighteen months after October 1789. The trappings of the old régime were still around: the government buildings, the street names of former heroes, the crowds of disgruntled European reactionaries in cafés and restaurants. Once I spent an extraordinary evening having drinks with a new Algerian government official on solitary chairs set in the middle of the vast, empty hall of the evacuated Prefecture.

As in France during this period of pause, there were those who had taken over the property of others who had left. I met an assistant at a garage who had assumed its ownership, and drove around in his *patron*'s new car. There were also people working into the night in new administrative posts they had inherited unexpectedly. I remember the recently appointed head of the telephone system in Algiers who had previously been a technician, never allowed inside a French house to install telephones. Like the 'canaille' in France before 1789, he had been despised and excluded, in this case because he was an Arab.

Once I went to a Press Conference given by Ben Bella, the new President. Talk was all of Liberty, reform and the great future of Algeria. Despite my knowledge of revolutions, I almost believed it. Why shouldn't this new Republic, owned by co-operatives and the people, work? Maybe similar revolutionary régimes had led to military dictatorships, but this, perhaps, would be different.*

If idealistic talk had this effect on me, a twentieth-century citizen, one can imagine how the French felt in 1790 with no previous experience of the bitterness and turmoil of a revolution. Both in Algeria and in France, the whole population gave themselves to endless talk of politics and utopian ideas. They felt they were living in the dawn.

In Paris, we now searched for traces of the more distant revolution, and explored what was left of the Palace of the Tuileries and of the site to which the Assembly had finally moved on arrival from Versailles. We were helped by meeting a M. Jacques Hébert, who worked in the French Railways. (He was no relation of the Hébert in the Revolution, the small, bloodthirsty anarchist who edited an extremist paper, *Le Père Duchesne*, accused Marie-Antoinette of incest with her son, and organized anti-religious festivals.) This M. Hébert had always been fascinated by the Tuileries, perhaps just because it no longer existed. 'What is so interesting,' he once said, 'is to imagine the Tuileries, there, in that gap, three hundred metres long, between those two surviving pavilions of Flore and Marsan. Imagining it is more rewarding than visiting a real building and being disappointed at all the new furnishing and redecoration that would inevitably have been perpetrated.'

As we stood in the Tuileries Gardens with its plain gravel walks, its straight rows of leafy trees and its round ponds sprayed by fountains, Jacques Hébert gave us a dramatic exposé of where the various places had been.

* In fact, within two years, Colonel Boumedienne, the Commander-in-Chief, had imprisoned Ben Bella and imposed a rigid military dictatorship which is only now being relaxed a little.

'From the end of 1789, this was the new centre of government,' he said, waving a thin arm around. He pointed to the end of the Gardens. 'There, was the Tuileries, the palace of the King.' The arm swung towards the Rue de Rivoli. 'There, was the National Assembly.' The arm swung again like a mobile signpost in the direction of the Place de la Concorde. 'There, was the Place de la Révolution, where many of those who belonged to the Assembly and the Court ultimately lost their lives on the guillotine.' The arm dropped suddenly, and twitched a little by his side, like a restless snake.

As we walked towards the empty space where once stretched the long narrow building of the Tuileries, we passed statues of gods and naked nymphs, with sea-gulls perched on heads or shoulders.

'Only the two end pavilions survive,' said M. Hébert, 'and they have been refurbished. You can see old photographs of the charred remains of the palace in the archives after it was burnt by the Commune in 1871. The outline is still clear. But the government of the day decided it wasn't worth rebuilding, and removed it.'

M. Hébert knew everything about the Tuileries from 1570, when Catherine de Medici had built it, right through to its occupation by Louis XVI, Napoleon, Louis XVIII, Charles X, Louis-Philippe and, finally, Napoleon III. 'It was after all, the home of all our last kings and Emperors – which is why the Communards burnt it down,' he exclaimed. 'Like so many people in the Revolution itself, they wanted to expunge the past.'

As we faced the small Arch of the Carousel, on which once reared the famous bronze horses plundered from Venice, which in turn had been plundered from Constantinople, Hébert motioned us to stop. 'We are now standing just inside the original entrance. Here, there were two fluted pillars on either side,' he said, looking into thin air. 'Within, was a large peristyle from which, on the right, mounted a grand staircase to the first floor of this central pavilion, called L'Horloge.' He looked up as if he could see it. 'This staircase opened onto a lofty reception room with windows looking out on both the courtyard and the gardens. A door on the left led to the King's apartments, arranged as at Versailles with antechambers, the King's official bed-chamber, and the Council room. Beyond this were the King's private apartments: the bedroom where he really slept, the Dauphin's bedroom, and a study-library.

'The Queen's apartments were on the ground floor, directly to

83

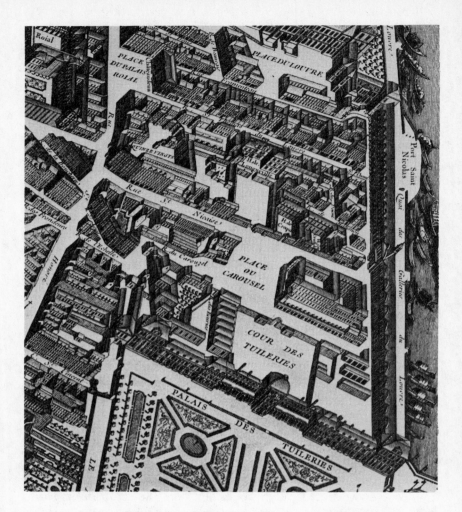

The Palace of the Tuileries in 1790. Only the two end pavilions remain and all the houses up to the Louvre have now been cleared. *Bibliothèque Nationale.*

our left. The rest of the building was occupied by other members of the royal family and the Court.'

As he spoke, work was going on behind us to complete the Pyramid which stands today in the open space before the Louvre. In front were the Gardens and the long, wooded avenue of the Champs Elysées, rising to the Arch of Triumph in the distance.

'Did the Court live very differently from Versailles?' I asked.

'Not as far as ceremonies went. The King still had his *Lever* and *Coucher* and all the other rituals. But the royal family were virtually prisoners. When they first arrived, crowds gathered in the gardens to catch a glimpse of them. People even climbed through the windows. Their only exercise was walks in the gardens, where the public were admitted after noon. The King could only go hunting in the Bois de Boulogne. In April 1790 they were allowed to go to St Cloud for Easter, but not the year after. The King, particularly, suffered from this lack of exercise, and became fatter and more sluggish. The populace and the Assembly were afraid they would escape, which of course they eventually tried to do.

'The Court itself was much the same, except it was without those who had emigrated. On one occasion, the King had to warn them not to make arrogant remarks about the new constitutional government and its officials. You can imagine all those young bloods, surrounding their King, always ready to pick a fight, or express their scorn for the new régime. The King's brother, the Comte d'Artois, had set up a centre of counter-revolution in Turin, and many at Court had relatives there, and were sure the Old Régime would shortly be restored.'

The whole thing was so extraordinary, I thought. Here, within a few months, people who had been able to do virtually what they liked were suddenly at the mercy of an elected Assembly which had the power to transform France, whatever King or nobles felt.

'And did the King accept everything?'

'I don't think so. He didn't want upheavals or bloodshed. He was prepared to temporize, and certainly gave no open support to his brother over the frontier. But at the same time, his pride was inevitably hurt, and he felt that his rights to which he had become accustomed over fifteen years of autocracy had been affronted. Now, he was no longer the Lord's Anointed, the sole autocrat, but simply the executive officer of the new government, paid from the Civil List. His title was changed to 'King of the French' instead of 'King of France'. Also, although he was popular, it must have been galling to be almost a prisoner. He had gone as far as he was prepared to go in his royal session in the States-General on June 23rd (see p. 29). Nevertheless, he went along with everything and hoped it would all work out. Don't forget he was a great optimist. He felt that sooner or later people would come round to his point of view. It was at this time that Mirabeau himself changed sides and worked secretly for him, with a salary from the Court of 6,000 livres a month. Although Mirabeau did little except give advice which the King and Queen rarely took, this was evidence to the King that the most outstanding revolutionaries could change their coats.'

'And the Assembly was only a few hundred yards away?' I asked.

'Indeed. Shall we go and see where it was?'

We left the thin line of empty air containing imaginary buildings, furniture, people, chandeliers, the muffled tread of footmen's steps.

As we crossed the Gardens the wind sprang up, jostling the leaves of the trees. There were flowers round the ponds but hardly any grass, and suddenly there was something bleak about these broad avenues of gravel. Everything was so formal and uncomforting, with the hard surfaces underfoot and those cold statues beckoning to nothing. It had none of the lushness of its nearest equivalent in London, St James's Park. The Tuileries Gardens were rigidly planned, brittle, almost ready to crack, it seemed. You could not even imagine dalliance in its sparse groves.

We followed the side of the Terrasse des Feuillants, a raised, flat bank between the Rue de Rivoli and the gardens. About halfway down, steps rose towards it. On either side were statues representing tigers, with their teeth buried in the flesh of a boar on the right and a rhinoceros on the left.

'These steps led to the Assembly,' said M. Hébert. 'It was called the Manège as it had been Louis XV's riding school when, as a boy-king, he lived in the Tuileries. The Rue de Rivoli, here, did not exist. Then it was turfed and used as a riding ground. All the remaining area was taken up by the monasteries of the Feuillants and Capuchins, with gardens, cloisters, churches, refectories and dormitories. It all became national property when the Assembly confiscated Church possessions in November 1789.'

'What happened to the monks?'

Jacques Hébert shrugged his shoulders. 'Oh, some returned to the world, and were given pensions. Others were collected together in monasteries that continued under the supervision of the State.'

'And what was the actual Assembly like?'

'Because it was originally a riding school, it was not very convenient. For one thing, it was ten times as long as it was broad. The deputies were ranged in six rows opposite the President's table. That's how the political distinction of Left and Right arose. Those who wanted to strengthen the King's position, and also have a

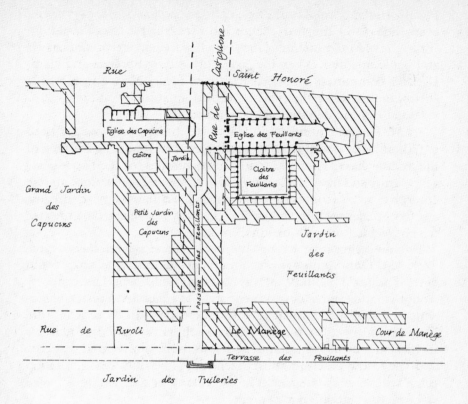

Area where the National Assembly installed themselves, with the 'new' Rue de Rivoli and Rue Castiglione imposed. Le Nôtre, *Carnavalet*

second Chamber of Lords as in Britain, sat on the right. Those who wanted one Chamber and a limited or non-existent royal veto, sat to the left.'

'And were the public admitted?'

'Yes – they had five hundred seats, distributed at either end of the long hall. The sessions were chaotic with their continual interruptions, with deputies walking and chatting in the space in the middle, called the "Piste", while the ushers and the President continually shouted for order. But the deputies worked hard: they attended long hours, starting at nine in the morning. And then there were thirty committees where much of the work was done.'

I looked out from the Terrasse at the Rue de Rivoli, with its heavy traffic. In front, was the elegant Rue Castiglione, leading up to the

Place Vendôme: solid buildings, arcades, expensive shops, cars on every side. Over the years, there had been a triple transformation. First, the old monastic buildings which were once resorts of prayer and contemplation. Then the Assembly, filling libraries and chapels with committees, frenzied with new ideas. Now a fashionable shopping centre for the rich. It seemed a natural evolution.

'What did the deputies actually achieve?'

As M. Hébert enumerated the legislation that was passed, I tried to fathom what was at its root. In simple terms it was the triumph of the middle class. There were now opportunities for the bourgeoisie in the army and navy and the administration, and restrictions on free enterprise were abolished. All municipal and judicial posts became elective. Juries were introduced so that it was an elected committee which decided on guilt or innocence.

From all legislative activity the working and poorer classes were excluded. Only those who paid a certain minimum of taxes could vote. The logic behind this was that only those who had property would vote for stable government and the general interest. Censorship was abolished, which gave free expression to those who were literate, and by 1792 there were over a hundred and fifty journals in the Paris area. Protestants and Jews were mostly middle-class, and they now received full citizenship. The only real hesitation came with freeing the slaves in the colony of San Domingo, who were neither literate nor bourgeois.

The structure the Assembly created was generally accepted. In any case, the new army of the National Guard under its commander, La Fayette, protected what had been achieved. There was a new emphasis on logic and order: metres and kilos were introduced to clear up the irregularity of different local measures. Eighty-three departments took the place of the old, irregular provinces. In many ways it was not very different from the modern State we know today, with government beginning to take over welfare and education from the Church which now was deprived of its wealth.

The National Assembly's great achievement was laying the foundation of modern democratic government. Today this achievement seems less remarkable, because over two hundred years we have got used to it and – especially in the last few decades – the conflict in Europe between 'workers' and the 'middle class' has been reduced, with more and more 'workers' becoming 'middle-class' as the economy has grown and wealth has been distributed more widely.

88

15. A contemporary playing-card with the Duke of Orléans as King of Spades (*Piques*). It thus emphasizes him as an alternative to Louis XVI and as leader of the mob which was armed with pikes. *Bibliothèque Nationale*

16. The Palais Royal Gardens today, empty and formal in contrast to the 1789 centre of revolutionary activity. (See p. 40–1) Author's photograph.

17. A lady of quality being whipped in the Palais Royal Gardens for spitting on the portrait of Necker, the popular Finance Minister. *Bibliothèque Nationale*

Une Femme de condition, fouettée pour avoir craché sur le portrait de M.ʳ Neker.

18. The Place Louis XV, before the Revolution. Later Place de la Révolution, and now Place de la Concorde. Note the Gabriel buildings which are still there, and the statue of Louis XV where the obelisk now stands. *Carnavalet*

19. The first armed clash of the Revolution, when, after dispersing a procession, German hussars swept into the Tuileries Gardens. The horses by Coysevox, the ramps and the pond are all still there. (See p. 42) Lallemand, *Carnavalet*

20. The mob's attack on the Invalides, which today is identical. They were in search of arms, and found muskets, but the gunpowder was in the Bastille. (See p. 44) Lallemand, *Carnavalet*

21. Attack on the Bastille. (See p. 52–5) Cholat, *Musée Renan-Sheffer*

LE S'QUELETTE au MASQUE de FER,
Trouvé, Par la Nation, Ce 22 Juillet 1789.

22. Discovery of the skeleton of the Man in the Iron Mask in a cell in the Bastille after its capture. This, like so much else, was a myth. *Carnavalet*

23. Destruction of the Bastille which began immediately after its capture. Robert, *Carnavalet*

24. The Queen's Staircase of the Palace, up which the mob swept in their attempt to murder the Queen.

25. The Marble Courtyard of the Palace where the mob assembled in front of the balcony.

26. Confrontation between the mob and the royal family at Versailles before the King decided to go to Paris. *Bibliothèque Nationale*

27. Louis XVI wielding a pick in the preparation of the Champ de Mars for the Feast of the Federation in 1790. (See p. 89) *Bibliothèque Nationale*

28. Dance on the site of the Bastille for the Feast of the Federation. Note the stumps of the towers holding seats for spectators. *Bibliothèque Nationale*

29. The Feast of the Federation on the Champ de Mars with the Altar to the Patrie in the middle. The Eiffel Tower now stands behind the arched building at the end. *Bibliothèque Nationale*

30. Satire on nationalization of Church lands. The fat *abbé* on the left has become the thin one on the right. *Bibliothèque Nationale*

AIR *Où courez vous M.^r L'Abbé.*

Ne redoutez plus les Brocards
Gentes Nonettes beaux frocards

De la Metamorphose

He bien

L'Amour rit et pour cause

Et vous mentendez bien .

31. 'I'm shaved in the morning
and get married in the
evening.' Many clergy
abandoned their orders.
Bibliothèque Nationale

32. The village of Cluny with
the outline of the destroyed
Abbey imposed on roofs and
streets. Note that the only part
which is left is in the top right-
hand corner. (See p. 97–8)
Editions Combier.

In 1789–91, however, only four million out of about twenty-five paid the necessary taxes to qualify as electors, and even fewer had the means needed to stand for election to the National Assembly. The new State was threatened on both sides. On one, the mass of the people who had no more electoral influence on their destiny than they had had before; on the other, those who had been stripped of privileges which for centuries they had regarded as their rights.

Nevertheless, in the summer of 1790 divisions did not seem deep. The harvests of 1789 and 1790 were good, and the economy was thriving. There was cause for celebration, and Festivals took place all over France. The climax came on 14 July, when over a hundred thousand delegates came to Paris. The Champ de Mars, which a year earlier had been the camping ground of royal troops, was transformed into a great oval of seats with the banners of the eighty-three departments stuck into the ground, dividing spectators from 'actors'. Enthusiastic volunteers helped with the preparations. Even the King came to lend a hand with a shovel. A large marquee was put up for the Court and royal family in front of the Ecole Militaire, and an altar to the *Patrie* was built in the centre. While, over towards what is now the Eiffel Tower, a tall archway was built, on top of which spectators could also stand.

The ceremony began with a procession lasting two hours. Between the deputies and the National Guard was a contingent of children and another of old people, representing the two extremes of life. Mass was said by Talleyrand as Bishop of Autun. La Fayette was the main actor in his role of Commander of the National Guard, taking the oath amidst the roar of cannon and the acclamations of the crowd, while the King swore to uphold the new régime, within his marquee because it was raining.

It was a kind of delirium. The Revolution seemed over. Had not the King gone to the Assembly the previous February to show his support for the new principles? Had not all noble titles been abolished, scarcely a month earlier? Was not the new constitution almost completed? There was a new rallying cry, 'The Nation', which linked everyone to the idea of one free united country. Celebrations took place in towns and villages everywhere. Traditional practices were adapted to new requirements: painted angels waved tricolour ribbons; Phrygian bonnets hung from royal crowns. 'It was an exaltation such as one cannot imagine,' wrote Pauline de Tourzel, the governess of the royal children.

Wordsworth, a young undergraduate, arrived at Calais, where the population were rejoicing in the streets. With a friend, he walked through Artois and Burgundy, noticing the window garlands, the flowers on triumphal arches. By the side of the Rhône, he and his friend were invited to banquets provided by the local commune, and ate and drank in village squares under the stars, dancing with girls who wore tricolour sashes round their waists. Those they met were full of hope and enthusiasm. It is to this time that his lines from *The Prelude* belong: '. . . benevolence and blessedness spread like a fragrance everywhere, when spring has left no corner of the land untouched.'

However, two days before the great Festival in Paris the Assembly had passed a measure which was to split France, and which Talleyrand described as 'perhaps the greatest political mistake of the Assembly'. This was the Civil Constitution of the Clergy. As Don Quixote had said in alarm to Sancho Panza: 'We have collided with the Church, friend Sancho!'

[9]

THE BEGINNINGS OF SCHISM

'Families are divided among themselves, fathers disagree with their children, husbands with their wives, friends mistrust their old friends . . .'

CHARRIER DE LA ROCHE, October 1791, writing about
the effects of the Civil Constitution of the Clergy.

The Civil Constitution of the Clergy provoked the age-old conflict between a mystical, spiritual view of the world and more concrete concepts such as order and social usefulness. In the opinion of most deputies of the National Assembly, it seemed sensible that, as with other public offices, the clergy should be elected by those they served, rather than appointed from above. They considered applying this also to army officers, but conscious of the divisions this might produce, abandoned the idea. It was a pity they were bolder with the clergy.

The Revolution also saw the flowering of the belief, which continues to our day, that control by a State elected by the 'people' ensures impartiality and a kind of fairness above the tussles and self-seeking of individuals, or of groups. The effects of authoritarian bureaucracy and of self-interested groups within elected government had not yet been demonstrated. Was it not logical, therefore, that priests be paid like civil servants and swear allegiance to the State and to the new Revolutionary settlement?

It is important to emphasize that these assumptions did not derive from anti-clerical feeling in the Assembly, where most deputies were still Catholic. Neither was the Church, in these first few years, unsympathetic to the Revolution. True, the suzerainty and privileges of the bishops and archbishops were threatened by many of the reforms, but with the idealism at the beginning of the Revolution, the mass of the clergy saw reform as a return to the simplicity of the early Church. Much of the impatience with hierarchy and pomp which in England expressed itself in Wesleyanism, also existed in France. The curés in the States-General had played an important role by mass desertions to the Third Estate in June 1789 (see p. 31). 'It is those two hundred and eighty bastard priests who have wrecked the Revolution for us,' said the reactionary Comte d'Antraigues, who had hoped for a purely aristocratic coup.

The assumption, today, that the Church has always been an ally of reaction is partly an effect of the French Revolution rather than anything else. As the eminent French historian, François Furet, has written: 'The theocratic and anti-clerical schools (in the nineteenth century) spread the idea that there had always been a basic conflict between the Church and the Revolution, but the men of 1789 were certainly not aware of any such conflict.'

Even the confiscation of Church lands produced no violent reaction among the clergy, although in the Assembly the Abbé Maury warned that violation of the property rights of the Church might soon spread to those of the bourgeoisie. However, it was also argued that the land of the Church did not belong to the clergy, and that the pious who had originally bestowed it, left it to them as managers rather than owners.

In any case, it was not so much the mass of the clergy who were affected by the nationalization of Church property, but rather the monasteries and convents who were in a state of decay, with fewer novices coming forward every year. In the great Abbey of Cluny, the hundreds of monks at its apogee had sunk to a mere forty in 1789.

Initially even the Civil Constitution of the Clergy produced little demur, and the King signed it on the advice of two archbishops. Ever since 1516, there had been a Concordat with the Papacy agreeing that the King should appoint bishops, and through them, the remainder of the clergy. All that seemed to have happened was that the Assembly as well as the King had inherited this agreement.

However, Pope Pius VI was an Italian aristocrat who instinctively opposed the Revolution and disapproved of the Declaration of the Rights of Man. In Rome, he was influenced by the reactionary French Ambassador, Cardinal Bernis. Politically, he was disturbed by the French threat to the Papal territory of Avignon, which in June 1790 had demanded reintegration with France. He was also piqued that the Civil Constitution had been decreed without consulting him. Two days after Louis signed his assent, in September

1790, he received a letter from the Pontiff denouncing it. No public pronouncement was received from Rome for a further eight months, but in March 1791 the Civil Constitution was publicly condemned. This meant that those priests who had taken the oath were virtually excommunicated. According to Catholic doctrine, their sacraments were valueless. Some of the ousted priests who had refused to take the oath still lived in their parishes, and many of the congregations ignored the new 'intruder' as he was called, and heard Mass in the houses of their former parish priests.

Thus, throughout France, two layers of opposing loyalties were created. Over the frontier, the counter-revolutionaries led by Louis XVI's brother, the Comte d'Artois, had tried in vain to abduct the King and to rouse provinces, particularly in the south-east. Now the Assembly itself had given them their opportunity.

Much of the violence of the Revolution derived from paranoiac myths. We have seen this already with La Grande Peur: the fear of an aristocratic conspiracy and of troops coming over the frontier (see p. 62). How far these rumours were true was secondary to the effect they had on the minds of Frenchmen. The problem was psychological rather than real. Those who had always feared a counter-revolution now saw in their midst priests, with their flocks, who had openly refused to swear allegiance to the Revolution. The delicate balance created by the Assembly was disturbed by split loyalties to Pope or government, and by the antagonism between constitutional priests and nonjurors as they competed for the allegiance of parishioners all over France.

Where was the best place to search for the effects and traces of this divisive decree? I decided to go to Chartres to see M. Roger Joly, a local historian who had lived there all his life, and then go on to Cluny.

Chartres reminds me of Toledo, the heart of Catholic Spain. It has no dramatic gorge, but a quiet, narrow river which was once spanned by a whole church, that of St André, which now has vanished. However, the streets are also narrow, winding round the hill on which stands the magnificent Cathedral which has some of the most beautiful stained glass in France. Despite the destruction of so many churches in the Revolution, Chartres still has the feeling of a clerical town, perhaps because the Cathedral with its pilgrims and tourists still dominates it.

Shivering, feeling something of what it must have been like to wander through a medieval town in winter, I made my way over snowy paving stones to the Rue Grenouillère, where M. Joly lived. On the river, by an old mill and ancient wooden houses, ducks and geese had the temerity to dive into the icy water.

I rang M. Joly's bell, and soon we were sitting in his warm study on the first floor of his modern house, looking out at snowy roofs.

'Here in Chartres, the Bishop, Lubersac, was very much in favour of reform,' said M. Joly. 'He was a friend of Brissot, who later became the leader of the Girondin party, and who was a native of the town. Only the eighty canons in the Cathedral were against the Revolution at the beginning, partly because it was they who benefited most from the three million livres which the chapter possessed. It must have been extraordinary in those days to be prominent in the Church,' emphasized M. Joly. 'The eldest son of a noble family went into the army, and the second was often compelled to take orders, usually without a vocation. It had been like that since the Middle Ages. The higher clergy lived like lords, which most of them were, and did very little. In Chartres, many of the canons lived elsewhere and some had never even visited the Cathedral.

'For this and other reasons, the mass of the clergy welcomed the Revolution. Even the King wanted reform, perhaps just because he was religious. But the Civil Constitution of the Clergy went too far by failing to get the agreement of the Pope. Because of this, the new constitutional priests were often abused and shunned by their congregations.'

M. Joly began to ruffle through a book. 'Let me find it. Yes, here we are. A constitutional priest who comes to his new parish at a little place called Blaive, as early as May 1791.'

We read it together:

'Very far from being welcomed as a curé should be,' wrote the priest, 'no one even had the courtesy to allow me to speak. I only saw some women who heaped insults on me, followed shortly by men who seemed to me to have no object but to maltreat me, as one among them asked me if I was not already a devil.'

'Already a devil,' repeated M. Joly. 'You must remember that the mass of the population were superstitious and devoted to the Church, particularly the women, who influenced their men. It's fashionable to believe that the eighteenth century was the Age of

94

Reason. This might have been so, but such ideas were confined to the literate. In the villages, the priest was the peasants' main guide, the interpreter of scriptures which most could not read, and the holder of the keys to Heaven. He was intimately involved in all the rituals of their lives from baptisms to funerals. He was also the main link with the outside world. When the Dutch and the English were advancing on Paris at the end of the War of the Spanish Succession, Louis XIV rallied his people by sending out an appeal to their loyalty and patriotism which was read at the Sunday sermon all over France. The priest was an essential part of communication from government to people. His sermons were a guide to morality and political attitudes. Now, suddenly, there were two claimants to respect and loyalty. The division is with us still.'

'Yes,' I said, 'I remember an English historian, Denis Brogan, writing that the history of nineteenth-century France is really the same as that of the French Church.'

'Yes – and priests were also the great distributors of alms to the poor,' added M. Joly. 'They were our Welfare State condensed into one person.'

After further discussion, we decided to go out for lunch. Then we walked round the town. Roger Joly told me that the population of Chartres had been 18,000 at the beginning of the Revolution, compared to 80,000 today. The main problem in the eighteenth century had been hunger, although the Beauce district, surrounding Chartres, was known as 'the granary of France'. But the town's proximity to Paris meant that most of the corn was transported to the capital.

Side by side with the splendour of the Cathedral, Chartres was then as primitive as any small town. Street lighting consisted of oil lamps fixed against the walls. 'Lighting was not so necessary,' said M. Joly. 'Chartres was an agricultural community: people went to bed at sunset and rose at dawn. They had very little idea of time, apart from the chimes of church clocks and the position of the sun. About 75 per cent were illiterate. The sewage went into the river where clothes were washed, but the smell was not as bad as industrial pollution today.'

Before the Revolution, the town was permeated by the Church. In memoirs written before he was guillotined, Brissot explained why he left Chartres when a young man: 'Everyone was in a state of torpor which contrasted too strongly with the movement of my ideas for it not to sadden my existence.' There was a limiting sense of being cooped up within the walls and towers surrounding the town. In all there were eleven parish churches, as well as three congregations in the Cathedral. All for eighteen thousand inhabitants.

As we approached the Cathedral, the square outside was full of young people who had come on visits organized by religious groups. Banners floated among them. 'We still have crowds of visitors,' said Joly. 'In the Middle Ages, Chartres was on the pilgrim route to Santiago. Now, we get foreigners too. The pity is that they only stay a morning or an afternoon, and leave us little money. But we do have three thousand people employed in tourism.'

We entered the Cathedral. The glory of red and blue stained glass was all around us. Chartres had been one of the first Cathedrals where flying buttresses were used, which meant that the roof did not need to be supported to such an extent by the walls. Great areas could therefore be given over to stained glass. As we walked round, I remembered Hesketh Pearson writing that the difference between Shaw and Wilde in Chartres was that Shaw spouted historical detail and talked about methods of manufacturing stained glass, while Wilde told vivid, improvised stories about the figures in the windows.

'Was the Cathedral damaged during the Revolution?' I asked.

'There was talk of pulling it all down,' said M. Joly. 'As with other Cathedrals such as Le Mans. In Marseilles, a builder pulled down the Cathedral in a few days, sold all the materials, and made his fortune. Luckily, nothing happened here. The Revolutionaries wanted to smash the Virgin of the Assumption, but Sergent, a deputy from the Convention, suggested putting a Phrygian bonnet on her head and thus turning her into a revolutionary goddess. So she was saved. Some statues were found recently, buried in a bank near here, and are now at the Cluny Museum in Paris. The real damage was done to parish churches.'

As we left and walked through the streets, we crossed a square which had once held a church, and the outline of the former building was marked on the paving stones. By the Abbaye de St Pierre was another large square which had once contained a church. 'Later, during the real anticlericalism of the Revolution, they pulled down eight of the eleven churches,' said Roger Joly. 'Demolition was big business. You not only acquired all the building material: the beams, the stone, the lead on the roofs. But you could also sell or rent out the land. It was even better with the city walls because you also had the moat.

'It is all very sad when you think of the initial enthusiasm and idealism turning so rapidly to destructiveness. Before 1789, the town was very devout. Afterwards, in 1817, it was declared *terre de mission*, a place where missionaries were needed. Sad. Very sad.'

Some months later, we travelled to Cluny near Mâcon, where we also saw some of the châteaux burnt or attacked in La Grande Peur in 1789. Here once stood the great Abbey which in the eleventh and twelfth centuries was the centre of a network of over three hundred monasteries all over Europe. Its reforming rules had been followed by other Orders, and its Basilica had been the largest church in Christendom before the building of the present St Peter's in Rome. Now, only vestiges remain.

In Cluny we went to a café for lunch and suddenly realized that we were sitting, munching sandwiches, on part of the actual site of the old, vast church. Afterwards we went through a door on the right of what had been the Basilica, and wandered through the cloisters and original monks' cells which are now used as bedrooms for the Government College which has been installed here. We also visited the few remaining chapels. In one, we were confronted with an altar and great arching pillars, huge enough to be the end of a large church. However, when we turned, there was no long vista but only a broad recent wall, blocking the perspective.

From November 1789, everything had belonged to the State, and the sale of objects in the interior of the Basilica soon began. The invaluable books and manuscripts in the library were also dispersed and sold. Records show the first list of things seized, including crosses, statues of the Virgin, reliquaries, chandeliers, and two figures containing the bones of St Hugues and St Mayeul. The monks were given the option of their 'liberty' with a pension, or of joining another religious community. It is interesting that as many as thirty-eight chose their liberty and only two decided to continue the religious life. The last Mass of all those celebrated in the 796 years since the Abbey's foundation took place in October 1791, with only a dozen monks attending. All the vestments and hangings were burnt, and the considerable weight of 25,000 kilos of gold and 18,000 of silver was extracted. For several years the vast Basilica remained empty, stripped of everything, and no longer maintained or repaired.

Later, in 1797–8, it was divided into four parts, each of which was sold for a song. Builders started the demolition by smashing all the windows. The lead was taken out of the rose window above the entrance and it fell suddenly, splintering on the steps below. One of the belfries was mined and another, with most of its support removed, collapsed with an overwhelming crash and clouds of dust. The municipality of Cluny protested to the central government in Paris, but there was no response. By the Restoration of 1814, there was little left of this vast church and of all the treasures that had been accumulated for eight centuries. It must have been a little like the sacking of St Peter's in Rome by the Moors in AD 839, when all the early treasures were loaded onto ships which sank without trace in a storm off Sicily. At least in the case of Cluny, the objects were sold, and most still exist somewhere in France. But of the building, only the stumps of the pillars on the large empty space and the belfries of L'Eau Bénite and the Horloge still remained.

Most of the destruction took place under the Consulate and Empire, but as with other churches all over France, the momentum began with the Civil Constitution of the Clergy, which was to contribute to the fall of the monarchy and to the creation of two armed camps in France, bringing violence and devastation in its trail.

In Paris, the tension caused by the religious split affected not only the atmosphere in the capital but also the King, whose religious conscience had been stirred by the Pope's condemnation of constitutional priests. Louis had temporized long enough. In October 1789, he had written a letter to the King of Spain which showed his true feelings. 'I have chosen your Majesty,' he wrote, 'the head of the second branch of our family, as the person to whom I entrust my solemn protest against all the decrees contrary to royal authority to which I have been compelled by force to assent since July 15th of this year. I beg your Majesty to keep my protest secret until its publication becomes necessary.'

Now, anarchy was yet more prevalent. In April 1791, the royal family entered their coaches in the courtyard of the Tuileries to go to St Cloud for Easter, as they had done the previous year. Now, though, there was fear in Paris that they would escape, or at least take Easter Mass in St Cloud with a nonjuring priest, thus defying the new legislation.

In the courtyard, a protesting mob had gathered. The National Guard were supposed to clear a path for the royal family, but despite La Fayette's insistent orders, they refused, and it was the grenadiers of the National Guard who actually held the bridles to restrain the horses.

After two hours, the royal family yielded. 'Now no one can say we are free,' said Marie-Antoinette as they re-entered the Tuileries. The only way out of an impossible situation seemed to be to escape from Paris, a plan that had been mooted and prepared for over a year, and in which Mirabeau had co-operated before his death just at this time. Mirabeau had insisted that the King should go to Normandy, or some province away from the frontier, otherwise there would be the suspicion that the royal family were joining foreign armies and the émigrés. The flight itself, whether it failed or succeeded, was bound to be a further death-blow to all that the Assembly had tried to achieve in the last year. For how could there be a constitutional monarchy without a King who was respected and loved by his people, as hitherto Louis XVI had been?

[10]

FIASCO AT VARENNES

'It seems to me, M. de La Fayette, that it is you who are giving the
orders.'

LOUIS XVI when asked for instructions by La Fayette,
on his return to the Tuileries from Varennes.

René Claude is one of France's leading experts on the Revolution.
Although over seventy, he is as bright as a new franc piece and as
immaculate as Beau Brummel. His lively conversation and brisk
movements are those of someone half his age. As one of the directors
of '*Paris et son Histoire*', which takes members on historical trips all
round the world, he had arranged a special tour to follow the escape
route which Louis and his family took on those two fatal days of 21
and 22 June, 1791.

The royal family's escape began in the Tuileries which Jacques
Hébert had evoked for us so vividly. Their first problem was how
to leave without being detected, a complex undertaking as there
were no fewer than six people to smuggle out of the palace: Louis
and Marie-Antoinette, the two children, Mme de Tourzel, their
governess, and the King's sister, Mme Elisabeth. In addition,
three Body Guards were to act as coachman, outrider and scout,
while two maids were to leave in a separate carriage and meet them
just outside Paris. Axel Fersen, a Swedish count, almost certainly
Marie-Antoinette's lover, was to guide them out of Paris and then
leave them.

The complexity of this operation contrasted with the escape of
the Comte de Provence, Louis XVI's brother, at the same time.
He travelled separately from his wife; each had a single companion
in light chaises and reached Belgium without serious mishap within
twenty-four hours.

The escape from the Tuileries was a drama in itself. At 10.45
on the night of 20 June, Fersen brought an ordinary hackney

cab to the courtyard outside the empty apartment of a nobleman who had emigrated. The children, with the Dauphin disguised as a girl, were led there by their governess, Mme de Tourzel. Amidst the bustle of carriages in the courtyard, they entered the cab, which trotted off to the Place du Petit Carrousel, now absorbed by the wing of the Louvre at the side of the Rue de Rivoli.

Meanwhile, Louis XVI went through the formality of the *Coucher* in his state bedroom. La Fayette, who was there, dawdled and chatted. When the *Coucher* was over, Louis went into his real bedroom next door, was undressed by his valet, and climbed behind the heavy curtains of his bed. As the valet went outside to do his toilet, Louis slipped out to the neighbouring Dauphin's room, where he changed into the clothes of a valet: brown wig, bottle-green coat and a black hat. Casually, he descended the stairs, even stopping to adjust a loose shoe buckle, and walked boldly through the courtyard, past the sentries at the gate and into the Petit Carrousel, where the hackney cab was waiting.

To everyone's alarm, the Queen, who should have arrived first, was not there. She had had to wait while a sentry in the corridor moved away from the door of the apartments through which the children had already escaped. As she walked through the courtyard, she had another shock as La Fayette's carriage came past. He was so close that she could have touched the wheel, she said afterwards. In panic, she lost her way in the maze of streets behind the Carrousel, and only arrived at the hackney cab at 12.45, an hour later than agreed.

In our motor coach, we followed the route which the royal family had taken. First we drove up the Rue de l'Echelle to the Rue Ste Anne, which remains a narrow street with ancient houses. Here Rousseau once lived in an attic when he started his relationship with the washerwoman Thérèse Levasseur.

As we drove along, it was easy to imagine the clop of the hoofs under the dim street lights as the horse pulled the uncomfortable fiacre with its heavy burden.

'Here was the royal family of France,' said René Claude, 'no longer dignified centrepieces of a splendid round of ceremonies, no longer symbols of this whole vast country, heirs of a line of semi-divine Kings. They were now little more than an ordinary, worried family, refugees from their own people, huddled in a common fiacre.'

At the top of the Rue Ste Anne, the hackney cab turned left and up the Rue de la Chaussée d'Antin, then lined with noble houses. They passed the church of the Trinité, up the Rue de Clichy, to what is now number 54. Here, in the stables of an Englishman, Quentin Craufurd, was hidden the heavy berline which was to take them to Varennes. It should now have left for the rendezvous beyond the Porte St Martin, but Fersen had made a detour to check this – which produced further delay.

By the Porte St Martin, an archway commemorating the victories of Louis XIV used to be the barrier where papers had to be shown. The royal family got through by presenting the passport of Mme de Korff, a Russian noblewoman, under whose name they were travelling.

They then found themselves in the open countryside, with vine-yards and farmhouses. Today, one drives through the scrub of a big city, past shapeless houses and shops with plastic signs, under an overhead railway.

Here, on the high road to Metz, the massive berline had been left with one of the Body Guards beside the road. With relief, the passengers climbed into the enormous vehicle, drawn by six horses, with white taffeta curtains and cushions, cupboards, two cooking stoves, a little library and leather chamberpots.

Hurriedly, Fersen drove the berline to the village of Bondy, where they stopped to change horses, as they had to do every fifteen miles or so. This village has now grown into a vast bargaining centre for furniture, with placards on the walls and advertising banners swaying across the streets. The long concrete runway of an autoroute starts up here, close to the place where, until recently, the original staging post could be seen.

Here Fersen said goodbye, leaving the family alone, except for the three ex-Body Guards. Originally it had been suggested that the Comte d'Agoult, a fervent and able royalist, should accompany them, but Mme de Tourzel had insisted on precedence as governess to the royal children. So, were any unforeseen crisis to arise, every-thing was in the hands of these three loyal but incompetent men.

With our own coachload, we motored along the original high road which the berline had taken to the village of Claye almost two hours behind schedule. 'Here,' said M. Claude, 'the two waiting

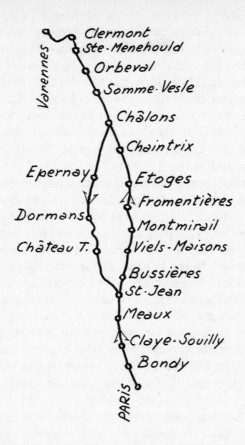

Clermont
Ste.-Menehould
Orbeval
Somme-Vesle
Châlons
Chaintrix
Epernay
Etoges
Fromentières
Dormans
Montmirail
Château T.
Viels-Maisons
Bussières
St.-Jean
Meaux
Claye-Souilly
Bondy
Varennes
PARIS

The route from Paris to Varennes. There was a deviation on the return journey via Epernay.

women had been sitting in a chaise for three hours. They joined the convoy, which now was anything but inconspicuous.

'You have to imagine this large berline drawn by no fewer than six horses trundling along at about ten kilometres an hour.' M. Claude suddenly whispered to the driver, who slowed so that we travelled at a snail's pace. 'That's their speed!' he said.

On the road, we passed a royal milestone, still there after hundreds of years.

'Do you know what Louis XVI had for breakfast?' asked M. Claude. Everyone shook their heads, except for a man in the front seat who always interrupted, and now suggested croissants. 'No.

He had four cutlets, a chicken, six pickled eggs in juice, and six slices of ham. In those days, meat formed a major part of the diet, and like most Bourbons, Louis had an enormous appetite.'

The road started up a long steep slope. 'Here,' said M. Claude, 'the loaded berline couldn't climb the hill. So the royal family got out and walked beside the straining horses. The children ran ahead. You can imagine their sense of release in the early sunlight, the cries of delight of the little Dauphin and his sister, Marie-Thérèse. Around them was the country air, the feeling that they were free, no longer imprisoned in the Tuileries.'

According to the memoirs of the governess, Mme de Tourzel, it was in the berline about this time that Louis read aloud a copy of the letter he had left behind for the Assembly. In it, he complained that he was a virtual prisoner, that all his concessions had been extracted by pressure, and that they had led to nothing except 'anarchy abroad and in the Kingdom'. In the berline, Louis also talked of his hopes of returning to Paris to establish a real constitutional monarchy where, now that the worst abuses of the Ancien Régime had been eliminated, the balance between Crown and Assembly could be achieved. However, it must be remembered that these memoirs were written almost thirty years later, and aligned Louis's hopes with the constitution granted by the subsequent Restoration. How far Louis would have returned to his previous absolutist rule is still unclear.

We came to Chaintrix, just before the Marne, where the original post-house still stands: two buildings with outhouses and an archway in the middle, rather grim and bare, beside the road. 'Here they were recognized, and the enthusiastic post-master invited them in,' said René Claude. 'You can imagine the awe of the post-master and his wife. It was like an unreal dream, with the King and Queen of France just dropping in for refreshments.'

Here, they wasted another half an hour, although they were already more than two hours behind schedule. When they left, the post-master and his son-in-law mounted the coachman's box and set off at maximum speed to compensate for loss of time.

When they got to the bridge over the Marne, however, a wheel broke and the harness snapped. It took another half an hour to repair the damage.

On they trotted, with gently rustling cornfields stretching to the horizon on either side, broken by clumps of trees which cast patches of shadow under the hot sun. Two hundred years ago, the wheat and barley probably grew more sparsely, without the benefit of modern farming. But even then, it was rich country.

In our coach we came to Châlons, and as we entered we could scarcely believe our eyes: two figures dangled from wires over the street. They were only effigies, suspended there as part of the electoral battle going on in France at the time. However, they seemed to bring us more closely into the Revolutionary past, when it would not have been surprising to see two corpses hanging above the street.

In Châlons, Louis was recognized. Unlike the Comte de Provence, who hid himself in his gig when horses were changed, and pretended to be an Englishman scarcely able to speak French, Louis was inquisitive and talkative. He believed now that success was certain. They were over nine hours from Paris. Who could catch up with them? Rashly, he put his head out of the window at the crowded staging post. People wished him God-speed. A man told the post-master that the municipality should be informed. But the post-master told him to do it himself. Fortunately, the royal family got out of town without being stopped. On their way, they passed an arch which is still there, put up by the loyal and enthusiastic citizens of Châlons to celebrate the arrival of Marie-Antoinette as a girl of fourteen, on her way from Vienna to marry Louis the Dauphin in 1770. One wonders if the royal family saw this arch and, if so, what memories and nostalgia passed through their minds.

An hour and a half later, they arrived at Pont-Somme-Vesle, where a first contingent of troops should have been waiting to escort them to Montmédy on the frontier. When they arrived, they looked out expectantly at the one street of the village. All was quiet. There were no troops anywhere.

Later, Louis recalled: 'I felt as though the whole earth had fallen from under me.'

The problem lay in their lateness. The commander of the hussars at Pont-Somme-Vesle was the Duke of Choiseul, who had been waiting apprehensively for the King ever since 11.30 that morning. The arrival of his troops had created alarm among the peasants in the vicinity, for the agent of their absentee landlord had been trying in vain to collect back rents, and they presumed the unusual influx of troops was connected with this.

The King was supposed to arrive by 2.30, and as the afternoon drew on and the armed peasants became more restless and
aggressive, Choiseul grew worried. By 4.30, it seemed the royal
family would not be passing that day. He therefore decided to
return to the army commanded by the Marquis de Bouillé, which
was camped beyond Varennes. With the Duke, however, was a
surprising individual called Léonard, who was the Queen's hairdresser, an excitable, effeminate man who had helped initiate those
hair styles which supported whole farmyards, or ships in full sail,
on top of ladies' coiffures at Versailles. He was yet another of those
retainers whom Marie-Antoinette felt she could not do without on
arrival in Montmédy, and for that reason he had accompanied the
Duke from Paris. Before Choiseul set off on the short cut through
the woods to Varennes, he told Léonard to take a carriage and tell
the troops along the way to disperse, as the King was not coming that
day. As a result, the escorts provided for the King were scattered
by a message borne by a hysterical hairdresser whose excitement
added to the feeling of crisis.

After the shock at Pont-Somme-Vesle, the royal family continued
to the town of Ste Menehould, where, had they known it, their
fate was to be decided. The town remains beautiful today, with its
brick and stone façades, its squares, its town hall built in 1732. It
has a feeling of the countryside, with a green, tree-covered ridge
overlooking the houses in the main street.

It was here that the post-master Drouet worked. His staging
house has not survived: bombed in the First World War, there
is now a gendarmerie. Nearby, on the other side of the square is
the Soleil d'Or, a restaurant which specializes in pig's trotters. On
a wall in the bar, it has a revolutionary poster depicting Louis XVI
eating pig's trotters at an inn called Le Fuyard (The Fugitive). The
owner is also a specialist in the '*pédalo*', and once pedalled over the
Channel to London and was fined for leaving his machine in the
Thames, outside the Tower of London.

As it happened, Drouet was furious with the competition offered
by the Soleil d'Or, whose proprietor had hired horses to some of the
dragoons passing through to escort the King the previous evening.
When the berline stopped outside his posting station, he may or
may not have recognized the King from a coin. What is sure
is that he noticed d'Andouin, the commander of the dragoons,
talking surreptitiously to the King by the berline, that he was

highly suspicious, and that after the King left he went to the
mayor, who arrested the troops remaining in the town, while
Drouet and a companion were sent off in pursuit of the berline.
Part of the personal tragedy of the flight to Varennes is the way
the King and Queen went on to their fate with no idea of what
was happening. There is something infinitely pathetic about this,
and it is still reflected in the feelings of some of the inhabitants of
Ste Menehould, who seem highly aware of what happened in their
town some two hundred years ago. When Brita asked the daughter
of the proprietor of the Soleil d'Or what she thought of the King's
flight, she answered passionately: 'Oh, we are Republicans. But
with the King. After all he was guillotined in the end. *Et ça ce
n'est pas normal!*'

From Ste Menehould, the berline entered the Argonne forest.
Dusk was falling and the setting sun was veiled by the tops of trees.
Today the countryside is rolling and bare, with copses of young
trees, for the forest and all this area was fought over bitterly during
the First World War. There are still parts where it is dangerous to go
because of unexploded shells, and there are old dugouts into which
you can fall. They say that after 1918, firewood spat in the hearth,
and bits of metal were left in the grate. At the time of the flight to
Varennes, the forest must have been thick and silent. Perhaps it
reminded Louis of a long day's hunting near Versailles. With the
tall trees on either side, this may have seemed the peaceful end of
another tiring day, with only a short time to run before they found
rest and shelter with Bouillé's army beyond Varennes.

The next stop, Clermont, is a small village. As you climb the
hill, smoke from chimneys drifts over the roofs and, as in Ste
Menehould, trees crane over a ridge above the houses. When the
berline climbed laboriously up the slope, the village was also in
ferment, stirred by the unexpected presence of troops commanded
by a Colonel Damas. When Léonard had arrived, Damas, unlike
d'Andouin in Ste Menehould, did not dismiss his troops. However,
when the berline trundled to the posting station, it occurred to him
that following it might excite the villagers further. So, despite his
orders, he decided to leave it to the dragoons at Varennes, which
was only an hour and a half away. So the berline continued on its
way, unescorted, but sheltered at least by growing darkness.

Then occurred one of those extraordinary strokes of bad luck
which mark the whole journey. The Greeks would have blamed

the gods; we can only wonder. The post-mistress at Clermont presumed that the berline was on its way along the high road to Metz. However, as it went through the village, Drouet's returning postilions heard instructions being given to turn left to Varennes. Thus Drouet, galloping in pursuit, was informed where the berline was going. Instead of continuing to Metz on a wild-goose chase, he decided to take a short cut through the forest. He was thus able to make up the valuable minutes which, in the end, were all that separated the royal family from safety and success.

As the berline trundled through the darkness on the last stage of the journey, the royal family slept.

In our coach, we drove through a broad valley with trees crowning the ridges on either side. After twenty minutes, or so, we saw the sign 'Varennes'. A modern museum appeared on our left and the road began to slope down ahead of us. We stopped, got out, and looked around.

Today, Varennes seems hardly even a village. Razed in the First World War, it is little more than a road sloping down to a bridge. There are a few newly built houses, a church tower without a church, some more houses beyond the bridge. On the right, a sheer bank covered with grass drops down to a green, sluggish river. It is moving to see the smallness of this scene of tragedy and farce, an insignificant theatre dwarfed by the extraordinary drama on which depended the future of the Revolution and of monarchy in France.

'*A moi!*' shouted René Claude, and we gathered round him. 'We will try and re-create,' he said. 'You must imagine!' He indicated a group of new houses beside the Mairie from which hung the tricolour flag of the Republic. 'At about eleven, the berline stopped here in the darkness. As elsewhere, there should have been troops and horses waiting. But the commanders, notified by Léonard, had gone to sleep in the Hôtel du Grand Monarque, there, beyond the bridge. The troops had also been quartered in that part of the village. Had the royal family gone straight down the hill and over the bridge for no more than a hundred metres, they would have been safe. But the postilions refused to go on. Their horses were needed for the harvest early next morning, and the post-mistress at Clermont had said they should be brought straight back. So after arguments, the King and Queen got out and knocked at the door of houses in the darkness, asking if the

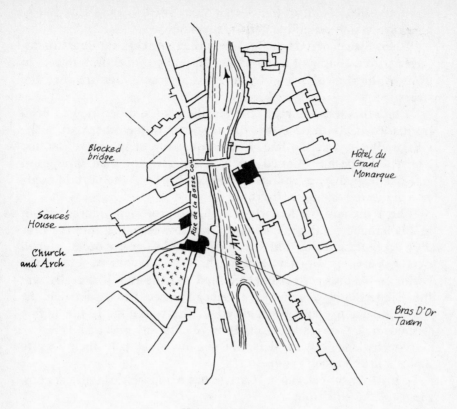

Varennes in 1791.

inhabitants had seen any horses. You can imagine their voices, which had made speeches at royal celebrations, now rousing the inhabitants who replied with sleepy imprecations, telling them to go away.

'Meanwhile, two shadows slipped past in the darkness. It was Drouet and his companion. They went to a hostelry called the Bras D'Or which used to be here.' We moved down the road past the church tower and looked over the grassy slope. 'The Bras d'Or was part of a row of houses which once stood above the river. Inside, there were several late drinkers who were astounded to hear Drouet's news.

'One of them went down to the house of Sauce, the deputy mayor, which used to be there' – René Claude gestured towards a little platform of brick with a monument behind it. 'Meanwhile,

Drouet rushed down to the bridge beside which was a cart full of furniture which he pulled across, blocking it.

'When Sauce arrived, he and the other drinkers stationed themselves with a couple of muskets just here, by this church tower, in front of the Bras d'Or and by an archway which then spanned the street.

'While this was going on, the postilions on the berline had been persuaded to continue a little further down to the other part of the village. But it was too late. Only a question of minutes. But too late. As the berline slipped through the arch, the men sprang out and challenged it, grasping the horses' bridles.' M. Claude made as if he were tugging at invisible reins.

'The King and particularly the Queen protested vigorously but finally handed over their passports, which were taken into the Bras d'Or to be examined. They seemed to be in perfect order, signed by the Foreign Minister, and Sauce was in favour of letting the berline go. However, Drouet pointed out the risk if it really was the King. Better to temporize. Sauce came out and said that the whole question could be resolved in the morning. If the family wished to stay in his house, they were certainly welcome.

'One by one, the royal family got out and made their way to Sauce's little grocer's shop.'

In his *French Revolution*, Carlyle has a superbly rhetorical comment on the situation:

Not the King shall ye stop under your miserable archway . . . to me Bodyguards; Postilions, en avant – one fancies in that case the pale paralysis of these two . . . musketeers; the drooping of Drouet's underjaw; and how Procureur Sausse [sic] had melted his tallow in furnace heat.

However, Louis would never risk the safety of his family, and muskets were trained on them. Besides, he wanted to maintain his disguise, which saved him from confrontation and – who knows? – perhaps made him feel a normal man for once. Presumably, he felt this was only a last-minute hiccup. Bouillé's troops were, surely, a few hundred metres away. It was only necessary to wait until they came. Marie-Thérèse, their daughter, the only survivor of the family, relates in her memoirs how, as they went down to Sauce's shop, they could see dragoons passing on the other side of the road. Yet in this moment of crisis, Louis did nothing to rally them. Versailles had made him unused to action and personal initiative. It was always someone else who arranged things.

René Claude now took us down to the stone platform which was once Sauce's shop. On it was a plaque inscribed in golden letters, relating briefly what had happened. Behind, in the garden, a black dog barked at us, perhaps defending his old master's grave.

'The family went through Sauce's shop, past the cheeses, bundles of candles and sausages hanging from the ceiling,' said M. Claude. 'It is difficult to imagine now, but can you see this small house with its wooden stairs leading up to two bedrooms above?' There were nods from those gathered about him.

'Upstairs, candles were lit and the children were put to bed. Marie-Antoinette sat on a chair, and Louis paced up and down the small room. The tocsin began to toll. Its deep clanging resounded through the village and over the countryside. People hurriedly put on their clothes and rushed out to see what was going on. Where we are now standing, stood the empty berline, a solid black shape amidst the flicker of moving lamps and burning torches.

'Sauce fetched a bottle of Burgundy and bread and cheese. Then he brought up a man called Destez, who had been at Versailles. As he crossed the threshold, Destez dropped to his knees. "Sire," he exclaimed. Louis now admitted who he was and, overcome, embraced Sauce, Destez and the others in the room. He explained that he had not intended to cross the frontier but to stay in Montmédy with his army. He had fled Paris because, if he had stayed, he would have been murdered. At this, Sauce and the others began to weep. Louis wept in turn and Sauce promised that next morning he would provide a hundred National Guards to escort him to Montmédy.

'Suddenly, there was the clatter of horses' hoofs outside. Louis started expectantly. Was it Bouillé and his army? However, it was Choiseul with the forty hussars who had just emerged from the forests of the Argonne where he had lost his way. Choiseul came up the stairs, saluted, and talked to the King in a low voice. Escape was possible, immediately. The royal family had only to mount horses and ride off through a little lane at the side, which you can still see, with an escort of hussars.

'Louis, however, looked out of the window at the streets now thronged with people, some of whom were armed. One of them might fire as they tried to escape and kill the Queen, or their daughter, or the Dauphin. He shook his head. They would wait for Bouillé.'

Looking back at the scene from two hundred years' distance, I find that it is here that I become impatient. After all, Louis could have appealed to the people from the window, as he had to Sauce and the others, whom he had moved to tears. Or at least he could have talked to Drouet, explained his situation and asked for help. He could have offered money to men who had very little. Everyone would have been overawed by an address from the King who had appeared so unexpectedly among them.

Why did he not send Choiseul and the hussars to push the furniture cart off the bridge, and fetch the dragoons on the other side of the river?

Was it that he was cowed by all that had happened in the last two years? Of course, the safety of his family was important, but at stake too was the whole future of the monarchy. Would his family be safe if they were forced to return to Paris? In fact, all but Marie-Thérèse died in the most horrific circumstances. Was it that Louis was so optimistic that he was sure Bouillé's army would arrive? Yet he could at least have sent one of the bodyguards to find out what was happening across the river, which could easily have been forded: when we were there, also in June, a small boy was standing fishing in water up to his calves.

Of course we can never really know what was in the King's mind, and perhaps the whole passivity, the extraordinary indecision of the aristocratic officers along the route was just the symptom of a decaying ruling class. This was summed up by the Marquis de Bombelles in his Journal: 'We have lived too long an easy life and no longer have the energy and resolution of our forefathers . . . now luxury and the *douceur de vivre* have succeeded in corrupting us. The word "honour" is always on our lips but not sufficiently graven in our hearts to dictate our actions.'

The British were probably no better, as is shown by their extraordinary incompetence in provoking rebellion in America and then blundering, largely through negligence, to defeat. When one looks round Europe, there seems to have been a crisis of talent among monarchs at this time: George III on the brink of madness, Ferdinand of Naples almost illiterate, Charles IV of Spain passively allowing himself to be cuckolded by the Guardsman Godoy, in a country where a reputation for virility has always been at a premium.

It is as if absolute monarchy at this time were blighted by a strange disease. Probably it was the complacency which a century free of major civil strife had worked into their bones, binding them with the rituals of their idle Courts. Their condition was similar to that of the Roman Catholic Church just before the shock of the Reformation. Régimes stumble like old men when they repeat the same formulae, when luxury and riches make them happy simply to exist.

'It was now two or three in the morning,' continued René Claude. 'The street, here, was like a fair. Stalls had been set up under the light of burning torches. The Bras d'Or was crowded. Inside Sauce's house, the children slept and Marie-Antoinette dozed on her chair.

'At five, there was a further clatter on the stairs. But it was not Bouillé. It was Bayon, the emissary of the National Assembly in Paris, who had at last caught up. He told Louis that the Assembly had put him and the royal family under arrest. They must return to Paris. Louis asked Bayon for written confirmation and was handed a note signed by La Fayette. Under the Constitution, all decisions had to be signed by the King, and the note has rightly been regarded by historians as a coup d'état.

'The King looked at it and gave it to his wife. "There is no longer a King in France!" he said, mournfully. He took the note back and let it fall on the bed beside the children. But Marie-Antoinette snatched it away. "I will not have such a thing soil my children," she is reported to have said.

'Bayon went out to talk to the people, as Louis should have done earlier. He told them the King was under arrest and that if he did not return to Paris soon, Bouillé would arrive and massacre everyone. All Louis and his family did was to try and postpone departure, which after Bayon's eloquence the people of Varennes were anxious to see as soon as possible. One of the waiting women pretended to be ill, and they dawdled over breakfast. However, at seven no further excuses were possible. One by one, the royal family descended the creaking staircase, and climbed into the berline.

'Only half an hour later, Bouillé arrived with his army on the other side of the river. He could actually see the slow procession and the yellow wheels of the berline, as it edged up the slope. But nothing could be done now. Rescue was impossible with the royal family held as hostages, surrounded by ten thousand armed National Guards.'

We walked over the bridge to the Hôtel du Grand Monarque for a drink. Like everything else, the original hotel (where Bouillé's son had been asleep when Louis arrived) had been rebuilt after the First World War. From a large, open bar, dark corridors ran off to bedrooms.

'Extraordinary!' said Brita to René Claude. 'With your description, you make me feel I was here at the time. I can see it all so clearly, although so little remains. That view down the narrow street, the bridge at the bottom, the river.'

'It was all such a near thing,' said René. 'All those coincidences coming together: Léonard's role, the importance of keeping to the timetable, the lack of initiative of the officers in command.

'To me, the moving part is when one considers the family as individuals rather than royals,' I said. 'They were so much on their own, ever since Fersen left them at Bondy. What would have happened had they joined up with Bouillé's army, one can never know. But it's the way they humiliated themselves, and the hatred their failure generated, which led them to their terrible death, which really grips the bowels.'

I asked the bar lady how the people of Varennes felt about the distant drama. 'Well, the young people are not much interested. It's just history, and it's too far away. Television has made youngsters more involved in what goes on today. For everyone, too, the most important event here is what happened in the First World War, which annihilated the village. But particularly among older people there's still a lot of fascination. After all, it was so dramatic.'

As we sipped at our drinks, Brita asked René Claude what happened to Drouet and Sauce afterwards.

'Both were rewarded by the Assembly, and Drouet later became a member of the Convention and voted for the death of the King. Later still, he was captured by the Austrians and tried to escape from the castle where he was imprisoned by making a parachute and throwing himself out of the window, breaking a leg in the fall. The most extraordinary thing, though, is that he was then exchanged for no less a person than Marie-Thérèse, the only survivor of the royal family.

'Sauce, poor man, was blamed by both sides: by the royalists for arresting Louis XVI; by the patriots for giving him hospitality and being so courteous. Popular pressure forced him to move from Varennes, and he became a morose clerk of the local court in a nearby town, hardly speaking to anyone till his death some thirty years later.

'Another figure in the drama, Léonard, was one of the few people who have ever "died" twice. Officially, he was guillotined in the Terror, but then reappeared and died in his bed in 1825.'

As we stood by the bar, my thoughts returned to the King and royal family. I imagined what they must have felt on their way back, going through the same places, remembering their own curiosity and optimism only twenty-four hours previously.

The journey was a Calvary although, for most of it, they were protected by two Deputies, Barnave and Pétion, who were sent to accompany them by the Assembly. It took almost four days. Some of it was by a different route. At Epernay, they descended from the berline for lunch and were almost torn to pieces. At Dormans, a local nobleman, the Comte de Dampierre, who came to pay his respects, was shot and his head waved on a pike in front of the berline window. Those who would probably have cheered if the royal family had been successful, now reviled them with impunity. Because of the heat, they had to keep the windows of the berline open, and on the last lap of the journey, between Meaux and Paris, a man spat in the King's face. When Marie-Antoinette proffered the little Dauphin as a plea for gentleness, another cried: 'Everyone knows the fat hog isn't his father!'

The entry to Paris was routed through the Champs Elysées as it was felt the shorter way through the streets in the north of the city was too dangerous. The Assembly had plastered Paris with an order which ran: 'Whoever insults the royal family will be beaten. Whoever applauds them will be hanged.' The berline with the Body Guards strapped to the roof made its silent entry down the wooded avenues of the Champs Elysées and into the Tuileries Gardens. It must have been like a surrealist dream with the guards holding back an enormous crowd, with no sound except the horses' hoofs and the noise of the wheels on the gravel.

The fall of the Bastille had demonstrated the hollowness of royal power. The removal of the Court from Versailles to Paris had shown the helplessness of the monarchy and reduced much of its pomp and dignity. Now, the way the royal family had been stopped at Varennes, with Louis disguised as a valet with brown wig and bottle-green coat, had made them ridiculous.

Politically, the Assembly had shown it could run the country with remarkable efficiency without the King, and Louis's assertions of loyalty to the Constitution had proved so much hypocrisy. The existence of a counter-revolutionary conspiracy was now confirmed: somehow, the whole royal family had managed to steal out of Paris, undetected for nine hours. And why had they been travelling towards the frontier, close to which the émigrés and the armies of Marie-Antoinette's nephew, the Emperor Leopold, were massed?

'No more kings!' wrote Hébert in his journal, *Le Père Duchesne*. 'But above all no more Capets, no more Louis the Traitor.'

11

PARIS: THE END OF
CONSTITUTIONAL MONARCHY

'The suppression of the clubs will restore peace; all that is necessary
is to destroy the machinery of insurrection.'

DUPONT DE NEMOURS

Because constitutional monarchy was supported by the majority in
the Assembly, a face-saving formula was found: Louis had only
fled to Varennes because abducted by foreign and reactionary
forces. However, this absurd explanation was not accepted generally. On 17 July an enormous crowd gathered on the Champ
de Mars to sign a petition for the King's deposition, and was
dispersed by the National Guard with Bailly and La Fayette at
their head. Fifteen people were killed. Martial law was declared,
and some of the agitators responsible for the petition went into
hiding.

In September, the King signed the completed Constitution. Once
again, the Revolution seemed to have come to an end. However,
the King's flight had changed everything. In the Tuileries, the
little Dauphin asked his father why his people now hated him
when they had once loved him so much. The conflict over the
constitutional priests, and the resentment of the poorer classes
against the property limitations which prevented them being elected
to the new Legislative Assembly, were also continual irritants.

In September Marie-Antoinette's brother Leopold, Emperor of
Austria, invited other European powers to support Louis XVI.
The émigré armies on the frontiers grew. In France, there was an
increasing fear of betrayal, and a weakening of trust in those who
had initiated the Revolution. New centres of power and influence
grew up, apart from the Assembly, particularly in the Jacobin
and Cordelier Clubs and in the District Assemblies – now called
Sections – of Paris.

In the 1970s, Brita and I lived on the Left Bank in Paris for almost a year. We were trying to develop a *'Village Anglaise'* with its theatre, pub, library, school of English, and bookshop in a picturesque alley called the Passage Dauphine, which had once been the vegetable garden of an Augustinian monastery. Unfortunately, only part of our original plan came to fruition. However, we lived right in the centre of the old Cordelier district, with its narrow streets, small squares and medieval buildings whose ancient cellars are now used as restaurants and discos.

One side of our international club was part of the wall which, in the thirteenth century, had surrounded Paris, and beyond the buildings opposite one of its towers could still be seen. At the bottom of our sloping alleyway, the Rue Mazarine followed what had once been the old moat of the city. At the top was the Rue Dauphine, which Henry IV had cut through after threatening to do so with cannon if the Augustinian monks did not concede passage – which, of course, they did.

Here, amidst this medieval maze of lanes, passages and dead ends, lived many of those who were now to become prominent revolutionaries, among them Danton, Desmoulins, Marat and Hébert, none of whom had been elected to the first two Assemblies and thus represented another wave of the Revolution. We explored what was left of their houses. Near us, that prim, moralistic intriguer, Mme Roland, was brought up in a flat which still looks onto the Seine and the Pont Neuf from one of the buildings at the end of the Place Dauphine. From 1791, she and her stolid husband installed themselves at the Hotel Britannique, which was somewhere in the neighbouring Rue Guénégaud. Here, she increased her influence by holding revolutionary salons, attended by the new Girondin members of the Assembly and by Robespierre and Danton. Primly, sugar-water rather than wine was served for refreshment.

Danton came to Paris in 1785 with a law degree from Reims, easily acquired and easily paid for. He was one of a mass of novice lawyers who arrived from the provinces in the hope of making their fortunes. For them, the Revolution was a welcome opportunity to escape from mediocrity and the drudgery of a legal office. Danton had already been fortunate in marrying Gabrielle Charpentier, who was the daughter of the wealthy owner of the Café du Parnasse, much frequented by lawyers. She is described by a contemporary, Rousselin de St Albin, as 'a most respectable woman . . . charming

St Germain – Revolutionary centre.
1. Danton's flat;
2. Marat's flat;
3. Café Procope;
4. Cordeliers.

as she is obliging'. Gabrielle was the cashier, which enabled Danton to speak to her whenever he paid his bill. The café was on the opposite side of the river, just beyond the Pont Neuf. One misty March morning, I went to find its exact position in what used to be the little Passage du Café du Parnasse, between the river and the Rue Prêtres St Germain l'Auxerrois, which still exists. However, a new block had been built over the café, probably in the nineteenth century.

By the time the Revolution broke out, Danton and his wife had settled in a first floor flat at the end of the Cours de Commerce. This is entered from the Rue St André des Arts, and is still a narrow, cobbled alleyway, now occupied by restaurants and pubs, with a men's outfitters at the upper end. The room where the guillotine was tried on sheep could be seen there, fifteen years ago, but has now been absorbed into a pub. To one side, Marat's old printing house still survives. It is a long, low, empty building with boarded windows on the ground floor and broken glass above. Shortly, it is to be turned into a Museum of the French Revolution. Here, Marat printed his journal, *Ami du Peuple*, which even before the King's flight to Varennes threatened that 500,000 'dishonest French heads' would fall by the end of 1791.

Marat himself was a small, croaking journalist with a Sardinian father and a Genevan mother. Formerly a doctor, with an MD from the University of St Andrews, he believed that anyone who disagreed with him was 'dishonest'. When he was not hiding from the police in cellars and sewers, where he caught an itchy skin disease, he lived in a house which used to be where the Rue de l'Ecole de Médecine joins the Boulevard St Germain.

Danton's first floor flat was near Marat's house and has also been destroyed by the creation of the Boulevard St Germain. It stood by what is now the Odéon Métro, where the upturned arm of his statue rallies passers-by to defend their country.

In Danton's day, you went to the end of the Cours de Commerce and then up a curving staircase to the front door, which led to an antechamber. This opened onto a dining room on the left, and a bedroom and two large sitting rooms on the right. The rest of the flat contained a kitchen and another bedroom where, presumably, Danton's two maids slept.

Here, Danton found the domestic bliss he treasured. He loved his wife Gabrielle so dearly that when she died in March 1793, during one of his journeys to Belgium, he had her dug up seven days after her death, and sobbed with her crumbling body in his arms.

Desmoulins lived further up towards the Luxembourg Palace, in 2 Rue de l'Odéon, just opposite his beloved Lucille, whom he could court from a window of his parents' apartment to one of hers. He, Danton and Marat had easy access to two revolutionary meeting places close by. One was the Café Procope, which is still on the Rue de l'Ancienne Comédie, a restaurant where prices are reasonable and the walls are decorated with portraits of former clients, from Voltaire to the Revolutionaries.

The other, more important, was the Club des Cordeliers, which was one of the largest monastic enclaves in Paris, within which were pleasant gardens, surrounded by cloisters. One sunny day, I explored what remains. The Ecole de Médecine has absorbed most of the monastery. The present courtyard, whose walls are peppered with notices of seminars and arrows pointing to different lecture rooms, follows the approximate lines of the former cloisters, using the old stone for pillars. On the south side stands the twelfth-century refectory, which is being restored.

When I enquired about this, the concierge of the Ecole looked at me with that indifferent remoteness which 'authority' in France so easily assumes. 'The Town Hall has run out of money for the restorations, and the building is closed,' she said. 'You have to get authorization to visit it.'

I left the concierge and crept surreptitiously round the side. Sheets of plastic draped the pointed windows. In a drab garden with earth in concrete borders, a faded placard announced 'Société de Biologie'. The wind blew, flapping the plastic, and I noticed a hole through which I peeped. The hall where the monks had eaten was bare, with earth floor and wooden pillars supporting a newly constructed plank ceiling. Even with the sunlight, there was a feeling of desolation amidst this partly completed restoration.

However, from outside you can still see the approximate boundaries of the Cordeliers: a rough triangle with the Rue Ecole de Médecine on the northern side, the Rue Racine as its southern border and the Rue Monsieur le Prince joining the two.

In the hall of theology, which used to be beside the refectory, the tumultuous meetings of the Cordeliers were held. Roussel de l'Epinay gives a contemporary description of one of them:

Despite the mutilation that has been perpetrated, there were still traces of religious devotion under the great roof. The enclosure was oval in shape, truncated at its extremities, and furnished with wooden benches in the form of an amphitheatre, with galleries. The oval was cut on one side by the President's desk and by the speaker's rostrum on the other. About three hundred people of every age and sex [sic] filled these premises. Their dress was so ragged and filthy that they could have been taken for an assembly of beggars. Behind, the Declaration of the Rights of Man was stuck on the wall, crowned by two crossed daggers. The plaster busts of Brutus and William Tell were placed on either side, like guardians. Opposite, above the rostrum, were the busts of Mirabeau and Helvétius with Rousseau in the middle. Great rusty chains were wreathed above their heads, crowning them. I was told that they were chains taken from the Bastille. But I learnt that they had been bought on the quay where they sell scrap iron.

At the beginning of the Revolution the Cordeliers housed the District Assembly, which was in continual conflict with the Town Hall led by Bailly and La Fayette. Danton was for some time the District's President. An eye-witness describes him in action when the assembly was protesting against the calling of the Flanders regiment to Versailles, just before the royal family were compelled to come to Paris:

Danton was in the chair; I had often heard of him and now I was seeing him for the first time . . . I was struck by his harsh and resounding diction, his dramatic gestures and expressive features, his penetrating and confident regard, by the energy and daring of his attitude and movement . . . He presided with the decisiveness, agility and authority of a man who knew his power. He drove the assembly of the District towards its goal. It adopted a manifesto.

Danton's tactics at this time are worth considering briefly. Repeated in tumults down to our day, they are one of the keys to understanding the Revolution. In the increasing chaos of different centres of power and of mobs ready to march behind the most eloquent demagogue, they were rooted in two evocative phrases typical of the kind of rallying cry which often goes unquestioned in times of social upheaval. In this case, these phrases were 'The Sovereignty of the People' and 'The Right of Insurrection', derived from the work of that illogical and masochistic prophet, Rousseau.

Who were the People?

'Factions misuse the word to persuade two hundred ignorant men that they are the people and, therefore, the sovereign power in the land,' wrote a contemporary right-wing journalist. To repress, though, would smack of the old régime – just as more recently in Italy, the fall of Mussolini's dictatorship brought reluctance to be strong because of the government's fear of being labelled Fascist.

From 1792 on, disturbances increased because those without power were continually intriguing against those who had it. This is true of any political situation, but established régimes have acknowledged rules of the game, and failure to observe them does not often lead to success. Here, though, was a situation where the sudden dislocation of a monarchy which had been the central authority for a thousand years meant that no one – and everyone – had a *right* to govern.

Danton, in the midst of his district of printing presses and newspaper offices, was shrewd enough to realize that power could only be achieved through agitation, expressed in the language of extremism, which alone rallied support.

His first clash as President of the Cordelier District was with his immediate superiors at the Town Hall, who had asked his District to elect their representatives to the Town Council. His great voice resounding through the hall, Danton insisted that their District represented the 'Sovereign People' and they would not send 'representatives' but only 'delegates'. For, should they not remain responsible to their own 'Sovereign Assembly'? The clash was inconclusive, but Danton's name became well known in the Assembly, and in the Town Hall, and all over Paris through reports in the widely read journals of the Cordelier district.

There was a further clash with the municipality when they issued a warrant for Marat's arrest for libellous articles in his *Ami du Peuple*. La Fayette sent 3,000 troops to the Cordelier District to arrest Marat. There, Danton met them in the street and quibbled about the legality of their warrant. Marat, meanwhile, escaped for a time to England as a 'Martyr to Liberty'.

In the re-organization of Paris, the Districts were replaced by forty-eight Sections whose powers were limited. With Desmoulins, Danton therefore founded the Cordeliers Club as a forum of political debate, similar to the Jacobins, north of the river. However, Danton's original power base had been eroded. So, he joined the Jacobins, whose members included more national figures.

After the King's flight, the Jacobin club had split. Those who supported the King's re-establishment departed to found a new club, the Feuillants, near the National Assembly, leaving the radicals behind.

Jacobin, like Cordelier, was the name of a monastic order whose buildings had also been nationalized in November 1789. Off the Rue St Honoré, opposite the buildings of the Assembly, an archway opened into a courtyard, beyond which was the church. Meetings were held initially in the chapter, and when the club grew larger it was moved to the library above the church. After the fall of Robespierre, it was razed to the ground and replaced by a market. Now, there are few traces left. The courtyard has become a narrow street, the Rue du Marché St Honoré, lined with a number of pastry shops. At the end, where stood the church, now squat the formless, massive offices of BP.

The Jacobin Club in a church off the Rue St Honoré. *Bibliothèque Nationale*.

One should imagine the club preferably at night, when most of the meetings took place. In a long, narrow hall, with a stove in the middle whose flues went straight up, and then diagonally to the roof, rows of benches faced each other and were also arranged at the end. Oil lamps cast the moving shadows of excited listeners and speakers on the walls, creating an atmosphere of intimate conspiracy.

Threats, enthusiastic proposals, denunciations, the evocation of Roman heroes, sounded from the rostrum. Ragged sansculottes descended from the gallery. Wild shouts of applause or cries of fury echoed through the semi-darkness as if this were a midnight meeting of demons.

Through their clubs founded all over France, the Jacobins rallied those who now sniffed power. *'Ote-toi que je m'y mette'* (Get out of the way so that I can take your place) has been one of the main drives of any revolution. Now, with the discrediting of the King, the divisions caused by the Civil Constitution of the Clergy, and a new economic crisis induced by the inflation of assignats, the new paper currency issued on the security of Church lands, discontent found expression in the streets, the local assemblies and the clubs, in what was really an alternative structure of power.

Something then happened which was to crystallize and heighten these divisions and give them an additional element of frenzy and fear. In April 1792, France declared war on Marie-Antoinette's nephew, the Emperor Leopold II. Louis XVI had appointed his ministers from among the group called Girondins, who centred upon a deputy and journalist from Chartres, Jacques Brissot. The Girondins were in favour of war because they felt it would confirm their influence, and they wanted to disseminate 'liberty' all over Europe.

The King was in favour because he saw his only hope in an invasion of France, led by Marie-Antoinette's nephew, which would re-establish him. Only Robespierre and the old liberal bourgeoisie were against. Robespierre, with his usual pessimistic caution, believed that a disaster for French arms would restore the Old Régime, while the others foresaw their beloved Constitution tumbling under the pressures which war would bring.

As we know from our own recent experience, war can produce an almost hysterical reaction against anyone suspected of being connected with the enemy. In 1914, Germans were so feared and hated in Britain that dachshunds were stoned as German dogs in the streets. The royal family even had to change their name from Saxe-Coburg to Windsor. In the Second World War, all enemy aliens and German sympathizers were imprisoned in the Isle of Man, while all over the world quite innocent people were suspected of being spies, often for the most ridiculous reasons.

In France, this hysteria was compounded by the fact that the hated Marie-Antoinette was Austrian, just as in Russia in 1914–17 the Tsarina's German origin contributed to mistrust of the Tsarist government. In France in 1792, fears and suspicions were heightened because the war began badly, with open treachery on the frontier, where many officers deserted and the French army would not fight. Plans for attacks on Belgium, then the Austrian Netherlands, collapsed. In early July, the Prussians also declared war.

In the capital Louis, with his terrible sense of timing, adopted a firmer policy. He vetoed two decrees approved by the Assembly. The first proscribed priests who would not swear the oath, the second proposed the establishment of a camp of twenty thousand volunteers from the provinces in Paris. On 20 June a mob invaded the Tuileries. The King, insulted as 'M. Veto', put on a red bonnet and drank to the Nation. But he stood firm.

Louis also fuelled antagonism by dismissing his Girondin ministers and replacing them with a group that came to be known as the 'Austrian Committee'. At the beginning of August, a manifesto from the Duke of Brunswick, the general leading Prussian troops into France, was sent to Paris. It threatened to raze the city to the ground if the royal family was harmed. This was the last spark, clearly identifying the King and Queen with the advancing enemy. Preparations in the Sections and the Town Hall were begun for an attack on the Tuileries. Excitement mounted. The provincial volunteers who had arrived despite the King's veto had sung a new patriotic song as they marched from Marseilles to Paris, composed by an officer in Strasbourg, Rouget de Lisle.

The atmosphere in the city must have been similar in our own recent history to Madrid at the beginning of the Civil War, when armed civilians stormed the Monteverde barracks which had come out for Franco.

In the early 1960s, I used to take tours of Americans round Europe, which always ended in Paris. I shall never forget those hot nights in August with the streets still reflecting warmth, the people moving around till early morning, the feeling that everyone was like fish swimming lazily in water at the right temperature. When dawn rose over Montmartre, the whole city began to stir, glowing under the heat of the new day, with the spires of churches topped with gold and the markets and squares bustling with early risers. Voluble, gesticulating, joking, they welcomed the new day, although at that time the Algerian crisis was at its height, with rumours of possible army putsches, and clashes between supporters of Algerian Independence and those of the colonial OAS.

So it must have been, this blend of heat and alarm, on the night of 9–10 August 1792. In the early morning, the tocsins sounded all over Paris, as if for early Mass. In the Tuileries, the black-coated gentlemen who had come to defend their King tried to name the churches from which the tolling came. At the Town Hall, a new Committee of three delegates from each of the forty-eight sections replaced the old municipality. They summoned Mandat, the Commander of the National Guard, who had placed contingents of cavalry and cannon on the Pont Neuf and in the Rue de l'Echelle, blocking possible insurrection. They arrested him, slaughtered him on the steps of the Town Hall, and his troops were removed.

In the Tuileries, Louis went to Mass. There is a painting by Robert of such an occasion, at about this time. Few evocations are more poignant, with the colour and ceremony, and yet the underlying sense of disorder and improvisation, as if the Mass were being held in a ship which was already sinking. The hurriedly prepared drawing room, instead of the chapel, the altar obscuring part of a picture, the royal family kneeling before arm chairs, the courtiers streaming in with their powdered hair, the splendidly robed official standing, self-importantly, with staff of office in his hand, form one of the most evocative representations of the dusk of the old régime. Supremely ironic are the paintings depicted on the wall: battle scenes of Louis XIV's time, with rearing horses and riders in plumed hats, pointing to victory.

At five, Louis went down to the gardens to inspect the National Guard. Cries of '*Vive la Nation!*' and '*A bas le gros cochon!*' reached Marie-Antoinette who was looking from a window, and she wept.

When he returned, flustered and out of breath, Louis gathered with his family and his Ministers in the Council Room on the first floor, just by his state bedroom. Perhaps he was reminded of that day, not three years ago, when the women had attacked Versailles. What were they to do? Persuaded by Roederer, a municipal official, the royal family decided to take refuge in the neighbouring Manège with the National Assembly. You can still see the way they took by the side of the Feuillant's Terrace, through the gardens, with the Pavillon de Marsan in the background, and the long line of trees on their left. From the garden they walked up the steps to where the Assembly was. A Grenadier took the little Dauphin and placed him on a table, and the President, Vergniaud, gave a cautious speech of welcome.

Meanwhile, armed masses of Parisians had crossed the Pont Neuf and were crowding the Pont Royal. From the district of St Antoine, a horde arrived to join those flooding in from the south. They massed in the Place du Carrousel, and entered the main courtyard in front of the Palace, from which the royal troops retired.

How the battle started is uncertain. One report states that the Marseillais fired their cannon which, badly aimed, sprayed the roofs of the Tuileries. Another says that the mob entered the main doors into the peristyle. Some of the 900 Swiss defenders were grouped on the main staircase and fired when two of their soldiers were captured and manhandled.

A devastating fusillade from the windows decimated the serried crowd in the courtyard. Napoleon, who was there, said that properly led, the Swiss could have won the day. The battle continued for about half an hour, until the Swiss ran out of ammunition. From the Assembly, Louis sent his last order as King, instructing his troops to cease fire, but it arrived too late.

The Swiss tried to escape. A group were overpowered in the Rue de l'Echelle and slaughtered, their naked bodies piled up for all to see. The mob ransacked the palace, throwing the furniture out of the windows, pillaging the valuables in drawers, writing desks, cupboards, killing any servants, Swiss or courtiers they could find. The wine cellars under the Pavillon de Flore were strewn with broken bottles, staved casks and bodies, while hags danced round the severed limbs of Swiss soldiers burning on a brazier in the courtyard. Three hundred attackers had been killed, and the people wanted their revenge. Yet another cycle of outrage and reprisal had been set in motion.

In the Assembly, a deputy protested that constitutionally they could not debate while the King was in the hall, and the royal family were removed to a little box provided for journalists behind the President's chair. Mobs came to jeer, shouting for the King's dethronement. The royal family remained in this cramped enclosure for three days. Meals were brought from a neighbouring restaurant, and at night they retired and slept on mattresses in the apartment of the architect of the Assembly.

On the third day, in the evening, they were taken through Paris to the Temple, which was almost an enclosed town in itself, a walled relic of the medieval Knights Templar. There had been talk of them going to the Luxembourg Palace, but it would have been difficult to defend against further attack. Through a vast crowd, the royal family rolled up the Rue St Honoré and into the Place Vendôme, where Louis XIV's huge statue lay shattered on the ground. Then, along the boulevards to the Temple, their last residence together.

12

MURDER IN PARIS

'I am the rage of the people.'

MARAT

With the King suspended, Danton was made Minister of Justice and virtual head of the new government. For six weeks, he and Gabrielle moved out of their flat in the Cour de Commerce and into what is still the Ministry of Justice in 13 Place Vendôme. The magnificence of this building must have dazzled at least Gabrielle. Built in 1699, it had been the Hôtel de la Chancellerie throughout the reigns of Louis XV and XVI. Apart from the splendour of the great rooms with gold decorations on the white walls, the Aubusson carpets and chandeliers, there was the view of the harmonious Place, designed by Mansart. In the middle was not a column, as now, but the immense equestrian statue of Louis XIV, which as we have seen was overturned by the mob, killing a woman newspaper vendor, leaving only shattered pieces on the paving stones below the great empty plinth.

When I visited the present Ministry of Justice, there were few traces of Danton's short stay there: an office which was closed and, for some reason, was known as Danton's room, and a clock which is still working, although Danton threw something at it in a rage. However, despite the inevitable partitions, dividing large rooms into small offices, and Napoleon III's ubiquitous redecoration, there is still a sense of grandeur about the building. A dining room, with polished wooden floors and chandeliers, still looks out onto the Place Vendôme. There are still ancient staircases with florid iron banisters, and rooms with tall ceilings and long windows with wispy curtains.

'Of course, the building has changed much over two centuries,' said the bright young man who kindly took me round when I arrived without an appointment. 'Justice is always expanding,' he said with a smile. 'Space not beauty is our real priority.'

In this building, Danton showed himself a statesman, not a mere demagogue, uniting France against the Prussian invader. It was when he lived here that he made his great speech, a phrase of which has been engraved on his statue in the Boulevard St Germain, where his flat once stood: '*L'audace, toujours de l'audace et encore de l'audace, et la France est sauvée.*' It is also at this time that he may have played a part in organizing the September massacres. As Minister of Justice, he certainly did nothing to prevent them, any more than did the National Assembly, or Roland, who was Minister of the Interior. If the account of Louis-Philippe, the Duke of Orléans' son, who became King of the French in 1830, is to be believed, Danton justified the massacres because it ensured the loyalty of young army volunteers by 'putting a river of blood between them and the émigrés'.

The September massacres were the first mass slaughter of the Revolution, the start of that period of savagery for which, unfortunately, the Revolution is best remembered. They were organized by the various committees of the Commune and were a natural, or unnatural, sequel to the attack on the Tuileries. Essentially, they represented vengeance on the Swiss survivors, on a few remaining aristocrats who had defended their King, and on the 223 imprisoned priests whose refusal to swear the oath to the Constitution seemed to mark them down as dangerous counter-revolutionaries.

In all, somewhere between 1,250 and 1,400 prisoners were murdered by about a hundred assassins, who were each paid 24 livres a day. Over 70 per cent of the victims had nothing directly to do with the Revolution, but were unfortunate enough to be in prison at the time, accused of common law offences.

The massacres were justified with stories of a conspiracy in the prisons to break out and slaughter revolutionaries, although how arms would be collected and an escape organized was not explained. As so often, the exigencies of the war were also used as a reason. In a circular to the Departments, inciting them to follow the Paris example, Marat wrote: 'All the French people cry out as did the Parisians, "We will march on the enemy, but we will not leave brigands behind us to murder our wives and children."'

'After all what does most of the media live on if it isn't murder, rape, and massacre?' asked Marilyn. She took a sip at her wine. 'I, like most people, find the bloodshed in the Revolution fascinating if horrifying, although I'm one of the few to admit it. Of course it's a mystery why we are interested in the gruesome details of other people dying. Probably, it's part of our aggressive instinct which we needed as primitives to attack others for food, or territory. Or at least it allowed us to applaud those in the tribe who were bold enough to kill our enemies for us. Also, of course, it's got sexual links, a paroxysm of abandon, a flouting of all restraint.'

Brita and I had met Marilyn, who was American, in a restaurant when, as usual, we were discussing aspects of the Revolution. Sitting alone, nearby, she had overheard us, and so the conversation began.

'One of the reasons I'm staying in Paris is that the French Revolution intrigues me,' she told us. 'The idea of all these people suddenly going mad, eliminating each other. The smashing of the Tuileries, the September massacres, the execution of the King and then the Terror, the civil war all over France. Why, it's really a blueprint of what's been going on in the world ever since. Suddenly, mannered, humanistic people, with their belief in Reason and Utopias, turn into wild beasts.'

'Not all of them,' I said. 'Even those directly involved in the Revolution were at most ten per cent of the population.'

'Could be. But most of the rest approved, or didn't come out against it.'

'It was also like Nazi Germany. Most people got on with their lives. They were afraid.'

I liked the way that, as happens with many Americans, Marilyn revealed what she felt without ambiguity, or apparent worry about what one might think of her. Of course I also accepted that we all had something primitive and uncontrolled beneath our 'civism'. However, as far as the French Revolution was concerned, I felt tired of people who only saw it in terms of massacres and the guillotine. Of course these things had existed, but it was also full of human dilemmas, and ideas and attitudes which had formed us for the last two centuries.

'I suppose you know revolutionary Paris backwards?' ventured Brita.

'Sure. D'you want to come on a tour?'

'That'd be interesting. We're just researching into where the September massacres took place.'

'Just my line. D'you want to go now?'

'Tomorrow would be better.'

'OK. Tomorrow afternoon? Meet you in the Place de Buci. Three o'clock?'

As the meal continued, Marilyn told us about herself. She must have been in her mid-thirties, slightly blowsy with generous but not unpleasing folds beneath her summer dress, and one eye slightly bigger than the other, which gave her a mocking, surprised expression. She was from Arkansas, she said, but now lived in Los Angeles, and worked in the media herself. She had come over to research magazine articles and maybe a book on the French Revolution, now that the bicentenary was round the corner. Originally, she'd intended staying for three weeks but had got so absorbed that she'd been living in Paris for the last four months. Despite her interest in bloodshed, she seemed delighted to hear we had three children and a dog.

The following afternoon, we waited on the corner of the Rues Dauphine and Mazarine when a hand waved from a passing Renault. Marilyn was with a man who grinned up nervously at us. 'We're just going to park,' she called merrily. 'See you in a moment.'

We sat down in the café on the corner, certain that parking a car in this area would take a long time. Around us flowed the usual crowds of students and tourists, while cars avoided each other with breath-taking skill, just missing our precarious chairs.

'Well, here we are. This is Raoul. He doesn't speak much English but he knows a lot.' Marilyn indicated a rather sheepish, wiry man with sprouts of blond hair emerging from his open shirt, like the fronds of a creeper.

'So,' she said, looking round the Carrefour de Buci with its five streets branching off in different directions. 'This is where it all began in the afternoon of Sunday, September 2nd, three weeks after the storming of the Tuileries. There was a recruiting centre here for the army, just a table and benches with a tricolour draped on the wall behind. Lots of noise with sergeants encouraging the young men to join up and save the *Patrie*. Presumably, there were the usual jokes about escaping from wives, and cheers from the crowd when groups of volunteers enrolled.

'Suddenly, four hackney cabs threaded their way through. They were crammed with priests, and were on their way to the Abbaye prison over there.' Marilyn pointed vaguely down the Rue de Buci towards what is now the Boulevard St Germain. 'The mood of the crowd changed suddenly. People started jeering and shouting abuse.

133

The Abbey of St Germain des Prés.
1. Abbaye Prison;
2. The gardens where many of the September Massacres took place.

There was a scuffle and one of the prisoners, a tall young man, was
pulled from a carriage. You could see the tonsure mark in his dark
hair. One of his escort raised his sabre and wounded him. The crowd
went mad and followed the carriages up to the end of the Rue de
Buci, round the corner of what is now the Boulevard St Germain

and into the courtyard on the far side of the church of St Germain des Prés. There, they dragged out the other twenty-three priests, and killed them all, except one. Then they roared back down the present Boulevard St Germain to the prison of the Abbaye, which contained over two hundred prisoners, many of them priests.

'They invaded the prison and set up a court at the entrance with a few so-called judges. The prisoners came in one by one, and were interrogated briefly. Then, the "judge" either ordered their release, in which case they were cheered by the mob and often taken back to their houses in a triumphant procession, or else the judge ordered their transfer to another prison. This was a subterfuge to indicate that they were guilty. They were then pushed out of the door and were either massacred in the street, or else dragged to the garden-court of the Abbaye, where they were bashed to death with sabres, pikes, axes, or even with carpentry tools.

'When night came, bonfires were lit, casting a hellish glow over the scene, and the "work" went on.'

'Can one still see where it happened?'

'Sure. We've left our car up there, anyway.'

We walked up to the end of the Rue de Buci, where the vegetable and flower market was being dismantled, and into the Boulevard St Germain.

'The prison itself was just about there, at the side of the present Boulevard, opposite numbers 135–7, in front of where those mod. dress shops are. Before the street was widened into the Boulevard, this was the Rue Ste Marguerite, which stretched down the side of the enormous enclosure of the Abbey. You can still get a sense of what the Abbey was like if we walk through all these little streets on the right.'

We went through a maze of curving medieval lanes with names like Rue de l'Echaudé, or Bourbon-le-Château. The Rue de l'Abbaye went straight by the side of the church which still stood, massive and uncleaned, with its two tall spires, amidst ecclesiastical buildings. To our left, now, was the entrance of the church with a little garden surrounded by railings. In front of us, at the end of the Rue Bonaparte, was a square.

'The massacres took place here,' said Marilyn. 'The gardens of the Abbey stretched over this square, which was surrounded by a high wall. Prisoners had been crowded into the neighbouring chapel and refectory. Another tribunal sat in the entrance to the Abbey guest-house, which gave onto the garden by way of a glass door. A man who survived described the turmoil of his interrogation. It was interrupted by another prisoner who, interviewed briefly, was pushed through the open glass door and slaughtered. Then a turnkey rushed in to say that a prisoner was trying to escape up a chimney. They lit a fire in the hearth so that he fell down, and he was also killed. There's another account of a notary's clerk who was returning home in the evening and saw the glow of the fires and heard the shouts of those being battered to death. He noticed the gutter was running with blood, and ran off home as fast as he could. And yet all over Paris, life on this Sunday evening was going on as usual. Couples were walking up the wooded avenue of the Champs Elysées, and the cafés were full. Only seven days later, the Fair of St Cloud was opened and everyone flocked to it and amused themselves. It's an extraordinary story.'

Raoul, I noticed, was looking a little green as he gazed distractedly down at the paving stones.

'But was it organized?' asked Brita. 'Or was it just the mob getting out of hand?'

'No – it was certainly organized by the Commune who, after all, engineered the attack on the Tuileries. There's not a lot of evidence, but enough. It was the various Sections in Paris who carried out the killings, mobilizing their members and using the Fédérés who had helped to storm the Tuileries.'

'Who were the Fédérés?'

'They were mainly from Marseilles and Brittany. They came to Paris just before the attack on the Tuileries, on their way to the front. But in fact few ever got there. After the September massacres, most just went home. Anyway, let's go to the Carmes, which is just as it was when the massacres took place there.'

'More?' questioned Raoul. 'It's horrible. I never realized it. I had heard of the September massacres. But only vaguely. To think French people did that.'

As we climbed into Marilyn's Renault, which was parked carelessly on the pavement, just where piles of corpses had once lain, she turned to him. 'Well, it's been repeated since. Look at Algeria. Klaus Barbie's defence lawyer at his trial in Lyons said that first they should try those who had committed crimes in the Algerian war before accusing Barbie of Gestapo activities.'

'Or Vietnam,' I added tactlessly. 'Or Cromwell in Ireland, or the British suppressing the Indian Mutiny.'

'It isn't a question of nationality,' said Brita. 'Unfortunately, it often happens when people are afraid and are manipulated by those in power, or want to take their revenge. It happened in Stockholm, too, when those supporting Gustavus Vasa were massacred by the army of the Danish King.'

'It comes from a division into two camps,' said Marilyn. 'Each is afraid of the other and only feels secure when those who threaten them are eliminated. That's what war's about, too.'

Raoul didn't look too convinced.

'Anyway,' said Marilyn firmly, 'you asked me to show you the sites, so I will. On this afternoon of September 2nd, another section of the mob went up to the Carmes, which was a Carmelite monastery, just here.' We skirted a large nineteenth-century building, all red brick in Gothic style, and went down the broad Rue de Vaugirard. We stopped at the open gates of a courtyard with a church beyond.

Marilyn parked and we got out. 'I'll have to square the concierge,' she said, and disappeared through a small door obscured with white paper so that no one could see through.

'OK,' she said, reappearing cheerily. 'Let's go.' We advanced towards a little corridor at the side of the church, with a door at the end. 'That goes straight into the garden, where most of the massacres took place.'

We moved left through the door of the church, built in 1613–20, and decorated in Renaissance style with chapels set on either side. Above, was one of the first domes made of wood in Paris, where Elijah soared up in his fiery chariot. 'This was used as a prison,' said Marilyn, 'like a lot of churches and monasteries in the Revolution. The Carmelites themselves were very popular in the neighbourhood because they gave a lot of alms to the poor. As a result, many refractory priests were welcomed as refugees in local homes and were arrested in the neighbourhood.

'On this day of September 2nd, a lot of these priests were imprisoned here, including an archbishop and two bishops. They slept on mattresses on the floor, held regular Masses, prayed, confessed, and gave each other absolution. You can imagine them speaking in those hushed voices so common to priests.

'Suddenly there were cries and the sounds of running feet outside.

Then the terrible yells of those who had gone out to walk in the garden and were now being pursued and killed.' Marilyn paused and looked round at the rows of chairs. 'Several men suddenly came into the church and announced that the priests were being moved elsewhere. First, though, they would be interrogated to see if any should be released. One by one, the priests shuffled through this door here, past this statue of the Virgin, sculpted in imitation of Bernini.' The angelic face of the white statue seemed to lighten the gloom as we walked through the same door and into a sacristy with low, wooden cupboards round the walls. Then, into what had once been a cloister, roofed over, with the pillars covered in a green coating, now forming a large lecture room. Finally, we found ourselves in a little corridor which led to an open garden door. Narrow stairs climbed up to our left.

'At the bottom of the stairs, here,' said Marilyn, 'a man called Violetti installed a simple table and a chair. As the priests passed, he asked them whether they had taken the oath. The majority, who hadn't, were pushed towards the garden door, there.

'Imagine being pushed along, knowing from the cries outside what was going to happen,' said Marilyn in her deep voice. 'As they came out on top of these six steps, they were hit on the head and reeled against the railing and down into the garden, where they were finished off. By six o'clock, a hundred and sixteen corpses lay on the grass, under the trees, or against the wall which, then, was much further down the garden. One man escaped and climbed to the top of the wall and was killed by a pistol shot in the head. Others succeeded in getting over the wall, although it was ten feet high. A few were released.'

We walked through the garden, and then went back to the narrow corridor. A telephone sat on a shelf, like a large, black insect, beside the place where the priests had passed.

We followed Marilyn up the narrow stairs to the next floor and entered a long room. Plaster had been removed from a section of the wall, and trickles of ancient blood streaked the faded surface. 'This is where the assassins leant their axes and sabres when they came here for a rest and wine,' said Marilyn. 'Also, Joséphine de Beauharnais, Napoleon's future wife, was imprisoned here in the Terror. You can see her signature there.' Marilyn pointed to a scrawl on the far wall.

We paused a moment and slowly descended again. Everything

was so silent, with the dusty church smell as I remembered it in clerical houses in Spain and Italy, the feeling of the static, of time heavy on hands. One violent September afternoon it had been disrupted for a few hours. Now it had resumed its silence.

We descended to the crypt, which was ice-cold. In dark glass cases, bones and skulls were strewn untidily. 'Look at the craniums. They're shattered round the temple. The jaws are broken.' The skulls looked like the tops of large mushrooms, greenish, almost mouldy, dented by axes or swords. 'They found them in a well,' said Marilyn. 'In the nineteenth century, they decided to look for the remains in the garden. They searched everywhere in vain when an old man pointed to a patch of grass. "They're there," he said. Probably, as a youth he had taken part in the massacres. Soon after, he disappeared. But they found the well, crammed with over ninety corpses and masses of rubbish such as earthenware plates, stamped with the Carmelites' coat of arms.'

We climbed again to the street. 'Well, there are many other places,' said Marilyn. 'There's Bicêtre, where they killed children of twelve; La Salpêtrière, where they violated and murdered young girls; or the street outside the old prison of La Force in the Rue Roi de Sicile, where they butchered Marie-Antoinette's friend, the Princesse de Lamballe, and dragged her dismembered corpse round Paris at the end of a piece of rope.'

'Did they show her head to Marie-Antoinette in the Temple as they intended?' I asked.

'I'm not sure. Some say they did, and that the Queen collapsed in a faint. Others that the royal family were warned not to look. Anyway, it was a diabolical way of announcing her death.'

'It's barbaric,' said Raoul, almost whimpering. 'It makes me ashamed. At school we were told that the Revolution was the birth of modern France, the beginnings of Liberty, the Rights of Man.'

'It was, as well,' said Marilyn.

13

DECISIVE SKIRMISH

'It was already the army of the REPUBLIC.'
MATHIEZ

The September massacres coincided with the gradual advance of the Prussian armies and the émigrés towards Paris, which inevitably increased hysteria in the capital.

At the same time, the Piedmontese advanced into south-east France and the Austrians besieged Lille. France was now faced not by war against a single power but by a European coalition.

Nothing seemed to stand between the Prussians, commanded by the Duke of Brunswick, and Paris. At Châlons, Luckner, an old general, had a camp which was mainly a disorganized mass of new volunteers being trained to carry arms. Otherwise, a professional army of some 16,000 men led by Kellerman was at Metz, while another general, Dumouriez, who had fought in the Seven Years War, was at Sedan on the Belgian border with some 30,000 men, many of whom were raw recruits.

Brunswick advanced steadily. On 2 September, the day when the massacres started, he took Verdun with little resistance. Some of the inhabitants were later guillotined for having welcomed the King of Prussia with a present of dragees. The French commander, Colonel Beaurepaire, committed suicide in despair, and his memory is now being commemorated in his birth-place, Angers, with a statue.

On came this army, with the émigrés exultant as they returned to their '*douce France*'. They travelled in their ornate coaches with all the usual appurtenances of campaigning officers of the Old Régime: their sumptuous tents and furniture, their valets and often their women. They were surprised and disappointed that the local French did not welcome them with open arms and that there was no peasant uprising in their favour. Still they squabbled about precedence, and the Austrians and Prussians were infuriated by their complaints, their arrogance and boastfulness. In many ways, they must have resembled Shakespeare's depiction of French nobles before the battle of Agincourt in *Henry V*, vaunting their horses, crowing over their yet undefeated enemy, describing these perhaps, as did Orléans in the play, as 'Foolish curs that run winking into the mouth of a Russian bear and have their heads crushed like rotten apples.'

The only major barrier between this army and Paris was the forty-mile wooded plateau of the Argonne, close to Louis XVI's escape route in June 1791. On 4 September, Dumouriez marched his army south and occupied the defiles at Grand-Pré and on the road between Verdun and Paris at Les Islettes. However, at both places Brunswick's troops beat him back and forced their way through.

Dumouriez's staff were in favour of a retreat to Châlons to join Luckner. But Dumouriez himself rejected this and took up position on high ground between Valmy, with its windmill on a hill, and Ste Menehould, from which, little more than a year previously, Drouet had galloped off to arrest the King at Varennes. Although Dumouriez was actually behind the Prussians, who now had an open path to Paris, he calculated that the invading army would never advance with the French straddling their supply lines and escape routes.

On the morning of 20 September, a bombardment opened between the French on the crest of Valmy and the Prussians on another slope, the Heights of La Lune. About 40,000 shots were fired and a few hundred soldiers were killed, but the Prussians managed to hit some ammunition caissons which exploded thunderously, filling the French levies with panic and provoking the flight of a German mercenary brigade which was serving with the French army.

Brunswick, the Prussian commander, decided to attack. As the last shrouds of mist cleared, the French could see about 30,000 Prussian infantry forming into columns. Slowly, they advanced up the green slopes. Here were Frederick the Great's renowned infantry, professional veterans, victors of many battles in the Seven Years War, the most highly disciplined infantry in Europe. They were approaching a French army which, deserted by many of its officers, was a hurriedly collected ragbag of inexperienced troops, demoralized by continual defeats.

The Prussians advanced to the lower slopes of the hill, on which stood the windmill which was to become renowned throughout the world. Then, for no apparent reason, they halted, turned about and retreated in good order. The battle was over. The cannonade went on till nightfall, but in the next few days the Prussians began a retreat to the frontier without being molested by the French. Paris was saved, and with it the Revolution. The monarchy was doomed. This trivial victory marked the beginning of French expansion all over Europe, and of a series of wars which were to last for over twenty years. Indeed one of the most amazing things about the Revolution is the long-lasting effects of apparently insignificant events.

We visited Valmy on our way to Varennes with René Claude. A reconstructed windmill stands on the hill, visible from the motorway to the south, like a single sailing ship on the crest of a green wave. Monuments to the victory stand around it. On them is no mention of Dumouriez, because six months later he betrayed the Revolution and went over to the Austrians. It is Kellerman who is inscribed everywhere as the victor, although it was Dumouriez's energy and judgement that made a triumph possible. This deformation of history remains evidence of the way passions about the Revolution still run high.

As we stood on the hill and looked over the gentle green slopes in the afternoon sunlight, I asked myself why the Prussians retired so suddenly and retreated over the frontier so meekly. No one seems really to know the answer. Some point out that the Prussians were ravaged by dysentery, as supplies from Verdun had not got through and the troops had had to subsist on an uncomfortable diet of green grapes and mushed wheat. But would that have caused the sudden decision at the last moment to withdraw? If dysentery-racked soldiers could get that far, would their ill-health have prevented them advancing those last few yards and probably pushing the French off the hill? Others say that the slopes were muddy after the heavy rain and the Prussian artillery fire could only cover their own troops until they arrived at the edge of the French position. But this surely might well be true of any frontal attack in warfare at the time, and the Prussians did retire in good order. It is more likely that Frederick William II, King of Prussia, who accompanied the army, was reluctant to risk his troops when yet another partition of Poland was about to take place, with Austria and Russia competing with Prussia for the spoils. Unless the campaign was swift and easy, Prussia would be bogged down in France, unable to assert her claims with force. Better perhaps to make a demonstration of force, and if the French did not panic and run, to retire again in good order.

Why, though, did the French allow the Prussians to retreat unmolested back to the frontier when they could have sniped and chivvied them? Certainly it all smacks of some prearranged plan, with the Prussians agreeing not to finish their attack so long as they were allowed to leave France unharmed.

A more fantastic theory has it that Brunswick, the Prussian commander, was bribed with diamonds. A week before, robbers had broken into the Garde Meuble in Paris and stolen the royal diamonds on display in a glass-fronted cabinet (see p. 44). They climbed up onto the colonnaded gallery in the present Navy Ministry, which overlooks the Place de la Concorde. There you can still see a section of the wooden shutters which has been repaired since it was smashed in those distant days of 1792. The robbers were not intercepted. They lowered the King's diamonds in baskets attached to a rope to accomplices below. Then they escaped, though some of them were later caught and guillotined.

The two opposing generals, Dumouriez and Brunswick, were good friends and they are believed to have met before the battle. Brunswick was the liberal ruler of a Germany duchy and is known to have sympathized with the early phase of the Revolution. He had even been suggested by some French deputies as an alternative constitutional monarch to Louis XVI. He was also passionately fond of diamonds, and had a valuable collection in his castle in Brunswick. When he died in 1806, killed fighting another French army at the battle of Jena, the Blue Diamond of the Golden Fleece, which belonged to the French Crown, was found in this collection. How did it get there?

Even in a historical climate where it is believed that only trends are significant, it is still extraordinary to think that the survival of the Republic and the future of the Revolution may well have hung on the venality of a German Duke who was over-fond of diamonds.

14

ROYAL DEATH IN PARIS

'I felt republican virtue wavering in my heart at the sight of the guilty man humiliated before the sovereign power.'

ROBESPIERRE

Meanwhile, the royal family waited in vain for deliverance in a gloomy medieval tower in the Temple. This tower was part of a great enclosure of gardens, chapels, palaces and houses which had once belonged to the Knights Templar, an order of soldier monks who had enriched themselves by acting as bankers, police and escorts to those going on the Crusades. The enclosure formed almost a separate city, which had been expropriated by King Philip IV as long ago as 1310, when he filled his coffers by extracting confessions of heresy and sacrilege from the Knights Templar by ghastly tortures. He was thus able to eliminate the Order and confiscate their treasure and property. Now, things had come full circle and it was the buildings of these tortured soldier-monks which imprisoned the descendants of the monarch who had persecuted them.

At the time of the Revolution, no fewer than 4,000 people lived in this enclosure, with its narrow alleyways and ancient medieval buildings. Today there is little left: Napoleon demolished it in 1808, fearful that the prison of the royal family and of Louis XVI before he was guillotined would become a royalist shrine. Now the area is bounded in a broad rectangle by the Rue Béranger to the north and the Rue de Bretagne on the south, with the Rue du Temple on the west and the Rue Charlot to the east. Today, much of it has been taken over by shops selling costume jewellery, all close together, as in a souk, while to the north there is an indoor market and shops selling leatherware clothing, displaying shiny black trousers and goatskin coats.

Of the gardens, only a little patch remains. At the end of it,

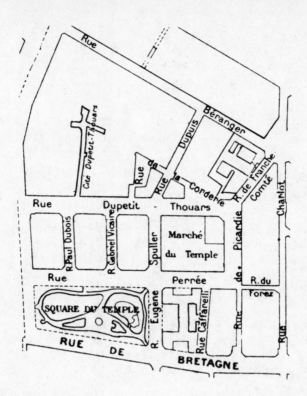

The area of the Temple today. The Tower was to the right of the Square in the left-hand lower corner.

fringing the Rue du Temple, was the Palace of the Grand Prior, which in the eighteenth century had been the elegant residence of the Prince de Conti, a doyen of the arts, who created a musical and literary salon there, attended by Rousseau and Prévost, where Mozart had given concerts as a child.

Here, in 1785, Marie-Antoinette attended a banquet to celebrate the birth of her son, who was also to be shut up in the Temple to die there alone, after his parents' execution, in 1795. Opposite the palace, to one side, there was a tall medieval tower with a turret on either corner. Massive and dark, it glowered down on the festivities like an evil giant. Marie-Antoinette besought her host to have it pulled down. It seemed so sinister and overpowering in contrast to the tasteful palace. Her plea, though, was ignored.

The Temple in 1792. *Bibliothèque Nationale.*
1. The Tower.
2. The Grand Prior's Residence.

Today, when you go to this little garden, you have difficulty finding exactly where this tower was. Children play near a bandstand. There is a small pond with ducks, and scrubby lawns. I asked the old guardian where the tower stood, and he answered in stately, concise French: '*Je ne pourrais vous dire.*' Finally, I went to the end of the gardens into the district town hall, and the receptionist pointed through the walls and said: 'It was just there. You're almost standing by it.'

It was here that the King and Queen, still legally sovereign, arrived under close guard on the night of 13 August 1792, after the sack of the Tuileries, with their two children and Madame Elisabeth, the King's sister. First they were given dinner in the Grand Prior's residence, not by lackeys with powdered hair and to the strains of music, but surrounded by their sansculotte escort, who watched them eat.

Then they were taken to the tower, lit by scores of oil lamps in the garden. Someone started a chorus from the old song *Malbrouk s'en va-t-en guerre*, which was taken up by everyone:

> *Madame à son tour monte*
> *Qui sait quand descendra?*

The royal family were led up to the apartment of the archivist of the Temple while their prison was prepared.

After a few weeks, they were moved to the second and third floors of the tower, which had been divided into different rooms. The King, the little Dauphin and the valet, Cléry, occupied the second floor. The ladies were above. In each wall were two narrow windows, giving little light as they were at the end of recesses nine feet deep, which was the actual thickness of the walls.

Each floor was closed by two thick doors, one of wood and one of iron, and access was by way of a spiral staircase in one of the slim secondary towers which was blocked by no fewer than twelve doorways between the ground and third floors. The guard room was on the first floor, and the palace at the end of the gardens was also full of soldiers.

In this sad, ancient prison, the royal family led a routine life. They dined at ten, and afterwards the King gave lessons in geography and history to his son. Then they walked in the garden which is the only part of this vast enclosure to survive, and spent the rest of the afternoon playing chess, or reading until dinner.

A newspaper vendor stood outside the walls and shouted out the news, which the royal family could hear. From him, they learnt of the September massacres, and of the battle of Valmy, which extinguished their hopes of rescue. From the vendor, too, came news that the King's locksmith, Gamain, had revealed the existence of an iron chest in a wall in the Tuileries. In it was all the correspondence held by Louis and Marie-Antoinette with the Austrians and counter-revolutionaries. It was proof of the King's treachery, although could the King actually be treacherous to himself? Certainly, though, Louis had betrayed the Constitution, the army fighting in the field, and the Revolution.

In the Convention, the debate about the trial of the King got under way. According to the Constitution of 1791, the King was inviolable. But if the people could decide this, could they not also take it away? Was it wise to try him anyway? The young Jacobin, St Just, thought Louis should be punished simply because he was a King, like crushing a poisonous snake.

Just before his interrogation on 11 December, the little Dauphin was removed upstairs, and Louis was totally separated from his family. No more lessons to his son, no more games of chess, nor meals together. Louis was not to see his family till the evening before his execution.

On 26 December, he was driven in a green carriage to his trial. Mary Wollstonecraft, later William Godwin's wife, caught a glimpse of him on his way to the Convention:

About nine o'clock in the morning, the King passed by my window, moving silently along (except now and then a few strokes of the drum, which rendered the stillness more aweful) through empty streets, surrounded by the national guards, who, clustering around the carriage, seemed to deserve their name. The inhabitants flocked to their windows, but the casements were all shut, not a voice was heard, nor did I see anything like an insulting gesture. – For the first time since I entered France, I bowed to the majesty of the people, and respected the propriety of behaviour so perfectly in unison with my own feelings. I can scarcely tell you why, but an association of ideas made the tears flow from my eyes, when I saw Louis sitting, with more dignity than I had expected from his character, in a hackney coach going to meet his death . . .

He was not actually going to his death – that was to come three weeks later — but it is interesting that from the back windows of 22 Rue de Temple where Mary Wollstonecraft lodged, you can still see the Boulevard St Martin along which Louis travelled.*

Imprisonment had made Louis pale and flaccid. He had been allowed to chose his own defending lawyers, and among them was Malesherbes, a former minister of his. De Sèze, a young lawyer, was the spokesman and gave a speech which lasted two hours, challenging the Convention's right to try Louis. However, his argument was legalistic when the issue was really political.

Then Louis was taken back through the mists of a winter's evening to the solitude of his medieval prison.

In the Convention, each deputy was allowed to give his opinion, but as this went on too long, voting began. In the tense atmosphere of the Manège, which already had witnessed so much, each deputy came forward to give his verdict, with the galleries cheering those who voted for the King's death, and execrating those who did not. Fear and excitement stirred Paris. There was betting in the cafés on the result, and rumours had it that the Comte d'Artois was back, and that there would be a royalist insurrection.

The verdict of guilty was almost unanimous, but how should Louis be punished? Proposals for a referendum on this question were rejected, partly for fear of civil war. Some deputies voted for death but with a stay of execution, others for banishment. After the second count, there was a majority of only one for death without qualification. Haplessly, Egalité, the King's cousin, once Duke of Orléans, had cast the decisive vote for death without qualification, shocking even the Jacobins. He was the one deputy whose vote against Louis XVI's execution would have been accepted even by the mob in the galleries. His vote was dangerous also for him personally. The Republic was unstable and only three months old, and Egalité himself was bound to be a close candidate for the throne if the form of government was changed back after a new convulsion. His vote, therefore, could be construed as a Machiavellian attempt to make his prospects brighter. Before going to the Assembly, he had actually told his family he would vote against Louis's death. But the timidity and lack of integrity which had prevented him following up his early success in the Revolution were too strong.

Louis was woken at two in the morning to be told he was going

* Researched by Richard Holmes and discussed in his fascinating book, *Footsteps*.

to die. He asked for three days' delay and for a confessor who had not sworn the oath to the Constitution. The first request was refused, and the second granted. Louis spent the day and evening preparing himself for death.

In January 1987, on the nearest Sunday to the anniversary of Louis XVI's execution, we made our way through the snow to the Chapelle Expiatoire, near La Madeleine in Paris. The chapel was built in 1826, over the cemetery where many of those guillotined on the Place de la Révolution had been buried; the altar is supposed to lie over the exact place where Louis XVI's body was dissolved in quick-lime, his head between his legs, on that other January, almost two hundred years ago.

About a thousand people were gathered in this bright chapel with its coffered ceiling and polished stone. Many were young, crowding into insufficient space, standing in dark suits and the ladies in sober hats. On either side were the statues of Marie-Antoinette and Louis XVI, standing opposite one another on large plinths, like side altars.

Everyone waited while the Duke of Anjou, the Legitimist Pretender and a direct descendant through the Spanish line of Louis XIV, entered with his son of twelve. Simultaneously, two other Masses were going on in Paris, each representing different royal claimants: that of the Comte de Paris and the supporters of the Orléans line; that of the Comte de Paris's son, who has been disinherited by his father. And this service we attended in the Chapelle Expiatoire.

By the altar, a Bishop gave a sermon. He talked of those crowned by God as His Representative on Earth, and how the Jews had waited two hundred years in Egypt, forgetting their religion and traditions, until their reawakening by Moses, which led to their triumph over the Egyptians and the Exodus. So had the royalists in France lost their traditions and beliefs. But the hour would come.

While he talked, I looked at the statues. Louis XVI was falling backwards with his arms out and one leg folded beneath him, sustained only by an angel. His face, with its big nose and powdered hair, looked upwards in bewilderment: without the spiritual support of the angel, he would collapse. By his foot lay his hat, curiously like a beggar's cap – as if he were asking for charity. Marie-Antoinette was erect, with an angel looking into her eyes, her small crown fallen and lying upside down on the fringe of her skirt.

There was a loneliness about the couple, isolated in this chapel, amidst people they could not know, who were singing and praying in memory of the burden both had carried, of their agony and gruesome execution in hostile Paris.

The service came to an end, and I went to read their last testaments, inscribed on the plinths. Louis's was a will in which he forgives those he had been kind to but who had not treated him well. He besought his son, 'if he is unfortunate enough to be King', not to avenge his death. Marie-Antoinette, in a later letter to Madame Elisabeth, Louis's sister, expressed her agony at leaving both her children orphans, but was comforted by the illusion that Madame Elisabeth could still look after them.

'Terrible, isn't it?' said a thick-set Frenchman with glasses, beside me.

'Yes – are there many people in France who think a King will come back?'

'More and more. After all, we're in such a mess. France has been in a mess since the Revolution. Glory went out with our legitimate kings. The restoration of monarchy in Spain is a great encouragement.'

We went out towards the snow, which was falling heavily beyond the columned porch. People crowded into a thick queue to greet the Duke of Anjou (who was killed in a skiing accident in 1989). As I passed, his hand was being kissed. There were gasps of '*Monseigneur.*'

Outside, they were selling royalist leaflets and magazines in the snow. The Duke of Anjou came out and walked to his car. '*Vive le Roi!*' the cry went up, and then almost in the football style: '*Le Roi! Le Roi! Le Roi!*' There was frantic waving.

We walked into the streets, which suddenly brought us back to normality, with a few people tramping through the snow to lunch. We walked down to Concorde, where there was a Republican demonstration with groups standing about and a procession on the pavement where the guillotine had stood, shouting '*Vive la République!*'

The division goes on, harmlessly perhaps, outside the present current of French lives. But there is still a reflection, a shadow of the events which split France two hundred years ago. In changed and evolved forms, it splits her still today.

The evening before his execution, Louis said goodbye to his family, sitting with them for two hours, the little Dauphin standing between his legs, the women weeping.

Then he slept peacefully till five in the morning, and said Mass with his confessor, the Abbé Edgeworth, who was a nonjuring priest of Irish extraction.

He did not see his family again that morning, although he had said he would, but climbed into a coach, borrowed for a King's execution, and was borne through a silent Paris, with window shutters closed and eighty thousand soldiers lining the route, through a slight drizzle and wisps of mist.

His carriage followed the line of the present boulevards, laid out on the old walls of Paris, past the Portes St Martin and St Denis, along what are now the Boulevards des Italiens and Capucins, finishing with that of the Madeleine and the Rue Royale, into the Place de la Révolution, which now is Concorde.

The guillotine, surrounded by soldiers, had been erected between where the obelisk now stands and the entrance of the Champs Elysées. In his coach, Louis waited a few minutes, seeming to the spectators to be asserting his last prerogative, but in reality reading the Prayer for the Dying.

Slowly, he descended with the Abbé Edgeworth, and mounted the steps of the scaffold. He took off his coat, revealing a white waistcoat, but then resisted having his hands tied. He had followed everything submissively so far, but this last humiliation he could not bear. Charles I of England had himself placed his head on the block, and then raised his arms of his own free will as a sign of readiness. However, the Abbé persuaded him to relent.

Louis advanced to the edge of the scaffold and tried to speak. He had always failed to do this when a speech might have saved him, as at Varennes, but he responded now to the last ceremony in which he was the leading figure.

'Frenchmen, I die innocent . . .' he began, but drums drowned his voice and he was hustled onto the plank. The knife fell, and he let out a little cry, perhaps because his neck was so fat that the blade cut through with difficulty.

Samson, whose ancestors had been the royal executioners in Paris for a hundred years, held the King's head up for the people to see.

Some witnesses said that there was a numbed silence. Others that cries of '*Vive la République!*' and '*Vive la Nation!*' resounded

33. Sauce's house (with downstairs shutters) in the main street of Varennes before the First World War.

34. The small room in Sauce's house where the royal family spent the night (see p. 111).

35. View of the church, the Bras D'Or next to it,
and other buildings. Varennes before 1914.

36. Same view as 35 today. The church has been rebuilt
and the adjoining houses were destroyed in the First World War.
Author's photograph.

37. The Jacobin club. The Royal Ministers, announcing the declaration of War, have the heads of beetles and a linnet. *Bibliothèque Nationale*

38. Louis XVI wearing a bonnet of Liberty during the invasion of the Tuileries Palace on June 20th, 1792. (See p. 126) *Bibliothèque Nationale*

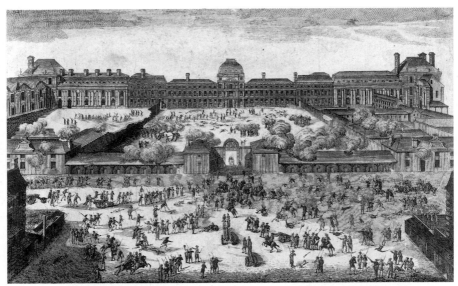

39. The attack on the Tuileries, 10 August 1792. (See p. 128) *Bibliothèque Nationale*

40. The royal family escaped along this side of the Tuileries gardens, and went up the steps on the left. On top of these stood the National Assembly. (See p. 127) Author's photograph.

41. The royal family in the journalist's box in the
Assembly, where they took refuge for three days.
(See p. 128–9) *Bibliothèque Nationale*

42. The Tower of the Temple where the royal family
were imprisoned. (See p. 147) *Bibliothèque Nationale*

43. English satires:
(a) 'A Limited Monarchy'
where the mob 'persuades'
Louis XVI not to
use his veto.
Bibliothèque Nationale

A LIMITED MONARCHY,
or, the *NEGATIVE* power of France
surrounded by the patriotic Furies
of the 20th Ult.

(b) 'An Unlimited
Democracy', where Satan gathers all
the contending
political parties
in his arms.
Bibliothèque Nationale

AN UNLIMITED DEMOCRACY,
or, the *ACTIVE* power of France
Reconciling contending Parties
by a General *HUG* on the 7th Ins.

44. The old Abbaye prison, now destroyed, where many of the September Massacres took place. (See p. 135) *Carnavalet*

45. Guillotining of Louis XVI. Notice Gabriel's buildings on the left and the Tuileries Gardens ahead. Also the caps on pikes in the background. (See p. 152) *Bibliothèque Nationale*

46. The new 'King Louis XVII', who remained in the Temple until his supposed death at the age of ten in 1795. Vien, *Carnavalet*

through the Place, and that the people danced the farandole around the scaffold. Others reported that people came with their handkerchiefs to stain them with the blood of the dead King, as if turning them almost into religious relics.

The effects of this execution were to be long-lasting. Only five months had elapsed since the King had ruled at the Tuileries. Now, a rift had opened between the whole idea of monarchy and popular democracy, which is still with us. The gradual evolution of kingship from an autocratic role to that of a powerless but resplendent symbol of national unity and of a stable democracy, which exists in so many northern countries, had been doomed in France by blood and violence.

15

PARIS: STRUGGLE IN THE CONVENTION

'The more I see of men, the more I like dogs.'
MME ROLAND, one of the most influential Girondins,
wife of the Minister of the Interior.

The execution of the King deprived France of that single sovereignty which had lasted a thousand years. The result was an inevitable tussle for power, heightened by the fact that the country was in danger, that a war had to be won, that many people were against the new developments, and that traitors, real or imaginary, had to be weeded out.

At this stage, those reading about the Revolution tend to throw up their hands in despair at the confusion. They probably know that the Girondins were guillotined and that the Jacobins were connected with Robespierre. But the rest is a complexity of events and names which seem impossible to decipher.

To add to the confusion is the uncertainty of what differentiated the two main opposing groups of Jacobins and Girondins. Both were mainly from the professional middle classes; both roughly the same age, in their thirties or early forties; both had been educated in the same kind of school, whether Oratorian or Jesuit. Many of both groups came not from Paris but from the provinces.

It is probably easiest if one starts with their tactical differences, which also illustrate their attitudes to government and the Revolution: the Jacobins used the Sansculottes and the Commune of Paris to serve their purposes, starting with the overthrow of the King, following through to the September massacres, and then to popular pressure for the King's death. Inevitably, they also responded, as quid pro quo, to the views of the Sansculottes: the need to weed out traitors, the sacrifice of everything to the war effort, and some control of prices, particularly those of food.

The Girondins, on the other hand, believed that only the Convention, with deputies from all over France, was the true organ of popular sovereignty. They therefore resisted the capital's attempt to dictate policy, and remained aloof from the mob which ultimately engulfed them.

Historians have also tried to divide Girondin and Jacobin into temperamental groups. The Girondins were on the whole more idealistic, more what we might call Romantics. The Jacobins were hard men, austere and determined, almost Calvinist in attitude, if not in religion and upbringing, seeing the world divided into the Elect, to whom they felt they belonged, and those who had not been 'chosen', who should be purged. 'Virtue has always been a minority on Earth,' Robespierre once said.

What is also important is that neither Jacobin nor Girondin represented a political party in our modern sense, but rather conglomerates of friends and sympathizers, who often disagreed with one another. They had no party system, nor manifesto of collective belief. They were even less defined than Whigs and Tories in Britain at the time, which is also why they seem so confusing to modern readers.

The Girondins, isolated in this turbulent capital, were motivated by fear of a dictatorship under Marat, Danton and Robespierre, abetted by the Paris Commune which controlled the forty-eight Sections, with their assemblies and armed Sansculottes, into which the city was divided. They were outspoken and aggressive, attacking Marat as a 'blood-drinker' and Robespierre as a sinister intriguer. Danton, temperamentally, was much closer to them, with his love of good living and lack of fanaticism, and he tried to bring the two factions together in the interests of the unity which was necessary for the war effort. But the Girondins, prompted by Mme Roland, who hated Danton for his crudity and aggressive virility, taunted him endlessly with corruption and his failure to produce accounts for his period as Minister of Justice. 'The Accounts!' they would shout, whenever he got up to speak. They also denounced him for his role in the September massacres.

The Girondins were handicapped by having gone along with the events they often deplored. Most of them had favoured the abolition of the monarchy; none protested against the September massacres until these were over; many voted for the King's death. They were young, talented and optimistic, but without any definite policy except fear and hatred of their opponents. Although they had a majority in the Convention for much of the time, this was fatal at a time of tension and war. Given the need for strong measures in a war which England and Spain had now joined, the Jacobins inevitably won the day.

The Girondins were helped initially by the triumphs of their friend General Dumouriez, with his victories at Valmy and, later, at Jemappes. But his desertion to the enemy after the defeat at Neerwinden in March 1793 compromised them hopelessly. Their rashness in bringing Marat before the new Revolutionary Tribunal in April was also disastrous, as he was acquitted and borne in triumph to the Convention.

Plans were hatched in an illegal Committee of the Commune to attack the Convention and remove thirty-two of the most troublesome Girondins, however much this might violate the ideals of 1789, and underline the domination of Paris in the Revolution. The time had come, Marat said, 'to organize a brief despotism of liberty in order to crush the despotism of kings'.

Back at the Tuileries once more with M. Hébert, we stood on the muddy patch which was once the courtyard, and looked through the non-existent palace, and over the gardens to the Champs Elysées.

'After the 10th of August, the palace was left devastated,' he said. 'The royal lilies were scratched out, the furniture smashed, the interior was full of debris. The outside, though, was unchanged, except for an enormous red Phrygian bonnet on top of the central tower of the Horloge, while "Liberté" was painted on a great banner on the Pavillon de Marsan and "Egalité" on the Pavillon de Flore.'

'A take-over of slogans.'

'Exactly. Then, in May 1793, the Convention and all its offices moved into the palace, just before the Girondins were expelled. They used a vast hall, the Salle des Machines, which was once a theatre and was now totally renovated. Imagine entering the main doors of the palace, which were here. You cross the arcaded peristyle and turn right to the staircase, which used to lead to the old royal apartments. You stop on the entresol and go through the door of what was once the royal chapel. This had been converted into an antechamber, and was very lofty because it went right up through the first floor of the palace. There were windows, high up on the walls, which were painted in imitation porphyry.

'Next, you went through the old sacristy of the chapel, which had been converted into the Salle de la Liberté. Its name came from a ten-foot figure of Liberty, made of plaster and draped with real cloth, all covered with bronze paint.

'Beyond it was the hall of the Convention, with galleries capable of holding fourteen hundred spectators. In front of the President's box, with the tribune just below it, the deputies' benches were set in lines. The acoustics were bad and it was poorly ventilated, but, from the tribune, an orator could see everyone in the assembly.'

'And it was here that the Girondins were denounced?' I asked.

'Well, not exactly denounced. I mean there had been furious accusations and counter-accusations between the two groups for months. Now, on this day of May 31st, it was more a question of resisting the armed mob which surrounded the Tuileries and demanded the expulsion of thirty-two Girondin deputies. The Convention resisted this challenge to their sovereignty and inviolability. Delegations arrived, protests were made. The tumult went on all day. You can imagine the furious debate in this enormous hall, the interruptions from the galleries. In the background, there was the tolling of the tocsin and the booming of the cannon on the Pont Neuf.

'The hundred thousand men round the Tuileries did not disperse till evening. On June 2nd they returned, and a deputy suggested they all go outside in procession, and try to persuade the mob to depart. They walked through the Salle de la Liberté, down the staircase, into the peristyle, and streamed through the main doors, their tall, black hats on their heads.

'But Hanriot, the newly appointed Commander of the National Guard, a former valet, ordered his cannoneers to get ready. The deputies returned to the Tuileries and went out into the gardens behind. They fringed the steps leading up to the Manège, which they had so recently left. But troops barred their way. They wandered down to the little drawbridge giving onto the Place de la Révolution. They may have admired the great days of the Roman Republic, but there was nothing Roman in this farce. Instead of standing their ground and defying those who threatened them, as the Romans would probably have done, they were like sheep trying to escape from their pen. But every exit was blocked.

'Marat came up and ordered them to return to the Convention

and decree the expulsion of the Girondins. Docile, they followed his command.

'In the Convention, they debated what they should do. Some suggested that the Girondins should resign voluntarily, in the interests of the Nation. But most of the Girondins refused. Finally, the Convention yielded, as authority always yielded to force throughout this Revolution. They decreed house arrest for the thirty-two Girondins. The Jacobins had won.'

'And what happened to the Girondins?'

'Some escaped and tried to rally an army in Normandy. But the pitiable force of only four hundred men, led by a nobleman who had no military experience, was crushed. Some Girondins wandered down towards Bordeaux and were captured and brought back to the capital. Condorcet, a marquis, one of their most eminent political philosophers, was arrested because, unused to preparing his own food, he ordered an omelette with twelve eggs in it, in a miserable country tavern where he had taken refuge. Others, like Pétion, the former mayor of Paris, died in the fields and their corpses were eaten by wolves.'

'Charlotte Corday assassinated Marat because of what happened to the Girondins, didn't she?'

'Yes, you could say that. Of course, the tragedy is that she made everything worse. It was Marat's assassination that really accelerated the Terror. It seemed proof of conspiracies, although Charlotte Corday planned everything alone. No leading Jacobin could now feel he was safe from assassination. The remaining twenty-two Girondins were guillotined at about the same time as Marie-Antoinette, in October 1793.'

'And of course civil war erupted.'

'Yes, sixty out of the eighty-three departments broke off relations with Paris, which seemed to be usurping government. The representation of the people had been violated. For the rest of 1793, you get civil war raging, not only in the Vendée, but in Lyons and Toulon, and throughout the South of France.'

'Was the insurrection in the Vendée caused by the expulsion of the Girondins?'

'No, it came earlier, in March 1793. It was fuelled by it, perhaps. But it had other causes.'

III

Counter-Revolution

16

THE VENDÉE: A HEROIC SAGA

THE BELIEVER: The dead, and what about them?
THE PRIEST: You can't use the intruders [Constitutional Priests]
to bury them any more than you can use them for anything else.
THE BELIEVER: Then we will be buried like vile animals.
From a pamphlet distributed in 1792 by the Mulotins,
an order of missionary priests.

If you drive down from Paris, via Chartres and Tours, to Angers, you find yourself in the Vendée when you cross the river Loire. One September, we criss-crossed this gently rolling countryside, which reminded us of Dorset. We went as far south as Niort and Les Sables d'Olonnes, and up to the Atlantic coast to the island of Noirmoutier and the country south of Nantes.

This whole area where the ferocious wars of the Vendée took place, between March and December 1793, is known as 'La Vendée Militaire'. Guerrilla skirmishing continued to flare and wane right up to 1802.

In those days, most of the Vendée Militaire, except the coastal fringe and the south bank of the Loire, was covered with hedges, small fields and patches of thick forest. Modern cultivation has thinned woodland and obliterated many of the hedges. To get a feeling of how it was two hundred years ago, it is perhaps best to see it in the early morning, with silence and the vague shape of trees etched vaporously around. Then you can more easily imagine peasant armies in sabots and ragged clothes moving through the mist to attack the *Bleus*, the Republican soldiers confronting them.

On the Atlantic side, which was reclaimed by Dutch engineers in the eighteenth century at about the same time as they were creating the Fens near Cambridge, the land is flat, with rows of poplars planted as wind-breakers. Canals break through with

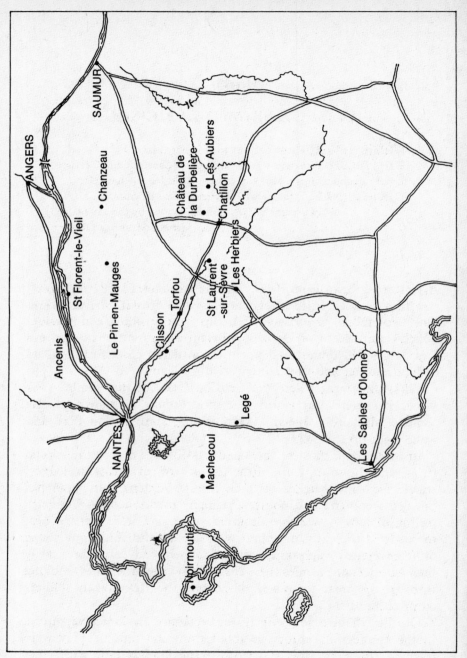

Map of La Vendée Militaire.

straight lines of silver water which the inhabitants used to vault with long poles. This landscape is less suited to the hidden march of guerrilla armies, but was difficult to invade for those who did not know the country well.

Few of the original buildings survived the insurrection. Just three old churches remain in the whole area. In Cholet, one of the biggest towns, only a fifteenth-century bridge survives. In the village of Chanzeaux there are few houses that were not burnt: one stands on a corner near the reconstructed church with a little window on the first floor.

The Vendée has always been fertile, but two hundred years ago most of the peasant sharecroppers lived humbly in small adjacent houses, few of which remain. Families slept several to a room, and ate a diet of thick, vegetable soup with rye bread and a little butter and milk. Only one metalled road crossed the whole territory, until Napoleon built others as a military precaution. Villages were connected by well-trodden *chemins creux*, as they were called: sunken tracks with high hedges which made travellers – or soldiers – almost invisible from the surrounding fields and woods.

The population was much as it is now, with approximately a million people. Villages were frequent, if isolated from one another, but there were few major towns apart from those on the Loire, such as Saumur, Angers and the sea-port of Nantes. Mainly, it was a land of big estates, rented to the peasants, where the nobles interfered little and feudal dues were lighter than in the rest of France. As the peasant communities were relatively isolated, there was little intermixture with the bourgeoisie of the towns – except for the fierce resentment these earned by buying the confiscated land of Church and émigrés which the poorer peasantry could not afford.

It is hard to believe that so much ferocious bloodshed could have taken place in this soft landscape. In paintings of the wars, only those showing ambushes or secret Masses reflect the dark, wooded countryside. Massacres seem always to have bleaker, more open settings.

Like most people, we knew little about the Wars of the Vendée when we arrived there. When I was specializing in the French Revolution at Oxford, the Vendée hardly figured, and I had read little about it since. However, we were soon enlightened. Talking to local Vendéans about the War is like discussing the rebellion of 1745 with Highlanders in Scotland. Indignation still boils, and stories are told which have been repeated round cottage fires for two centuries.

We first became aware of this when we were invited to a meeting of 'Le Souvenir Vendéen', a society founded in 1932 to put up memorials to those who had died on the insurgent side. The meeting took place in an old manor house near the village of Liré, south of the Loire. As instructed, we drove to it through small villages, until we came to the encircling wall of the manor house. We ignored the main gate, which was closed, and then turned left down a straight track of white pressed earth which went on and on through the dark trees, our curiosity roused by thought of what we would find at the other end.

Suddenly the wood cleared, and there was a long, grey manor house of stone, fronted by a bed of vivid white and blue hydrangeas. Inside, we entered a room in which maps hung on the walls showing neighbouring villages which had joined the uprising. Beyond, in the garden, about a hundred and fifty people were sitting at trestle tables, talking with French animation as they ate lunch. As we queued for hunks of bread, pâté and salad, we talked to a Dr Raymonde from Paris, who told us that there were no fewer than 3,000 members of the Souvenir Vendéen, who lived all over France but were descended from those who had fought in the War.

'How do you know if you are a descendant or not?' I asked.

'Oh, we don't exactly have family trees. But we know from family tradition that we come from here and that our ancestors fought in the War.'

'Before television, families would gather in the evenings and talk about how their *grands-pères* fought and died,' added a cheerful man with glasses, M. Grasse, a teacher from Fougères.

'But what's amazing is how little the wars are known, especially outside France,' I said.

With plates piled high, we moved towards one of the trestle tables. 'Well, of course,' said M. Grasse, 'the whole story was kept quiet by successive Republican governments, particularly in State school history books, where the Revolution was glorified as the birth of Liberty and modern France.'

'They were ashamed,' said Dr Raymonde. 'How could they justify a rebellion of peasants against a revolutionary government which abolished feudalism and preached equality? How could they justify the cruelty with which the Vendéans were repressed?'

'Only now is it all coming into the open,' said M. Grasse. 'There's a new book by a historian called Reynald Secher from Nantes University. He calls the massacres genocide and compares them to the Jewish holocaust in the last war.'

'The book's created a great scandal in France. Because of it, Secher lost his post at the University.'

'You must remember that until very recently the French Republic as a form of government was weak and threatened. After 1870, there were strong movements for the restoration of the monarchy. Then, in the 1920s and 1930s, there was the totalitarian threat of Communism and Fascism. After 1946, a succession of weak governments came in. They lost Indo-China and were incapable of ending the Algerian insurrection. It was really De Gaulle who established the Republic on a firm basis. Because of this, it is only recently that the Revolution can be viewed more objectively. Before, it was often a question of interpreting it through the dogmas of Left and Right, and of political propaganda.'

Later, M. L'Agniau, the President of the Souvenir Vendéen, told us that when he founded the association in 1932 there was local government opposition to the erection of memorials commemorating royalists martyred in the Vendée – even though these had occurred more than 130 years previously.

'But why did the insurrection break out here and not in other parts of France?' asked Brita.

'It did break out in other places,' said M. Grasse. 'In places like the Cévennes. But not as widely or as successfully.'

'If you want to find out the root cause of the Vendée insurrection you must go to St-Laurent-sur-Sèvre,' said Dr Raymonde.

'Where's that?'

'About forty kilometres south of here. Beyond Torfou, where the Vendéans won a great victory.'

Round the trestle tables, coffee was served and silence was requested as a sketch was about to be performed by local actors on the lawn. The drama was simple and straightforward. It concerned a priest who had sworn the oath to the Constitution in the early part of the Revolution. However, when the Pope condemned the Civil Constitution, he was persuaded by other priests to revoke his oath. Actors in white wigs and cassocks argued heavily in the sunlight about half-forgotten disputes which then were as vital as transubstantiation or consubstantiation, or any now obscure doctrine whose root importance was its influence on power.

'There – ' whispered M. Grasse. 'That was the basic cause of the revolt. If you go to St-Laurent-sur-Sèvre – '

Later, we met Jean Huguet, a distinguished historian of the Vendée wars, who also referred to St Laurent. 'It's still a remarkable place. It's really just a small town, but with two enormous churches. Two thousand priests and nuns still live there as if it were a tiny Rome. It's still a missionary centre which was founded a hundred years before the Revolution, commonly called Les Mulotins. Now they send missionaries to China. Then, they had enormous influence over the peasantry, particularly in 1791, preaching against the "intruders" as the new Constitutional priests were called.'

Jean Huguet, lively and fluent, is known by many Vendéans as a 'Republican' historian, although reading him it is difficult to see why. He is still a church-going Catholic, and he described a 'Mulotin' sermon he had known in his childhood, which scared him stiff:

'I remember as a child going to a church where Heaven was depicted in a chapel with golden figures of the Virgin, Christ and the Saints all bathed in celestial light. From this Heaven, a double row of candles reached down to Hell, which was a black turmoil of demons, reminiscent of a cobra pit. The alternatives were only too clear. I remember the lurid sermon of the preacher and my feelings of fear and exaltation, to this day. It's certainly not difficult to imagine the effect of displays of this sort on the peasants, three hundred years ago.'

We went to St Laurent on a Sunday morning. The small town lay on the river Sèvre, which was stagnant under the bridge with broad patches of weed lying on the greenish water. The streets were full of people, many of them young, hurrying to Mass in an enormous modern church with a tall spire. Nearby was the convent of the Grey Sisters, some of whom were walking quickly through the streets, like ants wandering in the vicinity of their heap.

We knocked at the door of the convent and were admitted. Inside, was a labyrinth of cloisters, corridors and courtyards, and we wandered until we came across the tomb of St Louis-Marie Montford, the founder of the missionary order. Born in 1673, St Louis-Marie had given the community its fervour and faith, sending missionaries all over the neighbouring countryside. Their influence was well established by the time of the Revolution, and when the clash between the refractory and the Constitutional priests occurred, they had little difficulty in persuading parishioners to reject the new priests, who often came from outside and did not speak the patois. In the isolated villages, the priests who would not take the oath often stayed on, holding Masses in their houses, continuing their parish work, denouncing their rival's services as invalid because they had been condemned by the Pope (see p. 92–3).

As we strolled through the streets of St Laurent and visited the church crammed with worshippers, we began to understand some of the reasons for the start of the Vendée Wars. To the peasants, roused by the missionary priests, the conflict must have seemed a repetition of those ferocious wars of religion which had rent the region in the sixteenth century and were also part of the collective memory. But how had the insurrection actually begun? What was the spark which set it off?

We were fortunate in meeting Dominique Lambert, who works as archivist in the Town Hall of Angers and also runs a weekly programme of interviews on the local radio. Dominique is a royalist, and his five sons are called after Vendéan generals. At home, he has thirty-six thousand names on a register of those who fought for King and Church in 1793. He also has seven hundred bottles of excellent wine in his cellar, which he intends to open when monarchy is restored in France. He, too, has an association of sympathizers with the Vendée wars, called 'Amis de la Vendée Militaire', which has about eight hundred adherents and competes with L'Agniau's Souvenir Vendéen.

When we asked Dominique about the start of the insurrection, he took us to the little town of St-Florent-le-Vieil, which is not far south of Angers (see map). Approaching it from the north bank of the Loire, we could see the houses jostling up the hill to a picturesque church with a spire. Most of St Florent was burnt in 1793. However, it was rebuilt shortly afterwards, and still looks much like old prints, standing beyond the flat islands in the river, on which tall poplars stand, their small leaves rustling in the breeze.

We stopped beyond the suspension bridge on the Place Maubert. 'It was here,' said Dominique, dramatically, 'that the war started.'

He looked round at the old houses in the little square. 'On Sunday March 12th, 1793, on this spot, the municipal authorities announced that lots would be drawn for conscription, as there were insufficient volunteers for the army. Hitherto, the Vendéans had accepted the Revolution passively, but they were certainly not prepared to leave their farms and fight on distant frontiers for ideals they detested. They resented, too, that the municipal authorities and the National Guard were exempt from conscription, and that the burden therefore fell mainly on them. Protesting, the crowd jostled the officials and several young men were arrested and taken to the local jail.

'The following Tuesday,' continued Dominique, 'more than 2,000 peasants marched into the town, wearing white royalist cockades. As they confronted the municipality and shouted to them to suspend the drawing of lots, the National Guard panicked and fired. The crowd then surged forward, and the Guard fled down the slope, just there, to the river.' We walked through a narrow passageway between an old chapel, now a museum, and an ugly, rectangular cinema, and descended a cobbled path through trees to the banks of the river. Before us, the Loire flowed swiftly past. 'The National Guards took refuge there, on those islands, and the town was in the hands of the insurgents.

'A delegation now set out for the local château to implore the Marquis de Bonchamps to be their leader. Bonchamps had seen service as a major in the royal army in India. Like most Vendéan leaders, he was reluctant to accept, as he regarded the cause as hopeless. However, after a few hours, he changed his mind and set up his headquarters at St Florent. From the church steeple floated the white banner of the Bourbons. The War of the Vendée had begun.'

'Did it erupt anywhere else, at the same time?' I asked.

'The first trouble was here, but as Sunday 12th March was the day on which volunteers for the army were expected to come forward all over the Vendée, several other groups of peasants gathered as they had at St Florent. Different leaders were recruited. Cathelineau lived at the little village of Pin-en-Mauges, where you can still see his house and where the old curé will take you round a small museum. Then Stofflet, a gamekeeper of German origin, was soon at the head of another band. As was d'Elbée, who had been an army officer in the cavalry. He was about to celebrate the christening of his new-born child when the peasants arrived at his château and asked him to lead them. While near the Atlantic, Charette, who had been a naval officer for ten years, began to play an independent and often triumphant role.

'Within less than a fortnight, most of the principal towns were taken, including the major administrative centres of Challans and Cholet.'

'But was there no resistance?'

'The Republicans had few regular troops and mainly local National Guards. Also, the ferocity of the Vendéans scared them. The royalists would emerge suddenly from the woods, emitting blood-curdling cries and shooting with great accuracy. They fought in the form of a crescent with their best marksmen on the horns so, before the Republicans knew where they were, they were surrounded.

'The Republicans called them "The Brigands" and their skill and boldness soon created a legend of invincibility. Towns and villages surrendered without a shot, and were full of ammunition, muskets, cannon and food – not to mention treasure chests – which gave the Vendéans the war material they lacked.'

We walked up the slope again, and to the church. Beyond, there was a stretch of grass with a column at the end, erected at the Restoration to celebrate all that had taken place in St Florent. From it, we could see the Loire, broad and shallow, sweeping down towards Nantes and the sea.

'And what about La Rochejaquelein?' I asked, naming one of the few Vendéan leaders I had heard of.

'Ah, La Rochejaquelein!' said Dominique, with a little sigh. 'A great man! No, he joined the Vendéans a little later. Let's go to the château where he was born.'

The courtyard beyond the archway is surrounded with low, grey buildings with green, tiled roofs.

'Henri de Rochejaquelein must have galloped through this archway thousands of times,' said Dominique. 'Imagine him on horseback with his fair hair and English face – the most gallant of men!'

As we entered, a bulky goat squatted on the grass of the courtyard, and two men were working diligently on vegetable patches.

In front of us, a tangle of broken buildings with crumbling towers presented a dramatic contrast to the sunny farmstead. A small bridge spanned the moat, while beyond it, a balustrade of low, chipped columns gave a sense of grace, evoking noblemen and their ladies leading over to talk to their newly arrived guests.

'Here it began in April 1793, when the peasants came to the château to ask Monsieur Henri, as they called him, to be their leader,' said Dominique.

'You can see the crowd standing in this courtyard with their muddy trousers and wooden sabots, carrying pikes and scythes. Their weathered faces looked up at La Rochejaquelein, who stood here where I am standing. There was the mumbled buzz of conversation. Then, silence as he spoke. He ended with the famous words: "If I advance, follow me; if I retreat, shoot me; if I am killed, avenge me."' Dominique flung out his arms, and then paused as if he could hear the roars of acclamation.

'He was only twenty-one. Yet, at the head of a peasant army which had never been under fire before, he defeated the Republicans at the little village of Les Aubiers. Then his small army joined the main force of the Vendéans and fought in almost every major battle till his death.'

We wandered round the courtyard. In the former riding school of grey stone, with delicate pillars supporting the roof, Monsieur Henri first mounted a horse. Straw is now stuffed to the eaves. A tractor stood to one side. By the château, the water of the moat was dark, glinting through the branches of chestnut trees.

We turned to look again at the shattered buildings. 'That is the tower where M. Henri was born.' Dominique pointed to a cracked structure. 'And that was the chapel.' He indicated the roofless walls with little Romanesque windows. 'No one does anything to preserve it,' he protested. 'In a few years, it will all be a heap of stones – like the glory of France.'

On the way back to Angers, we were silent and thoughtful. Amidst the old prejudices which still divide France on the whole question of the Vendée wars, it is often difficult to discover the truth. However, this struggle does appear to have been a heroic saga, similar in some ways to the Jacobite rebellion in the Highlands of Scotland in 1745. There is the same quixotic fight of a region against a central government, the same strong local support from rich and poor alike, which weakened as the armies got further away from their base, the same fervour for the Church and the descendants of an executed King.

The Vendéan rising also stirs associations with other romantic sagas: the Morte d'Arthur with its ideals of chivalry and loyalty, and the early Crusade of Peter the Hermit, with half the poor of Europe setting out to conquer Jerusalem.

By the beginning of June 1793, the rebels had advanced up what is now Route 160 towards Saumur, a town on the Loire with a fairy-tale castle, similar to the one portrayed in the medieval illustration of the *Très Riches Heures du Duc de Berri*. Still it stands, on a hill just outside the town, with its battlements and pinnacled towers. The town, too, is still full of eighteenth-century houses and narrow streets winding down to the river.

In Saumur, we had arranged to meet M. Denechau, a shrewd and eloquent local teacher of history with a black beard. Together, we stood on the Fouchard bridge, spanning the river at the southern end of the town. From it, a road goes straight up to a hill on which the Republicans were positioned in strength, as the Vendéans were reported to be advancing that way. Their artillery was posted in what is now a café by the side of the road, although the owner knew nothing of this when I went to enquire.

In fact, the royalists never appeared on the road: they outflanked the Republicans, infiltrated through the trees, took the Fouchard bridge in the Republicans' rear, and crossed the river into the town.

We wandered through the trees and then drove up to a hill in Saumur itself, which was covered with new houses with cream-coloured walls and dark roofs. In their midst was a solitary windmill, standing forlorn on a hillock. 'That is the only windmill that remains,' said M. Denechau. 'Then there were many. The Republicans put up their last resistance here, but their forces were hopelessly dispersed by this time. Again, they were outflanked and retreated down to the river to escape over the straight eighteenth-century bridge across the Loire, or up the road to Tours. Duhoux, the Republican commander, was on his sick bed giving orders in the Hôtel Blanclerc, which you can still see in the Place Bilange, when suddenly he was told that his nephew, a general on the Vendéan side, was advancing into the town, and he had to gather up his bedclothes and flee.'

The capture of Saumur was the climax of the rebels' success. The Republicans were shattered and disorganized. La Rochejaquelein and Stofflet were in favour of marching on Paris, and Napoleon was later to write in his memoirs (which admittedly were edited on

St Helena by La Cases, who was a friend of the Vendéan general, Charette): 'Nothing could have stopped the triumphant march of the royalist armies, the white flag would have floated on the towers of Notre-Dame before it was possible for the armies of the Rhine to come to the Government's assistance.'

This was one of the periods of greatest danger for the Republic. Foreign armies were advancing from over the frontiers, and the expulsion of the Girondins had alienated three-quarters of the departments.

However, one wonders whether the Vendéans themselves were interested in playing the national role which an attack on Paris would have forced on them. Regional attachments were paramount, and Paris probably seemed as distant as Istanbul appears to us today. The Vendéans had fought fiercely to clear Republican troops from their soil. Now to leave their territory and overwhelm the central government was another matter, even though they must have realized that they could never be secure until the Republic was destroyed in its lair.

With success at Saumur, the real weakness of the Vendéans became apparent. Like the Highlanders of Charles Stuart invading England in 1745, they were now anxious to get back to their farms and harvesting. Within a day, their army in Saumur had lost a third of its thirty thousand effectives through desertion. Two weeks later, the town had to be abandoned as the garrison had shrunk to eight men.

What kind of régime would the Vendéans have imposed had they taken Paris? About this time, they published a decree which eliminated the Civil Constitution of the Clergy and ordered the imprisonment of Constitutional priests and the restitution of confiscated land to Church and émigrés. Otherwise, their aim seems to have been to restore the constitutional monarchy of 1791.

However, had they captured Paris, the small provincial nobility who led the royalists would almost certainly have been engulfed by the reactionary cohorts of returning émigrés, and it is difficult to see who would have been strong and wise enough to create a compromise government capable of arbitrating between the two extremes. Louis XVII, after all, was only a child of eight. If, as Talleyrand said, the Bourbons had learnt nothing when they returned in 1815, how much less likely were they to have changed by 1793, the very year in which Louis XVI had been guillotined.

However great the heroism of the Vendéans, they were probably fighting for a restoration of much that was worst in the Ancien Régime, whether they knew it or not.

After Saumur, it was decided to push along the north bank of the Loire and capture Nantes. This vital sea-port would allow reinforcement from England, with regular supplies of guns, ammunition and food. From Saumur, we followed their route, first along the curving river to Angers, which still is a remarkable city with its towering, medieval fortress by the river Mayence, its narrow streets and large squares, many of which were then occupied by the monasteries and convents which formerly filled the town.

Angers yielded without resistance. Grillé, a local inhabitant, describes how aristocratic ladies began distributing white cockades to passers-by, rather like matrons in England on Poppy Day. A Te Deum was sung in the Cathedral. The leaders wore their best uniforms, and white doves were released in a fluttering cloud to fly up to the Gothic arches.

It was a commemoration of all the Vendéans had achieved in only three months, with music and prayers and the pews filled with peasant soldiery. Without fear, city society could display itself in front of the altar as they took Communion. Afterwards, everyone gathered outside to discuss the great events, and perhaps give brief congratulations to M. Stofflet, or M. d'Elbée, or the saintly M. Cathelineau.

The headquarters of the Vendéans in Angers can still be seen in 9 Rue de Volier. However, they were there for only a few days before leaving for Nantes. As soon as they departed, the Republicans returned, and the mayor, the Comte de Ruillé, who had agreed to continue in office under the royalists, was tried and guillotined.

From Angers, we continued along the route to Nantes on a fast motorway which only occasionally allowed a view of the river. At Nantes itself, we were caught in massive road works which delayed us for almost as long as the invading Vendéans were stopped when they tried to invest the city, on 29 June 1793. The town was small compared to today, but it was prosperous, largely on commerce with the Indies and, like Bristol, as a centre of the slave trade. Much later, in 1943, many buildings were flattened by air raids, but much also survives, or has been rebuilt in line with the original layout. A stroll round the centre, with its traffic-free walks, its squares, its

Cathedral and its imposing eighteenth-century theatre, still gives an impression of what it must have been like two hundred years ago.

The Vendéans had surrounded Nantes, and hoped that like Angers it would surrender without a fight. In the early morning, Charette started his bombardment from the south bank. However, as the progress of other divisions in the north-east was delayed, he soon withdrew. Bonchamps's men penetrated the city and were in sight of the Cathedral, but were hesitant because Charette's fire no longer protected them. An hour later, Cathelineau was badly wounded by a shot from a window in the present Place de Viarme.

In those days, the Place de Viarme was on the edge of the city, with countryside stretching to the north. Today, it is used mainly as a car park. You should be able to see the plaque marking the spot where Cathelineau fell. However, several of us spent time peering under cars in vain, attracting mystified stares from passers-by who probably suspected us of planting bombs.

The news of Cathelineau's wound spread rapidly, demoralizing the Vendéans. Another commander, the Prince de Talmont, foolishly stiffened Republican resistance by firing on the retreating columns. 'Comrades, if we must die, let us die gloriously, with our weapons in our hands,' General Beysser, the Republican Commander, is reported to have shouted to his men. The fleeing Republicans returned to the city and continued its defence.

The Vendéans retired in good order, but in Paris the Convention was spurred at last to action. Important was the need to rally Republicans in France against royalism, and try to unify those who had been divided by the expulsion of the Girondins. A leading member of the Committee of Public Safety, Barère, made a speech saying that the Vendée was devouring 'the heart of France'. More regular troops were sent, as were professional generals such as Kléber, who was to fight with Napoleon in Egypt, or Westermann, who brought a new element of horror and devastation into the struggle.

Nevertheless, victories continued. At Torfou on 19 September, the royalist army, whose initial retreat had been stemmed by women pushing their men back into battle, crushed a professional army under Kléber. When Kléber was reproached for his defeat, he said: 'Those devils in sabots fight as well as we do, and shoot better.'

However, the battle fought at Cholet on 17–18 October was a disaster for the Vendéans. If you go to the town today, it seems anything but historic. Most of it was rebuilt in the nineteenth century, and the suburbs are full of long, pastel-coloured offices and warehouses, with rectangular windows and 'franglais' signs such as 'PROMOCASH' or 'HOME SALON'. However, there is a museum where idealized portraits of the Vendéan leaders, painted after the royalist Restoration in 1815, can be seen: young La Rochejaquelein, almost girlish with golden hair, with one arm in a sling and the other outstretched with a pistol in his hand; Stofflet leading his troops into battle with a curved sword; Lescure standing on a mound, surrounded by his followers as he looks up to the sky with the liquid eyes of a visionary.

During the insurrection, Cholet became one of the royalist capitals. As in all the towns they occupied, the streets were full of elegant people in carriages, while balls, dinners and receptions were held. 'Revolution changes only 10 per cent of the way of living, and yet 90 per cent of people,' wrote a French historian.

The battle of Cholet was decisive not only because of the casualties and loss of war material, but because of the mortal wounds of three of the principal royalist leaders. Lescure was incapacitated by a musket ball in the skull. Bonchamps was fatally injured, and d'Elbée, who had been appointed Commander-in-Chief after Cathelineau's death, had no fewer than four major wounds. To help him recover, he was sent to Noirmoutier, an island on the Atlantic coast, then occupied by the royalists. However, in January 1794 the Republicans advanced along the causeway, which is still passable at low tide, although now mainly by cars whose owners stop to wade and collect mussels.

On a cold winter day, with the wind blowing in from the sea and ice underfoot, d'Elbée was shot with three other officers. He sat in an armchair, as he could not stand because of his wounds. The square where this happened can still be seen outside the castle, as can the filled-in moat where their bodies were thrown and never recovered. In the museum stands the armchair in which d'Elbée was shot, with five jagged bullet holes in the back. On a wall, there is a poem by Leblant. Two lines are as follows:

> *Maudites soient les guerres civiles*
> *Qui font par les vaillants fusiller les héros.*

('Cursed be civil wars, Which make brave men shoot heroes.')

After Cholet, the royalist army retreated to St-Florent-le-Vieil, intending to cross the Loire, and make for a port on the Channel where the British could reinforce them.

Sixty thousand ragged soldiers gathered in the town which we visited with Dominique Lambert. With them were twenty thousand women and children, for whole families had now abandoned their farms. Six thousand Republican prisoners were shut up in the church, and, excited by the massacres, the Council of War decided on reprisals, as it would be difficult to ferry them across the river.

Cannon were placed at the doors of the church, while soldiers waited to finish off those who survived the grapeshot. However, at the last moment the dying Bonchamps pleaded for the prisoners, and as most of the royalist troops involved belonged to his division, the captives were released. One of them was the father of the sculptor David d'Angers, who, in gratitude, carved the scene in marble. It can still be seen in the church, with Bonchamps raising himself from his deathbed to plead for the prisoners.

On the whole, the Vendéans were more merciful to prisoners than the Republicans, who regarded the rebels as reactionary 'brigands'. At the beginning of the rebellion, five hundred Republicans had been massacred by an unscrupulous individual called Souchou. Usually, however, the Republican prisoners were released after an oath never to fight again. Their heads were shaved, so that they would be recognized if captured again.

At St Florent, however, this deed of mercy was later described by Merlin de Thionville, a Deputy of the Convention, as an act of 'unbelievable hypocrisy'. He advised the Committee of Public Safety not to breathe a word about 'this indignity of free men owing their lives to slaves'. In the bitterness of this civil war, even magnanimous actions were seen as perfidious.

In two days, 80,000 Vendéans crossed the Loire with only one casualty. Napoleon again expresses the admiration which made him call the whole conflict 'the Battle of Giants': 'My engineers are able men, but at St Florent, the Vendéans were water sprites,' he wrote.

It was like the passage of the Red Sea. In a nineteenth-century painting the crowds wait on the slopes leading to the river; the rafts drift across, loaded with people and possessions; the women sit on the near bank beside peasant soldiers holding long scythes. Today, from the esplanade by the church, you can imagine it all.

The wounded Bonchamps died on the far bank in a little house near the present hotel of La Closerie des Roses. The house is still there, and you can visit the small room where he expired, and see the crucifix which was placed on his breast.

Fortunately for the Vendéans, there were no Republican troops on either bank. La Rochejaquelein was elected Generalissimo and the royalist army, with all the accompanying 'useless mouths', started its long trek to the Channel coast.

17

NORTH OF THE LOIRE:
THE END OF THE SAGA

'All these victims were transferred to another boat, where they were undressed, and their hands tied behind their backs. These women and children were drowned the same evening.'

GRIAULT, a sailor at Nantes.

North of the Loire, the Vendéan armies were joined by a few thousand Chouans, whose knowledge of the local countryside proved invaluable. 'Chouan' is a term applied to the guerrillas who fought in Brittany and Mayenne at the same time as the Vendée uprising, and continued for the rest of the century. The term has often been confused with the Vendéans. However, to take a modern parallel, the Chouans resembled the guerrilla movement in Northern Italy during the last war, as opposed to the Vendéans, who were closer to Tito's armies of partisans in Yugoslavia.

One of the most famous Chouan leaders was Jean Cottereau, a salt smuggler, who had been in prison under the Ancien Régime. His birthplace still stands off the road between Laval and Fougères, set in the trees beyond fields on which cattle graze and maize grows. No sign indicates where it is, and we only found it on a misty September morning after stopping and asking a man in a paratroop uniform who was going round and round a field in a one-horse carriage in a dizzy and almost surrealist manner.

The house is now falling down, because the owner still has Republican sympathies and is unwilling to sell it to the local 'Friends of the Chouannerie' as a memorial. If you peer through the empty windows of the simple stone cottage, you can see the whole roof collapsed in the gloom under a temporary asbestos cover.

In the Vendée, the royalists had fought in units formed by parishes, and had mixed freely with their officers. But now so many of these were dead. Now they were refugees in an unknown

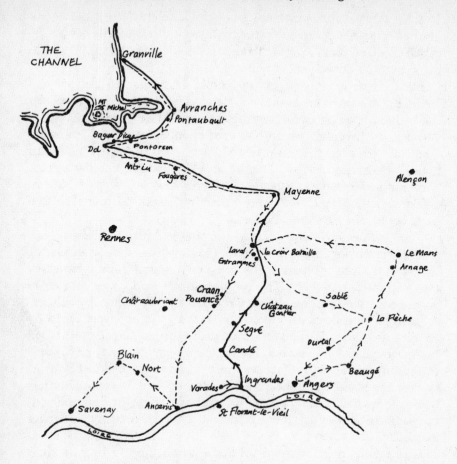

Journey of the Vendéan Army to Granville. Their tortuous return is marked by a dotted line, ending with the final defeat at Savenay.

country, and something of the old relationship between them began to change.

Yet, despite triumphant declarations in the Convention in Paris that the Vendéans were crushed, they continued their incredible victories, even when confronted by no fewer than three armies. These, however, were commanded by incompetent sansculotte generals like Lechelle and Rossignol. With the exception of Kléber and Marceau, the subordinate officers were not much better, acting impulsively against orders.

It should have been easy to overwhelm this ragged royalist horde

179

which stretched for twelve miles along the muddy road, taking six hours to pass one place. Only the advance and rearguards contained experienced soldiers. Simple flank attacks would have split up little pockets to be wiped out at will.

The countryside north of the Loire is similar to that of the Vendée, with small fields and woodland. The Vendéans marched up the gentle Mayenne river, past dreamy towns like Château-Gontier, Laval and Mayenne, which have not changed much in centuries. They all have castles on the hill, and Pied Piper of Hamelin houses clustering on both banks and divided by narrow streets with medieval names: Rue des Orfèvres and La Grande Rue in Laval which, despite its imposing sound, is so narrow that two carts could not pass one another.

The first decisive battle was at Entrammes, just south of Laval, where the airport now lies. Here the royalists were waiting for the assault, fully prepared through information from a treacherous Republican general. The Republicans were foolish enough to advance in two columns which were picked off, soldier by soldier. A young Republican who took part wrote: 'Victims were faced by an execution squad.' The attacking army turned and fled, pursued by the royalists who came so hot on their heels that they bayoneted the enemy as they ran. Only seven thousand of the original army of twenty thousand Republicans assembled beyond Château-Gontier. Most units had been broken up and were totally demoralized, particularly as they had been told that the Vendée army no longer existed.

As a result, only light skirmishes awaited the royalists on their march to Granville. The Republican General, Rossignol, was foolish enough to divide his remaining army into small units which were easily overwhelmed. Many of his troops were raw levies. 'I am in despair, Citizen Minister, at commanding men like these,' wrote a general, Lenoir, to the War Office. Despite Vendéan pillaging, the countryside was with the rebels: 'Practically all the districts here have only six patriots per commune,' wrote the Deputy Letourneur, attached to the Republican armies.

However, a new cruelty seems to have affected the royalists. Perhaps because of Lescure's death on the way to Fougères, they hunted out Republicans and killed them. Mme de Rochejaquelein, who was married to M. Lescure, wrote: 'I confess that on that day, finding on the road the corpses of several Republicans, a kind of involuntary and secret fury made me, without saying anything, guide my horse so that those who had killed M. Lescure were trampled on.'

The wounded left behind by either side were slaughtered mercilessly. Mlle de Gontard, a royalist lady with the army, talked to a Vendéan soldier who told her there were four hundred Republican wounded in the hospital, and he hoped they would soon be killed. She replied that he should no longer serve in the Christian army as he dishonoured its name.

'That's all very well, mam'zelle,' he answered. 'Our generals tell us the same thing, but my father and my brother were murdered in the hospital at Fougères, and I claim the right to avenge their death.'

According to Republican estimates, two thousand priests were still with the rebels. Mme de Rochejaquelein whose memoirs, unfortunately, were re-edited several times in the 1830s and are only partly reliable, describes a priest trying to rally fleeing troops:

'My children,' he said, 'I will march at your head, the cross in my hand; those who want to follow me should get down on their knees and I will give them absolution: if they die, they will go to Paradise, but the cowards who betray God and abandon their families will be murdered by the Bleus [Republicans] and will go to Hell.' More than two thousand men surrounding him got down on their knees; he gave them absolution in a loud voice.

Nevertheless, some Vendéans were cynical about capturing the port of Granville. Many believed their leaders would take ship to England from there, and abandon them.

Three and a half weeks after they had crossed the Loire, the Vendéan army found themselves before Granville, a small fortified town on a rocky peninsula which sticks out into the Channel, with the harbour on one side. Granville is now one of those Norman seaside towns which, at the turn of this century, were fashionable with English visitors. When we were there the local museum had an exhibition of Granville as a bathing place with ancient photographs of bathers in fussy costumes which went down to their knees. Along the ridge, with its solid stone houses, is a sudden gap known as the Tranche aux Anglais, cut defensively by Lord Scales in 1439 when, at the end of the Hundred Years War, he occupied Granville. The

Germans, too, fought here. In March 1945, right at the end of the last War when Berlin was beleaguered from east and west, they mounted a daring and unexpected raid from the Channel Islands which they still occupied. They captured some Americans in their pyjamas, and also took away a group of Germans who proved reluctant to exchange the comfort of being Allied prisoners for the shortages and near starvation of German-occupied Jersey.

Down in the town, below the ridge, there is a little museum with tableaux of all these events. One of them shows the Rue des Juifs, which still runs up to the battlements, with Vendéan soldiers on the roofs sniping at the Republicans on the fortifications. Now a plaque is attached to the main gate overlooking the harbour, which lists the twenty-five Republicans killed in the action.

The assault was brief and futile. The Vendéans had little artillery and no siege equipment. Most of the army was away foraging for food, or encamped in the lower town. Only a thousand of the bravest volunteers followed La Rochejaquelein into the assault. Many had been demoralized by the absence of the British fleet, which they had expected to see on arrival. In any case, they were used to towns surrendering without a shot. Rebuffed, their one aim was now to get back to their farms beyond the Loire. Within twenty-eight hours of their arrival they were once more on the move, streaming back the way they had come.

Even today, snide remarks are still made about how the British let the Vendéans down, although, as the French historian Loic du Rostu writes, this 'exists only in the minds of historians anxious to hold them [the British] solely responsible for the defeat.' The problem was organization. An emissary had left to ask the British to come to their assistance only four days before the army arrived at Granville. Few troops were available except for a regiment of émigrés, but the admiral in charge, Lord Moira, was an enthusiastic supporter of the royalists. His fleet arrived four days after the Vendéans had left and found the coast empty. If the royalists had been less impatient and more realistic about the slow pace of communications, if their generals had been able to persuade them to continue the siege, many disasters might have been avoided.

Once more, the royalists defeated the Republicans standing in their way at Dol and Antrain. They swept down to Fougères, with its enormous castle in the valley. Following their trail, one finds the countryside bleak and desolate, with a road going up and down hillocks under the grey cloud. The Vendéans swept through Laval and out towards La Flèche, with its quiet eighteenth-century streets, and swung back again down the road to Angers, which they hoped to use as a bridgehead. But Angers was fortified more strongly than Granville had been. Famished, they sought an area they had not previously stripped of food, and marched north-eastwards to Le Mans which, again like Granville, stands on a long ridge. Here are still narrow streets and ancient houses and a magnificent Cathedral where Romanesque arches lead to a wonderful Gothic structure round the altar.

In Le Mans, the Vendéans were decisively defeated after a night battle, and fled again like wounded animals searching for their lairs, back to Laval and down to the river which they could not cross because of Republican gunboats. Cavalry pursued this now desperate mass, slaughtering the laggards. A witness wrote: 'I myself saw hundreds of naked corpses by the road, piled on top of one another like pigs ready to be salted.'

Snow began to fall, and the weary royalist soldiers built great fires at night and huddled around them. But, weak and racked with dysentery and typhus, many were frozen to death before dawn. Indeed, the end of the Catholic army reminds one of the last stages of Napoleon's retreat from Moscow, with a trail of cannon, carts and bodies, the sudden, devastating raids by enemy horsemen, the lack of food and gradual abandonment of hope and energy.

One difference is that in Russia the army was not accompanied by this horde of women and children falling down weakly in the mud to be trampled by enemy hoofs. The difference, too, is that in Russia, the Grande Armée was fighting a foreign enemy, while here, just north of the gentle Loire, Frenchman was fighting Frenchman with all the ferocity of civil war, struggling mercilessly to eliminate those whom each side regarded as traitors to their country, and, for the Vendéans, to their religion.

Madame de Rochejaquelein describes their departure for the final battle at Savenay beyond Nantes:

We left in the middle of the night, with cold rain falling in floods. Nothing can express our despair and sense of being crushed down: the hunger, the exhaustion, the sorrow which transformed us all. To protect ourselves from the cold, to disguise ourselves, or to replace worn-out clothes, we were covered in rags; when we looked at each other, recognition, under this garb of the deepest misery, was difficult.

When we went to look at Savenay, we were welcomed by Mme LeCadre from the municipality. Together we climbed the tower of the church to survey the little town and the battlefield to the north. We struggled up a creaking wooden staircase, through cobwebs and disturbed bats, to the sound of buzzing flies which darkened the small window panes. At the top was a little metal balustrade, which we treated with respect, while Mme LeCadre pointed over the roofs to where the Republicans attacked what remained of the Vendéan army, two days before Christmas 1793.

'The royalists were drawn up there beyond those trees which form what is called the Bois des Amourettes,' said Mme LeCadre. 'The centre was commanded by Marceau, and the left by Kléber. The royalists put up a desperate resistance, but the Republicans advanced with the bayonet and drove them back through the town.' She pointed to our feet. 'Down there in the Place de l'Eglise a last royalist rearguard put up a strong resistance to help the others escape.' We looked southwards over the green marshes to the distant Loire. 'But there was nowhere to go. As you can see, the Loire broadens here before flowing into the sea. The marshes are treacherous and the river very difficult to cross.'

Over eight thousand royalists were slaughtered at Savenay, we were told when we descended to the Place de l'Eglise. Perhaps eighty thousand bodies now lay strewn over the fields and highways of Brittany, Mayenne and the Sarthe.

Westermann wrote to the Committee of Public Safety, with one of the most extraordinary references to 'Liberty' yet recorded in this most extraordinary of Revolutions: 'The Vendée is no more. It has died under our sabres of Liberty with its women and children. I have just buried it in the marshes and woods of Savenay. I have crushed the children under the hoofs of horses and massacred the women.'

Four months later, Westermann was to be guillotined in Paris, not for his brutality but because he was a friend of Danton's. The new Republic had been saved again, but France was devouring itself.

Singly, the remaining royalist commanders battled on. Below Nantes, Charette, who had held aloof from the march over the Loire, continued a desultory guerrilla warfare.

His headquarters was in Legé. At the end of a lane with tall stone walls, covered with Virginia creeper, we found his house. It was on the edge of the village, with large modernized windows looking over the fields. 'We had to replace the windows to get more light,' a white-haired lady told us. 'There was an old stone staircase, and we removed it to enlarge a room.' Despite the transformation, one could imagine the Vendéan officers walking across the small courtyard, the messengers hammering at the door, the hurried orders and the stamping of fretful horses.

A few kilometres away, Charette entertained at the dreamy Château de Bois-Chevalier, which looks a little like La Durbelière, Rochejaquelein's mansion, as it was before the Republicans burnt it. (see p. 169) An alley of plane trees leads to the house. By a little lake and surrounding moat, there is a conglomeration of small rectangular towers with pointed tiled roofs. Nobody seemed to be about when we entered it, and we blundered into the kitchen, where milk had been spilt on the floor, and talked to a lady with black-stockinged, matchstick legs, who took us round.

As she described the house, she spoke like an ancient gramophone record which came to a halt when you asked a question, as if the stylus had suddenly been lifted. Then she resumed her set recitation. 'Charette held his reception in this room,' she intoned. 'Louis XV chairs.'

Charette fought on till 1796, when he was run to ground in a wood with only thirty followers. Wounded, he was taken to the neighbouring Château de la Chabottière, where, if you can find someone to open the door, you can still see the bare kitchen with its stone floor where he was held prisoner. Then, with his arm in a sling, he was taken to Nantes, marched through the streets, and shot in the same Place de Viarme where Cathelineau had been fatally wounded during the attack of June 1793.

Charette refused to be blindfolded, and gave the order to fire himself. A cross, incongruous by a bustling petrol station, marks the event, and the local Musée Dobrée shows the bullet-holed garden door that stood behind him.

Stofflet, too, fought on until he was captured in February 1796 in a farm in La Saugrenière and taken to Angers, where he was shot on the Champ de Mars.

The Prince de Talmont, who was related to the royal family and was the noblest of the Vendéan leaders, was guillotined outside his family castle in Laval on the Place de la Trémouille. Now, the ground floors of the old houses have been turned into shops: a pharmacy, a vintner's, a bookshop called 'France Loisir', with the inevitable car park.

Fat, young and lazy, Talmont was over-conscious of his illustrious birth, and contributed to many of the squabbles among the Vendéan generals on the long march north of the Loire. He died bravely. 'How long have you been with the brigands?' a Republican asked him at his trial. 'Ever since I was captured by you!' he answered. His head was mummified and nailed below the little window above the narrow entrance to his castle – an example to the people of what happened to even a lord of Laval if he rebelled against the Republic.

Only twenty-two, La Rochejaquelein was shot by a Republican soldier. Tearfully Stofflet, who was with him, slashed his face with his sword so that his corpse would not be recognized. Then, he buried him, stripped of his uniform.

Meanwhile the Vendée was being systematically devastated in a way which has roused the historian Reynald Secher to term it deliberate genocide. General Turreau, the Republican commander in 1794, created twelve 'Infernal Columns' which crossed the Vendée, six from north to south and six from east to west, methodically burning houses and villages and slaughtering everyone they met. The plan derived, ironically, from Louis XIV's systematic devastation of the Palatinate a hundred years earlier, which was studied closely in the military academies of the Ancien Régime, one of which Turreau had attended. The Vendée was desolate and shattered, ready for pacification. By returning to the barbarities of the past, the Republicans roused the peasantry to further resistance and created scars which still are there today. Yet all was done in the name of Liberty, Equality and a new Utopia, even if its roots were really revenge and fear, and the ancient determination to kill or to convert.

Perhaps the most terrible massacre perpetrated by these columns was near the little village of Le Petit Luc. The old parish priest who went out to plead for his parishioners had his tongue and heart torn out, and 563 people, including 107 children under seven, were shot and bayoneted. 'The Germans never did anything as bad!' said a Frenchman we met when visiting the memorial chapel.

Later, we went to the small town of Chanzeaux with Dominique Lambert. Here, women discovered decorating their church were taken out and shot beside a stream. Ironically, we met a woman, her arms full of flowers for the church. She greeted Dominique with a seraphic smile, and it seemed suddenly good to be alive on this sunny day in the peaceful countryside, when, two hundred years earlier, she would have been pushed roughly down to the stream to her death.

Dominique also took us to the forest of Vezins, with the sun splintered by the branches, and the scents of autumn leaves underfoot. In the middle of a clearing there was a wooden cross with some of the lower parts nicked off as relics. Here, Stofflet had had a field-hospital which one afternoon was invaded by Republican soldiers, led by a traitor who knew the way. Fifteen hundred wounded royalists were butchered.

As we drove back to Angers, a car lurched out of a lane, almost crashing into us. 'I've taken his number!' joked Dominique. 'I'll prosecute when the King returns!' We started talking about the kind of monarchy Dominique wanted. He explained that he saw it in religious terms, with the King being also a spiritual leader and the father of his people. As legitimate sovereign he would have the confidence and dignity to act as arbiter of his people, outside the swing of politics, able to concern himself with the long-term interests of France. Otherwise, Dominique did not see this as conflicting with constitutional government, or democracy.★

Back in Angers, Dominique took us to the main Place du Ralliement. 'This was created by pulling down a church early in the Revolution,' he said, and pointed to where the guillotine had stood in the centre of the square. 'A physicist, Chevrol, lived on a street below this square and told how the blood gushed down in front of his door when he was a boy. In 1794, the massacres were horrendous. The captured Vendéans and their sympathizers were imprisoned in the Cathedral where only a few months earlier the Te Deum for royalist victories had been sung. Straw mattresses for hundreds of captives covered the floor.'

To the north of the town, a road called the Chemin de Silence

---

★ I go to Buckingham Palace every year to take part in the presentation of prizes to writers of books and theses in the field of English to Foreigners. This is organized by the English Speaking Union, and prizes are presented by its President, the Duke of Edinburgh. I am allowed to invite a guest, and in 1987 I asked Dominique to come over. He was delighted to be in a royal palace that was lived in, but felt our monarchy was too watered down and secular to be entirely admirable!

leads to Avrillé. A church stands beyond a wall. To the side is a gravel area where ten broad rows of earth are planted with flowers.

'This was a field owned by a member of the revolutionary committee, who offered it as a burial ground. So twelve hundred prisoners were brought out here in six batches. They were shot there, in front of open ditches. Then the onlookers stripped them, stole their clothes and valuables, and flung them in.'

The Vendée began to seem like one huge cemetery.

In Clisson, the ruined, massive château has a well in its courtyard, which was excavated in 1961. The caretaker, who also looked after a splendid garden in the moat, full of blue hydrangeas, remembered this excavation happening when he was a boy. 'A book published in 1910 gave the number of corpses in the well as sixteen, which was exactly the number found. How did the author know? Entirely through word of mouth coming down for more than a century. There were four children, eleven women, and one old man, all buried under cannon balls and stones. Rubbish had been added over the years. When they dug out the well, they found a tiny, rotted child's shoe among the bones.'

'But what had happened?'

'Soldiers saw a light one night. It was very cold, and a fire had been lit in the courtyard. The soldiers came over to see what was happening and accused those they found of being rebels, even though they were mainly women and children. Of course, women and children had helped in the war as scouts, even carrying arms. But the soldiers were probably drunk. All the wine-cellars in Clisson had been ransacked.'

We drove on to Nantes. The most infamous of the Representatives on Mission,* Carrier, ruled here from October 1793. He devised a new way of eliminating the thousands of Vendéan refugees by simply putting them in covered barges which were sunk in the river. Over two thousand were disposed of in this way. When he wrote to the Convention, explaining how efficiently he dealt with rebels, Carrier's letter was read out and applauded by the deputies.

In Nantes, an attractive lady, Mme Pierregat, was waiting at

---

* These were Deputies from the Assembly, sent to armies in the field, to ensure loyalty and effectiveness.

the tourist office to help us. She took us to Carrier's house, a massive eighteenth-century building with a courtyard and a staircase with wrought-iron banisters. 'Carrier lived here for some months,' she told us, 'giving orders, rarely going out. Women who had relatives they wanted to save would go up and try to persuade him, and he spent a lot of time with them.' As we came through the archway from the courtyard, she said: 'Thank God we live nowadays – not then!'

She took us to the church of Ste Croix, where Carrier would get into the pulpit and threaten the bourgeois of Nantes, assembled before him. Then to the Place du Bouffay, where the guillotine was installed under the windows of an eighteenth-century mansion. The inhabitants all left soon afterwards.

Finally, at the Rue des Martyrs, we saw a monument to those executed in the quarries which, then, were worked nearby. A cross and the monument stood incongruously, crammed into a small space, close to a block of modern flats. 'I've never seen this building before,' said Mme Pierregat in amazement. 'The cross used to stand on its own. It's incredible the way they are building everywhere in Nantes.'

'What happened to Carrier?'

'He was guillotined in Paris after Robespierre's death.'

'Good. At least Napoleon didn't appoint him an Ambassador, like Turreau!'*

'And where did the drownings actually take place?' asked Brita.

'Cheviré,' said Mme Pierregat. 'It's on the way out of Nantes.'

Next day, we drove out in the sunlight to Cheviré and walked by dock buildings to a quay on the Loire which here is very broad and deep. Cranes, like giraffe necks, and a generating station stood opposite. The deep water was full of mud, billowing yellowish in the current. Further downstream, the banks were lined with poplars and the river grew wider as it approached the sea. From here, two hundred years ago, the bodies floated down, sometimes snared on islands at the river mouth. I wondered if there were still barge-loads of bones on the river bed, in their rotting wooden containers.

---

* Despite his atrocities, Turreau was made Ambassador to the United States by Napoleon, in 1812. Then Louis XVIII gave him the Order of St Louis for surrendering a castle to the Royalists, just before the Restoration.

A man came down the gangplank of a steamer moored to the quay. I approached him to see if he had any information. One never knew.

'The drownings were here – ?' I began, speaking in French.

'Not know.' He said in English, pointing back to his ship, with its frayed flag. 'Romanian!' he said.

Later, I went to the fish market in the Place du Bouffay. There was a tray of tiny shrimps, some of them still moving. I asked the fishmonger about them. 'Oh, they can live quite long out of their element,' he said cheerfully. 'You can never tell. Sometimes though they die almost immediately.'

We passed the hill of the Alouettes with its windmill semaphores, set with the same signals as the Vendéans had used. Then we plunged down concealed country lanes until we arrived at the Puy du Fou, which houses the very evocative Museum of Vendéan History. We got there an hour before it opened, as summer time had ended the night before, without our knowing.

A group of young people were gathered round the stables outside, and invited us into a shed to have coffee. They were, they told us, among the 700 actors in the historical pageant of Son et Lumière which takes place here every August.

Inevitably, we talked about the Vendée. 'Although we are young and have many things to think about, we still find the whole story of the insurrection very moving,' said a girl with dark hair in a pony tail.

We sipped black coffee out of plastic cups.

'Of course it's just history,' said a man in a cap. 'And we do feel very much a part of France.'

'Maybe – but we still have a great sense of local pride. Thus, most young people like us don't want to leave and work elsewhere as they do in other provinces.'

I asked how most people voted.

'Still Conservative,' grinned the man in a cap.

'But not for Le Pen,' said the girl with the pony tail, alluding to the leader of the extreme right. 'You see, we get few immigrants.'

Outside, the mist curled round the remains of the eighteenth-century château, also burnt down in the Vendée war, and now being rebuilt.

In the courtyard, yellow flowers bloomed on the broad window sills of the caretaker's house. A bell was fixed high up on a wall. It swayed slightly in the strong breeze. But the chain attached to it was too short for anyone to reach it – even on tiptoe.

There was no need now to ring the tocsin to summon peasant armies.

[18]

DESTRUCTION IN LYONS

'I have visited many towns in France, Italy and Germany, and Lyons
seems to me certainly the most beautiful; its quays, its vast Place Louis
XIV, its old Town Hall . . . Where the natural setting is concerned, it
is incomparable.'

REICHARD, a Prussian, in 1792.

While the war in the Vendée was going on, insurrection broke
out in Lyons, the second city of France and one of the richest,
the centre of the silk industry. Ironically, it happened on 29 May
1793, at about the same time as the Girondins were expelled from
the Convention in Paris (see p. 157). In Lyons, though, it was a
revolt against the Jacobins, while in Paris it was in their favour.

Like most of France, Lyons had welcomed the Revolution.
However, fear of counter-revolution had started to agitate Lyons
from the middle of 1790. The city was not far from Turin across
the border, which was the centre of émigré plots. Here the King's
brother, the Comte d'Artois, had taken up residence, and the fact
that local government was mainly in the hands of the rich merchant
class roused fear and suspicion among the people.

A Central Club, affiliated to the Jacobins in Paris, with thirty-one
branches throughout the town, was founded with three thousand
members, just off the present Rue du Bat d'Argent, near the
Town Hall. This Club organized demonstrations, and infiltrated
the municipality. At its head was an extraordinary visionary called
Chalier. Like Marat, Chalier was a foreigner, born over the border
in Piedmont. Before the Revolution he had been a commercial
traveller for a silk merchant, and had visited Italy, Spain, Portugal
and Constantinople where, he wrote later: 'Everywhere . . . I saw
the people oppressed and when I remembered my reading of books
about the great days of Athens and Rome, the comparison was
odious.'

At the Jacobin Club, Chalier became renowned for his blood-curdling speeches, which sent shivers of fear through the bourgeoisie of the town. There is a print in the Musée Gadagne showing him standing on a table in the Club, leaning slightly back, pointing a dagger upwards as if he wanted to disembowel someone, while around him the other members cheer and wave their knives.

In fact, Chalier was much loved by the poor for his generosity and kindness, and he was never directly responsible for putting anyone to death. Nevertheless, his proposals included the erection of the guillotine on the narrow Morand bridge over the Rhône, so that heads would fall into the river on one side, and bodies on the other. His intention, so he announced to the cheering mob, was 'to purge the town of aristocratic vermin by cutting off fifty heads'.

As so often in the Revolution, threats induced a fierce reaction among those attacked – which led to further threats. By February 1793, just before the Vendée war broke out, the city was divided into two camps, each of which felt it necessary to suppress the other in the interests of its own security.

In March 1793, Bertrand, a friend of Chalier's and another Jacobin, became mayor. Like militants in any Conservative town, the new municipality succeedèd in alienating many of the citizens. House arrests were made, a Committee of Public Safety was created in imitation of Paris, a revolutionary army was formed. In the Place des Terreaux, behind the Town Hall, Chalier set up the guillotine, sent in a box from Paris, with a ring of soldiers round it. The object was to warn those who conspired against the 'patriots' what might happen to them. The irony is that Chalier, who put it up, was to be the first to die on it.

Like most first-time visitors to Lyons I expected a drab industrial complex. However, after penetrating the ring of modern factories we entered a light, dignified city, with broad streets and pale, tall buildings. The only sinister thing about it was a modern, black tower, slim and tall, with a prismatic roof like a helmet, which resembled a frowning Norman knight keeping stern watch over the city.

Lyons bestrides two rivers, and it is a delight to wander over a bridge above the Rhône from the modern, newly built area in the east, through the main peninsula. Then, over another bridge, to the older city, beyond the Saône. Here, narrow streets and medieval squares cluster below the hill of Fourvière, crowned by its nineteenth-century Basilica. Unlike so many big cities, Lyons rarely loses touch with the countryside. You never feel lost among buildings: views of Fourvière and glimpses of the rivers tell you roughly where you are.

'Lyons was a good place to murder people in,' writes the historian Richard Cobb, referring to Revolutionary times. Between the winding streets and little squares are the narrow walled alleyways called *traboules*, through which the criminal or refugee could find his way undetected from almost any place to any other. On the other side of the Rhône was the empty plain of Les Brotteaux and the village of La Guillotière, where inns and wineshops provided another refuge – particularly as they were in a different Department, the Isère, with its separate local government and police force. Another advantage was that the two rivers provided a convenient way of dumping corpses.

In those days, Lyons was a city of 100,000 inhabitants. As we discovered, living in Cordoba in southern Spain in the 1950s – a city then comparable in size and traditional class structure – there was a lot of direct contact between people, and everyone knew those prominent in the city. The poor lived mainly in their districts, which were almost like adjoining villages, with all the traditions and close family relationships of small communities.

In Lyons, at the time of the Revolution, the city walls meandered along the Rhône and crossed the high hill of the Croix Rousse at the landward end of the peninsula. They also stretched along the bottom of the hill of Fourvière. Some of the street names still remain: the Rue de la Charité, which used to run by a hospital of that name; or Rue St Hélène; or the Place Bellecour, built by Mansart under the name Place Louis Le Grand, and renowned as one of the most beautiful squares in Europe.

Some of the quays, too, like that of St Antoine, or the Célestins, recall the forty-eight monasteries, convents and houses of Penitence which crowded Lyons at a time when the Church owned a third of all the housing in the city.

However, the most significant building from before the Revolution is the seventeenth-century Town Hall, dominating the Place des Terreaux. It was this key nerve-centre which was stormed on 28–29 May by a force of rebellious National Guards. Against

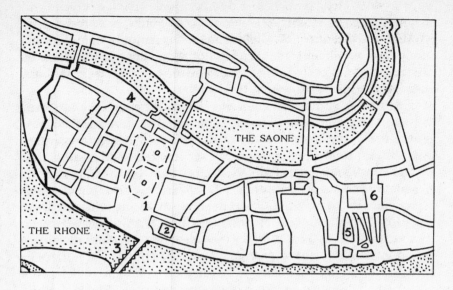

Lyons at the time of the Revolution.
1. Place Bellecour (Louis le Grand);
2. Hospital Hôtel-Dieu;
3. Pont du Rhône;
4. Arsenal;
5. Jacobin Club;
6. Place des Terreaux in front of Town Hall.

them were the Jacobins and the newly formed revolutionary army, consisting of 'patriots' and the poor, and directed by Deputies on Mission from Paris. The Arsenal was occupied and, after a fight which lasted all night, with heavy casualties, the Town Hall was taken, and the 'patriots' fled for their lives.

The new régime remained Republican, although inevitably percolated by royalists who, however, did not declare themselves as such. News of the fall of the Girondins strengthened their resolve, and Lyons became part of the movement in sixty out of eighty-three provinces which defied the Convention because its inviolability had been outraged and the Girondins purged.

For some time, however, there were no open hostilities between Paris and Lyons, largely because Danton was still a member of the Committee of Public Safety. Blustering, egocentric and shrewd, Danton was warm-blooded and human – if not humane. More far-sighted than most of his colleagues, he wanted conciliation with Lyons. However, on 10 July 1793 he left the Committee and abandoned power to his self-righteous and vengeful colleagues.

At about this time, the Lyonnais took an impulsive step which made civil war inevitable. On 16 July they revenged themselves on Chalier, that Savonarola of the Revolution, who had done so much to provoke the revolt against the Jacobins.

The official executioner in Lyons was called Ripet, and he came from a family which had held the post as a hereditary fief for generations. He was a jocular individual who had a teasing relationship with his assistant, Bernard, whom he called 'Mon Commis' (My errand boy), while Bernard called him 'Mon Bourgeois'. Despite Chalier's threats, the guillotine had never been used before, and Ripet and Bernard were uncertain how to use it. Furthermore, the crowds who came to witness the elimination of the man who had kept them sleepless at night swarmed over the platform of this unfamiliar instrument to examine it, and unbalanced it.

In the late afternoon, Chalier, surrounded by troops, walked from the Prison de Roanne, which was where the Palais de Justice now is. With watery eyes fixed on the sky, seeming the reincarnation of a martyr who had denounced 'heretics' too fiercely, he mounted the scaffold. Ripet and Bernard seized him, bound him to the plank, tilted him down, placed the top of the 'window' over his neck, and released the blade.

However, the guillotine wouldn't work. The blade stopped halfway. Ripet and Bernard tried again with the same result. The third time, the knife grazed Chalier's neck, and the fourth, cut it in half. Ripet had to detach the head with his knife and, as Chalier was bald, held it up by an ear, while the crowd shouted abuse at such incompetence.

Chalier's death decided the Convention in Paris. On 8 August Republican armies surrounded Lyons. Once the campaign got under way, the city was bombarded night and day. Even in modern Lyons, it is not difficult to imagine the buildings trembling and shuddering in the wedge between its rivers, pounded mercilessly from all sides.

At this time, the Arsenal was near the Saône, behind the present quays of Joffre and Tilsit. One evening, it was hit and blew up. A jet of flame, leaping into the sky, carried with it a hundred and seventeen houses. The red glow in the river formed livid pools and lit up Fourvière, which flickered like a volcano about to explode.

The rebels had hung a black flag on the enormous hospital of Hôtel-Dieu, which still stands beside the Rhône. However, this merely helped the enemy artillery to concentrate on it. The sick and wounded who survived were evacuated to empty, cavernous convents which, three years earlier, had echoed to whispered prayers and midnight Masses. At the Town Hall, the roof over the splendid Grande Salle was hit, and left open to the summer sky. The streets were full of rubble, and the black stains of fire marked the walls of ruined buildings.

'It was a spectacle which neither Vesuvius nor Etna have ever offered to mortal eyes,' wrote Dubois-Crance, the delighted Republican general, to the Convention in Paris.

The end came on 9 October. Because they were not officially royalists, no attempt was made to relieve them by the foreign armies invading France. Although Toulon had been captured by the English at the end of August, a Republican army had attacked in the south, capturing Valence and Marseilles, breaking up the rebellious movement against Paris. In the Vendée the royalists were embarked on their last desperate campaign which was to lead them to Savenay and extinction. There was thus no way of destroying the besieging army with help from outside and, as in the Vendée, many of the peasant soldiers who defended Lyons had returned to their farms to gather their harvests and had stayed there. The most terrible affliction was famine, as the Republicans had now had time to place a ring round Lyons through which supplies could penetrate with difficulty.

One of the most destructive periods of the Revolution was about to begin. In Paris, the exultant Convention decreed that Lyons should be destroyed. All the most luxurious and beautiful houses of the rich were to be pulled down. The egalitarian alternative of expelling the rich and allowing the poor to occupy their houses was not even considered. The object was melodramatic punishment which would always be remembered. Even the name was to disappear. Lyons was re-baptized 'Ville Affranchie' (Liberated Town), and over the ruins a column was to be erected, bearing the words: 'Lyons bore arms against the Republic. Lyons no longer exists.'

Couthon, the crippled Representative of the Convention, was carried in procession to the Place Bellecour. There, on the corner of the old Rue des Deux Maisons, he tapped on a wall with a silver hammer and said in a sonorous voice: 'The Law strikes thee.' Fourteen thousand workmen then began to demolish the beautiful, stately houses. Fortunately, Napoleon restored many of them in 1800, and today the Place Bellecour is almost as splendid as it then was.

The razing of buildings was accompanied by vengeance on those who had fought for their city. In his vitriolic Parisian newspaper, *Le Père Duchesne*, Hébert, who at this time embodied the current spirit of violence and anarchy, wrote: 'If I had been commander in Lyons, I would have hanged all the tribe of merchants, all the monopolists, all those who make a commerce in the exchange of assignats, all priests, all the rich, all the lawyers and I would have the bastards chucked into the Rhône by the Sansculottes.'

The Town Hall, stripped of its paintings of city councillors and mayors, which had all been burnt in an attempt to eradicate the past, now became the prison and the seat of the Revolutionary Tribunal. Today, much of its former splendour has been restored, and Paul Feuga, who has written a book on the building during the Revolution, took us round. Paul is yet another of these people one meets so frequently in France who are fascinated by the Revolution. In his case, it is probably because of love for his birthplace, Lyons, and the fact that some of his ancestors fought on the side of the besieged.

Together we went up the rather dull Grand Staircase of the Town Hall and made our way through splendid rooms with gold tracery on the walls and tall windows, to what is called the Salle de la Conservation. 'Before the trials,' said Paul Feuga, 'the prisoners were kept in convents and monasteries all over Lyons. Once every three days, long processions, linked together by a chain like galley slaves, were marched through the streets to the Town Hall. Here, they were kept in a large room like this one.' Paul Feuga looked round at the elegant emptiness. With no furniture it was easy to see it crowded with ragged men and women, chattering, weeping, trying to keep their spirits up.

'Every day, they were given a pound and a half of rye bread and, on arrival, issued with a blanket and a bale of straw. Their situation was similar to that in the old palace of the Luxembourg in Paris, with everyone herded together in what used to be splendid state rooms, with the walls disfigured with the graffiti of names and farewell messages.

'A turnkey supervised each room. At night, when he was asleep, occasional escapes took place. Once three prisoners let themselves down from the window with a rope made of straw.' We moved over and looked into the courtyard. 'One, however, was too fat. So he climbed along this ledge here.' A couple of feet below the window, a ledge, chipped at the edges, stretched along the building. 'He walked to another window, which was open. Inside, a National Guard gave a cry at sight of this sudden apparition, and ran from the room. The prisoner hurried down the stairs, past sentries who presumed he was a municipal officer, and escaped through the main door.'

We walked to a little antechamber, bare, with parquet flooring. 'Prisoners awaiting questioning sat here on a bench,' said Paul Feuga. 'Through the door, in what was once the Salle du Consulat, sat five to seven judges, resplendent in gold epaulettes and tall hats with red feathers. Round the room was a low, wooden wall, behind which spectators stood.'

I could see it all suddenly as if they were there, as in a surrealist dream.

'The prisoners were questioned for only five to ten minutes, as there were so many of them. Much depended on their answers to a few direct questions: Did you fight in the siege? What do you think of Louis Capet (Louis XVI)? Do you believe in God?

'To this last question, one timid priest answered hesitantly: "A little," and was immediately condemned. Another, when asked if he believed in Hell, replied: "Meeting you has confirmed my belief."

'The judges made signs to show their verdicts: if it was the guillotine, they touched a little axe which hung from the tricolour ribbon round their necks. If the firing squad, they touched their foreheads. If the prisoner seemed innocent, they stretched an arm along the table.

'The turnkey was supposed to decipher the final decision of the President of the court. Taking the prisoner by the arm, he led him, or her, over there.' We walked out of the room, turned left and descended an ancient, stone, spiral staircase whose steps, Paul Feuga told us, were held together by pressure rather than mortar.

At the bottom we entered a spacious reception hall, just behind the main door, which gave onto the Place des Terreaux. Then, down into the cellars. 'The turnkey took the condemned prisoners over to the left, into what was called the "mauvaise cave".' We looked round under naked light bulbs at the long, empty cellar with barred windows round the walls. 'The innocent were led to the "bonne cave", on the right.' Paul tried a door but it was locked.

'Inevitably, this complicated system was open to error,' he continued, imperturbably. 'No one will ever know how many prisoners were taken to the wrong "cave". The time the trials took place was also important: mornings from nine till twelve were fairer. In the evenings, from seven till nine, the judges were drunk, or irritable.'

We walked out, round to the Place des Terreaux, and stood by the steps leading from the Town Hall entrance. Ahead of us lay a simple square with a nineteenth-century bronze statue in the middle, depicting a woman with children being borne along by straining horses. On the left was the mass of the Palais des Arts, which before the Revolution had been a convent, and on the right a series of colourful eighteenth-century terraced houses.

'Those who had been released were marched out to stand on these steps, and were welcomed back to the bosom of the Republic with ceremonial speeches.

'The condemned stood in front of the same steps. When the executions first started, they were shot. However, the bullets also penetrated those barred windows you can see in the Town Hall basement. Sometimes the prisoners inside were wounded. Once, a guard had his arm shattered, so the fusillades were moved elsewhere.

'Two weeks after the end of the siege, the guillotine was erected here, just in front of the steps. There was a tradition that criminals should be punished on the site of their crime, and it was here that Chalier had been guillotined. The problem, though, was that the executioners, Ripet and Bernard, were in prison, accused of Chalier's murder. Ripet's brother took over.

'From the end of October 1793 until the beginning of April 1794, 850 people were guillotined.' Paul took a piece of paper from his pocket. 'Here's a copy of an article in the local paper of the time, which might interest you. It's the imagined correspondence between the guillotine of Lyons and the one in Paris.' He started reading:

'"Since the 12th October until the 22nd of December, I have already sent 777 heads to the Devil, except for a few who have escaped because of fusillades. To how many curés, vicars, host carriers, sacristans, beadles and dealers in 'Holy Bread', have I given a good 'Peccavi' with the edge of my revolutionary iron."'

'It's extraordinary how many priests seem to have been executed.'

'Yes, those who refused to take the oath were regarded as the most dangerous counter-revolutionaries of all because they could influence their flocks. However, the residents complained of the miasma of blood, spilt on beaten earth. So the guillotine was moved to the other end, in front of what is now that department store, the Galerie des Terreaux. From there, a ditch was dug along what is now the Rue Constantine, there, so that the blood flowed into the Saône.

'The executions were watched by two representatives from the first floor of the second house, which you can see on the right. It was then a café called Antonio, which shows that immigrant Italian restaurateurs also set up business in those days. Now, it's a chess club, there, above that café called "La Fleurie". Shall we go in and have a drink?'

We sat rather gloomily round a table. 'Who were the Republicans most responsible for organizing this Terror?' asked Brita.

'Oh, Couthon, a cripple who was a friend of Robespierre's. Collot d'Herbois, an ex-actor who is said to have taken his revenge on the Lyonnais for hissing him when he performed in a play here, before the Revolution. And Fouché, a cold calculating ex-priest who under Napoleon became head of the Police and Duke of Otranto.'

Among other things, we started talking about the forthcoming trial of the Gestapo chief Klaus Barbie, a more recent example of Richard Cobb's remark about Lyons being a good place in which to murder people. However, it was on the other side of the Rhône that the most gruesome reprisals took place, in an open space called Les Brotteaux. Now it has been built over, and the area is where the Rues Du Guesclin and Créqui are crossed by the Rue Louis Blanc.

Processions of prisoners crossed the bridge, now the Pont de la Guillotière. Then they marched along the bank with the long ruined façade of the Hôtel-Dieu on the other side. November mist rose from the river, and the open grass on their right was coarse and muddy. For a few hundred yards, the prisoners marched on, and then turned inland until they came to a row of willow trees. Between these a long cord was slung, to which the prisoners were tied in pairs. Opposite, were the snouts of loaded cannon. Not even cattle in the slaughterhouse have such clear signs of approaching death.

When all was ready, the cannon belched flame and grapeshot.

Corpses dangled on bits of broken cord, and soldiers went up and down, finishing off survivors. The bodies were flung into the Rhône, which carried the mangled remains past torrid southern towns, a macabre warning to those who might be thinking of defying the Republic.

One day, no fewer than 209 men and women were eliminated in a single cannonade. The official number of those to be executed was actually 210, but two men escaped just before the procession reached the bridge. The number should therefore have been 208. However, a police commissioner in mufti who was watching the procession was thought to be a prisoner, and was hustled in by the guards, despite his protests.

Some of the raving exultation which greeted these cannonades was quite extraordinary. Achard, Robespierre's agent in Lyons, wrote in a letter:

More heads and heads falling every day. What a delight that you saw the justice done to the 209 criminals! What majesty! What an impressive atmosphere! Everything was edifying! What a number of great scoundrels bit the dust that day in the arena of Les Brotteaux! What an event cementing the Republic together!

Collot d'Herbois justified the cannonades and was applauded in the Convention:

'We shot down hundreds of criminals at a time and now we are told that it was a crime. How can anyone not see that it was an act of mercy? When twenty culprits are guillotined, the last of the executed dies twenty deaths, but the two hundred we shot all died together.'

Apart from personal revenge and sadism, it is difficult, outside Belfast and Beirut, to understand the mentality behind these events. Revenge for Chalier's death and, in the Vendée, for dead Republican soldiers played a part. Why, though, were reprisals so merciless when in both places clemency might well have united France behind the Republic?

Perhaps, as happened in Nazi Germany, much can be explained by the way circumstances can give power to people who enjoyed slaughter. I remember talking to a psychologist in Italy who specialized in battered children. When I expressed surprise that Italy, where children always seem so loved, should also have this problem, he said: 'Well, I think all countries have the same strata of cruelty and sadism. It's just a question of whether it has been discovered and publicized, or not. But believe me, it's always there.'

Once public opinion comes to accept horror, people can always be found to carry it out, whether because obedience to orders is preferred to being victimized, or because many have a deep destructive instinct, born of continual frustration and hurt, which lurks in the shadows, waiting to emerge.

In Lyons, M. Blouson, a municipal officer, explained it in terms of the youth of most of the revolutionaries. 'They were mostly in their twenties,' he said. 'They had the energy, enthusiasm and intolerance of the young. I remember, when I was that age, I would happily have sent those who disagreed with me on certain issues to the guillotine.'

Certainly, it is difficult for us now to understand the assumptions about human life and pain in a society which had a low life expectancy and no anaesthetics.

Today, we tend to be blasé about the ideals the Republicans fought for. Most of us have had enough of ideological convulsions, and we have seen in practice that perfect solutions to social problems do not exist. It is therefore difficult to empathize with the almost religious faith which the new Republic evoked. Those executed were people who had betrayed that faith, who belonged to a past now so maligned that any attempt to restore it seemed depraved. St Just, Robespierre's henchman, once said: 'That which constitutes the Republic is the total destruction of that which opposes it.'

Of course some did oppose it, not on political grounds but on those of conscience. Colonel de Beaumont, who commanded the troops responsible for the cannonades, told Collot d'Herbois that he could not continue – and was arrested, a few days later.

On the site of the massacres, a *chapelle expiatoire* has been erected, in what is now the Rue Louis Blanc. Inevitably, it is a depressing building, kept by Domini nuns, with little blue kerchiefs on their heads.

Inside, the windows are frosted and darkened, as if to fill you with gloom as you wait for the nun to find the key. You go down a spiral staircase into a plain, domed chapel made of grimy blocks of whitish stone. At one end is the solid tomb of the Comte de Précy, the commander of the city during the siege. On either side is a neat pile of bones, about three feet high and ten feet long. They were disinterred from the ditches in which the victims were buried – once the Republicans had discovered that throwing so many corpses into the river could infect whole districts.

The bones lie in rough, straight lines, with skulls grimacing between them, like large eggs in a nest of branches. On either side of the rectangular tomb of De Précy, the insurgent commander, they seem frail and even irrelevant, the refuse of horror, dusty and brown in colour.

The Comte de Précy got away, breaking through the Republican lines with two hundred cavaliers to Switzerland. But each of these fragmented skeletons went through the agony of the guillotine, or a cannonade, with terror clawing at stomachs which now have withered away, with prayers and cries on lips which now show only bone.

In turn, they were revenged. When Robespierre fell, the counter-revolution began again in Lyons. The judge Lafaye was killed by the mob. The crippled Representative, Couthon, was guillotined with Robespierre; Collot d'Herbois was deported to Guiana, where he died.

Many others were assassinated mysteriously in alleyways, on bridges, in their homes. Much of this was repeated when Lyons became a major centre of the Resistance in 1943–5.

Perhaps it is no accident that Lyons is also the home of 'Grand Guignol', the horror puppet show.

BRITISH AND ROYALISTS IN TOULON

'Our Republic is based on all the virtues, and it will one day make
those who fight her blush with shame.'

> Letter from DUGOMMIER, the Commander of the
> Republican army at Toulon, to General O'Hara,
> rejecting the sixty louis which he had sent
> to those who had captured him.

On 28 August 1793, an extraordinary sight met the gaze of those
Toulonnais who had climbed Mount Faron above the town. In the
distance, fourteen warships could be seen, with launches laden with
troops. In the sun, the flash of bayonets was visible, even at that
distance. After centuries of battles with French ships, the British
were arriving as allies of the 30,000 inhabitants of the foremost
naval base in France. Many of the Toulonnais staring out at this
array of ships had fought the British, or had lost relatives in naval
engagements against them.

An even bigger fleet then appeared on the horizon: seventeen
Spanish men of war, sailing slowly, with a light wind behind them.
The biggest was the *Concepción* of 100 guns, a real 'cathedral of
canvas'. Behind them came yet other ships from Sardinia and the
Kingdom of Naples, until the sea below was covered with sloops,
frigates and men of war.

The fleet anchored in the mooring called Les Vignettes, which
now is surrounded by the suburbs of Toulon. The town shook as a
seventeen-gun salute was given and returned. Launches, crowded
with marines, approached the shore and marched into the town,
their band playing 'Lillibullero', which the Toulonnais had never
heard before.

Toulon was now defended against the tiny army of the Republic
which had just swept down the Rhône and occupied rebellious
Marseilles, only a few score kilometres to the west.

Yet another counter-revolutionary blow had been struck against the Republic.

The old town of Toulon is small, sloping down to the harbour and arsenal. Although it attracts few foreign tourists, it has the joyousness of the Midi, with its outdoor cafés, its fish restaurants, its yachts weaving their way along the numerous capes and inlets of the extended bay. During the summer, its inhabitants are protected from the hot sun by the shade of narrow streets. When we were there, a large, toy-town train, painted red, ran along the Avenue de la République and up the Cours Lafayette, spouting garish music, stopping for passengers, and advertising the local Galeries Lafayette.

Along the line of the demolished seventeenth-century city wall, the Cours Lafayette runs up from near the sea. It is a broad pedestrian way with plane trees and high old houses on either side. There, a morning market takes place with all the regional glory of fruit and vegetables, the cries of those selling melons and grapes, the *badinage* and flirtation of the South.

Amidst the stalls, a one-man band occasionally performs, wearing a tricolour bicorne hat and medals, and playing patriotic songs. A cannon-ball from 1793 is still stuck in the wall of a house, above a shop selling babywear, set in a decorated brass circle to ensure that it does not fall suddenly on pedestrians. It looks like a metal nipple in the ochre, rendered wall.

At the bottom of the Cours Lafayette stands a large, rather grim church, once St Jean, now St Francis de Paul. Here, the sessions of the revolutionary Jacobin Club were held. Their excesses included throwing the Bishop's coach into the sea and mobbing the Admiral of the Fleet, who was hung up, feet first, on a lamp-post outside the arsenal. As in Lyons, these excesses rallied support for a counter-revolutionary municipality which came to power in July 1793, after the Girondin deputies had been arrested in Paris. It was this municipality which, fearing the advancing Republican army, invited the Allies in.

Toulon was well equipped to resist the Republican siege which now began. Its fortified walls had been strengthened and redesigned by Louis XIV's great engineer, Vauban, who estimated that only an army of 140,000 men, with 200 cannon, could capture it. Forts protected the landward side on the heights of Faron. Other fortresses could ward off attacks on the outer walls: St Catherine, which has now been swamped by lapping suburbs, and Malbousquet, which can still be seen to the west, amidst scrub country which rises to the hill of Les Arènes. It has a ragged bulk of stone walls, set on rock, and visible from the road.

Forts also protected the other vulnerable point in the city's defences: the straits between the outer and inner harbour, which, if held on both sides, threatened ships entering or leaving Toulon. You can see one of them, the Tour Grosse, by going south-east, out of the town. Standing on the point of a peninsula, it is a round and solid tower, now a naval museum and meteorological station.

On the other side of the straits are the forts of L'Eguillette, which is closed, and Balaguier, which is another naval museum. Here you enter a garden with a dovecote and a round pond. On the battlements, cannon point dull, brass barrels to cover the narrow stretch of sea in front.

In fact, the cannon which stood there in 1793 could not have sunk a ship passing through. For their range was only 1,000 metres for reasonably accurate fire, and 1,500 as a maximum. They might have struck an insignificant blow if a ship were tacking against the wind, but with the wind behind it, a ship could hug the other shore, and would expose its vulnerable flank for only a few minutes. Cannon in those days were remarkably ineffective at a distance: during the Revolutionary and Napoleonic Wars, it took an average of 2,000 shots to kill one man.

So the young artillery officer, Napoleon Bonaparte, was not entirely right in believing that the key to Toulon was possession of these two forts, on one side of the straits. As we were to discover, it needed other circumstances to give him his first significant triumph.

The Republican army arrived only a few days after the Allied fleet. It was commanded by General Carteaux, a portrait painter. Ten years before the Revolution, Carteaux had resigned from the army and had painted Louis XVI on horseback, for which he received 6,000 livres from the municipality of Paris. At the beginning of the Revolution he had participated in the attack on the Bastille, and had joined the army once again.

On arrival from Marseilles, he established his army headquarters in the Château de Montauban, which is now owned by summer visitors who leave it empty all winter. We drove up to see it with Dr Barjeon, a naval doctor, who told us the well-known story about Napoleon proving Carteaux wrong. 'Carteaux is said to have decided to bombard the enemy ships in the bay from the terrace of the château,' said Dr Barjeon as we drove past the fortress of Malbousquet. 'He invited his officers to dinner to watch the great event. Of course, the whole idea was quite impossible, as Napoleon told him at the start of the evening. The sea was much too far away. But Carteaux insisted, and ordered the cannon balls to be heated till they were red-hot over a fire in the kitchen. The cannon were fired, but of course they did not even reach the sea. Carteaux was humiliated and Napoleon gained a reputation for expertise.

'The story is probably untrue,' added Dr Barjeon. 'After all, Carteaux had a lot of experience in the army before he resigned. Napoleonic legend has made him into a bluff, incompetent man, but he was actually a decisive, able soldier with, of course, a strong element of caution, which is not surprising when you consider how the Republic treated unsuccessful generals.* The story, anyway, originated with one of Napoleon's future marshals, Marmont, who was not even there at the time.'

We left the road and went down a narrow lane with villas on one side, and soon glimpsed the château, secluded in trees, behind a high wall. There seemed no way of getting in, so I contented myself, reluctantly, with climbing onto a wall on the other side of the lane. From there, it was possible to see the former Republican headquarters through the trees. The terrace itself, a long slab of yellowish stone, emerged under overlapping branches.

'From his headquarters, here,' said Dr Barjeon, 'Carteaux authorized Napoleon to push two batteries to the sea where he really could bombard the Allied ships.

'The first battery was called "Montagne", after the dominant party of Danton and Robespierre in the Convention. The second, a few hundred metres to the south, was called "Sans-Culotte".

'Both were within a range of 800 metres and fired on the royalist French frigate *L'Aurore*, and on various Allied gunboats. All the ships were hit and one of the gunships sank.

'In retaliation, Admiral Hood sent in men of war, equipped with

---

* Among generals guillotined in 1793, were Custine, La Marlière, Biron and Houchard, and, in 1794, Dillon and Beauharnais, husband of the future Empress Joséphine.

over 300 cannon. They bombarded the Republican batteries and pulverized the little village of La Seyne.'

Standing on the edge of the little bay, I found it easy to imagine the hail of metal flying from the ships tossing on sea roughened by the mistral, and the roar of successive salvos, shattering the ears of royalist and Republican alike, while the tall masts, bare of sail, bobbed up and down, visible occasionally through the shrouds of smoke.

During the next few weeks, there were attacks and counter-attacks, we were told. The Allies set out from Fort Malbousquet through the scrub to attack the Republicans on the hill above. However, after an initial success, the commander of the Allied land forces, General O'Hara, was captured when he fell from his horse. 'He was probably caught with his trousers down,' Dr Barjeon told us, 'for both sides were ravaged with dysentery.' Following the English custom, O'Hara offered sixty louis to his four captors, which were refused.

Meanwhile, in Toulon, the streets were full of tents. The guillotine had been publicly burnt, but a gallows was put up, made of the wood of the Tree of Liberty which was erected in all Republican towns. The Spanish army, bristling with chaplains, brought a religious flavour, with processions, the refusal to use churches for billeting troops, and their insistence on purifying the church of St Jean, which, as we have seen, had been used by the Jacobins.

On the Republican side, Bonaparte busied himself establishing new batteries closer and closer to Fort Mulgrave, which he regarded as the key to capturing Toulon, for the fort had been constructed on the hill to provide protection for the vital forts of Balaguier and L'Eguillette, which overlooked the straits. Capture of these forts, Bonaparte believed, would prevent the Allied ships sailing through the straits, and they would be bottled up in Toulon and the neighbouring roadsteads.

The closest of these batteries was 'Hommes Sans Peur', which was only 600 metres from the fort. We found it because of a visit to the Museum of Old Toulon in the Cours Lafayette. The museum had few exhibits of the siege, but the curator was very helpful and advised us to go and see a M. Vieillefosse, who lived right on top of what had been the battery. 'He has written a remarkable book about the siege from the point of view of an old artillery officer,' said the curator. 'He's in his eighties, now, and doesn't leave his house much. Wait a moment. I'll phone him.'

The next day, we followed intricate instructions on how to get to the Rue Pères Nonhortains, where M. Vieillefosse lived. After driving along various one-way streets, and retracing our route several times, we asked a pedestrian, and then a taxi-driver, where the house was. As, still confused, we stopped a lorry to ask the driver, we were approached by a lady who, seeing our GB plates, introduced herself: 'I am Mme Vieillefosse,' she said with dignity. 'I have been waiting for you.'

She led us along a lane, with a ridge on one side facing open countryside, then up some steps to a house perched on top of the rise, with a cannon-ball by the door. Inside, an erect, well-preserved gentleman was waiting in the sitting room, which gave directly onto the steps. Around the room were some of the twenty-eight cats which shared the house. Plied by Madame with cakes and beer, we started talking about Toulon.

M. Vieillefosse's grandfather had died in 1930 and was born in 1838, and had heard a lot about the siege from his grandfather, who had been a child in 1793.

M. Vieillefosse's youth had therefore been coloured by the stories he had heard. As he later became an artillery officer in the navy, he had often thought of the campaign in terms of the technical knowledge he had acquired. 'I looked at the siege,' he said, 'as if I were an artillery officer of the time, knowing what guns were capable of, how long it took to aim and fire a shot, and the range of different cannon. For instance, some say that when he captured Fort Mulgrave Napoleon could have turned the cannon round to fire on the English below. This I knew was quite impossible. Guns were carefully placed, and it would have taken at least twenty-four hours to adapt the emplacements and turn the heavy guns round.'

Napoleon's role, he felt, had been over-estimated. After all, it was not so difficult to see that control of the straits was the key to a defence which depended on naval power. It had already been suggested to the Committee of Public Safety in Paris by a Citizen Brune.

'Napoleon was also greatly helped because one of the Representatives sent by the Convention was Salicetti, a Corsican. Fréron, another Representative, was madly in love with Napoleon's sister, Pauline, and his assistant was none other than Napoleon's brother,

Joseph. So, through family and Corsican connections, Napoleon had support at the highest level. Of course, his drive and energy made a great contribution to the success of the siege. But it is wrong to think that Toulon made him famous. He was promoted general afterwards, but so were twenty-four other colonels. Had Napoleon not become Emperor, his role at Toulon would probably have been confined to a footnote in the history books.

'In any case, the siege ended not so much because of Republican assaults but because the political situation had changed. By December 1793, Lyons had fallen to the Republicans. The rebels in the Vendée were at their last gasp. And in November, the French armies in the east had won a victory at Wattignies, relieving pressure there.

'The Allies had only landed at Toulon the previous August because they believed the Republic was about to collapse. Admiral Hood hoped to use Toulon as a bargaining counter with the new government of Louis XVII for West Indian sugar islands, or a garrison at Dunkirk. In the changed circumstances, he needed at least 150,000 men, which he hadn't got, for an invasion of the Midi. The siege did not end just because Napoleon's attack was successful. After all, Hood could have pulverized Bonaparte after he took Fort Mulgrave with broadsides from his ships, and have retaken the fortress without much difficulty.'

We went outside to the top of the steps, and examined the cannon-ball, which weighed sixteen pounds. 'We found heaps of them here,' said M. Vieillefosse. 'The battery was right where our house is, concealed in the trees. The guns, weighing three to four tons, were dragged up at night by men, or horses. It took several days to prepare a battery. A platform of wood had to be built to steady and align each gun. The powder and cannon-balls then had to be brought up.'

M. Vieillefosse pointed to a tree-covered hillock, a few hundred yards away. 'That was another battery, Les Sablettes, which at one stage was captured by the English in the fierce fighting which swept back and forth through these woods.'

The sun was shining. 'The fine weather is deceptive,' said M. Vieillefosse. 'You must imagine this countryside wild and uninhabited, with the rain falling, the soldiers with wet uniforms, protecting their gunpowder, huddled under the eaves of the parapets, their boots squelchy when they walked.'

We shook hands, thanked Madame for her profuse hospitality,

and stroked a few cats. M. Vieillefosse promised to send me his manuscript, although he had only one copy: the others were in the Toulon Museum and in the Archives in Paris.*

We tried to assemble our thoughts. The key to the whole attack was obviously Fort Mulgrave, occupied by the British, and overlooking Balaguier and L'Eguillette, which dominated one side of the straits with their guns. The batteries, including 'Hommes Sans Peur', where M. Vieillefosse's house was, were placed to prepare the assault on Fort Mulgrave. We decided to go and see what was left of this fortress. We drove round and up a broad track in the middle of a pine forest, to a parking place under the trees. From there we climbed a dusty path, passing two men with a dog, followed a curve, and found ourselves facing the gateway of a squat fort, with grey, stone walls and a deep ditch round it.

This, we were told, was not the original Fort Mulgrave, named after Lord Mulgrave, who commanded the British infantry. It had been erected in its place by Louis XVIII in 1821 as a defensive fortification, and had been occupied by the French army right up to 1974. In 1984, it became a cultural centre, with jazz concerts, dances and exhibitions of paintings.

However, the fort was in the exact position of the one the Republicans had stormed. We walked round the ditch and the wall defending it. The lines were very similar. Fort Mulgrave, too, had had an outer rampart and a ditch. Inside it, there had been another wall with cannon loaded with grape-shot, and infantry with muskets.

Here also were the tents, field kitchens and a circular platform from which cannon could fire over the walls. The garrison was a mixed bag of two hundred Neapolitan, British and Spanish infantry, who presumably communicated badly with each other.

If one lies where the outer ramparts must have been, the wood in front is thick, with birds singing and the sun dappling the leaves. However, to see it as it was, one must remember that trees had been cut down to clear the arcs of fire. Continual bombardment must have made the wood look as if giants had trampled on it. In this chaos of broken trees, the cracking of dead wood would have heralded an assault. A day attack would therefore have been difficult, which is why operations were mainly at night.

* Much of the information I have used comes from M. Vieillefosse's scholarly manuscript.

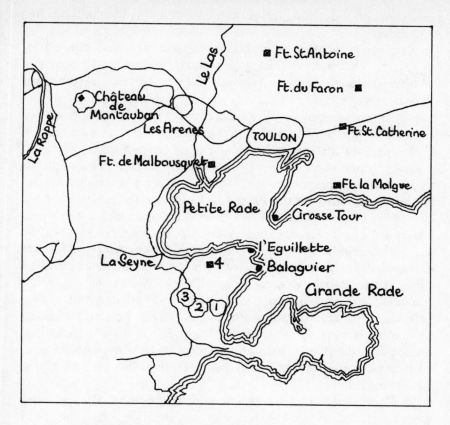

Toulon and neighbourhood during the siege of 1793.
1. Battery of Jacobins;
2. Battery of Chasse-Coquins;
3. Battery of Hommes sans Peur;
4. Fort Mulgrave.

So it was with the final assault on 17 December 1793. For two previous days the fort was bombarded from the Republican batteries, including the one where M. Vieillefosse's house was. At 1 am on a wet, squally morning, the assault began. The incessant rain was an advantage for the attackers, as the defenders' powder was wet. One Republican battalion assaulted directly from the landward side. Another swung round to scale the other. Shadows moved in the dark. Fighting was mainly with the bayonet. Napoleon was wounded by a bayonet in the thigh, and his boot filled with blood. After two hours' fighting, the fort was captured. What remained of the Allied garrison fled down to L'Eguillette and Balaguier.

Meanwhile, another Republican force had scaled the Faron mountain and had surprised the small garrisons. Although a counter-attack was likely, dawn saw the Republicans in command of two strategic positions.

In the early morning of 17 December, Admiral Hood held a Council of War on his flagship, the *Victory*. The cabin where he held it can still be visited in the ship, at Portsmouth.

Apart from his own officers, Neapolitans, Piedmontese, Spaniards and French royalists attended. They all spoke French, which the cultural domination of the Bourbons had made the language of the educated classes of Europe. Most voted for abandoning the siege. Particularly in this moment of adversity, they were resentful of the way the British had assumed command of the operations. This was especially true of the Spanish, whose forces were almost as large as those of the British. Because none of these officers shared overall responsibility, it was not they who would be blamed for withdrawing.

Admiral Hood alone was reluctant. However, he was persuaded by a wind favourable to withdrawal, and the courtly if somewhat dubious words of the Piedmontese general, De Revel: 'My Lord, all Europe knows that you have taken Toulon. No one will blame you for having lost it.'

In Fort Mulgrave, the weary and triumphant French were soon heartened to see the Allies evacuating Forts Balaguier and L'Eguillette, whose guns were spiked and all the horses killed.

In Toulon, itself, the inhabitants had heard cannon firing, but were not certain what was going on. To their consternation, they saw piles of officers' baggage accumulating on the quay, and sloops plied back and forth from the harbour to the ships in the bay.

That evening, they were told that those who wished would be taken on board the Allied men of war. By the early morning of the 18th, 2,500 citizens were camping on the decks, while the quays were full of the sick and wounded, lying on mattresses, waiting to be collected.

Those with money hired private boats to take them further down the coast to Leghorn, or Genoa. While there was no obstruction to those boarding the warships, those hiring private boats had to get a health certificate from the authorities, as the owners were unwilling to risk being put in quarantine when they arrived at their destinations. So confusion was increased by frantic crowds trying to get their certificates from the authorities.

In the streets, looters were beginning to pillage the houses of those who had left. The Neapolitans fired on them, which added to the fear and panic sweeping Toulon.

It had been agreed that all Allied troops would be evacuated by midnight on the 18th/19th. However, the Neapolitans had abandoned the fort of Malbousquet, and that of St Catherine, beyond the eastern city wall.* Fire from St Catherine now hindered access to the embarkation point on the coast just opposite Les Vignettes where the main Allied fleet was anchored.

As the Cathedral clock struck nine, the British embarked first, with the Spanish taking up the rearguard. Round the walls of Toulon, the Republican camp-fires were a circle of flickering lights, while a few shells and mortar bombs fell on the Arsenal, doing little damage.

As the Allies departed, an inferno of destruction was lit. First, a Sardinian frigate was hit by Republican mortar bombs and set on fire. This was followed by two enormous explosions. The Spanish had set alight two royalist French ships which had been used to store powder, thus preventing them falling into Republican hands. The town was shaken as if by an earthquake, and the very sky now seemed aflame. Debris fell, and set alight another French ship, the *Thémistocle*, which contained some two hundred and sixty political prisoners. Some of these broke their chains, and those who could swim jumped into the sea.† Most of the others were rescued by two English gunboats.

The explosions were taken as a signal by the British naval officer, Sydney Smith, who had been charged with blowing up the Arsenal. Flames began to envelop buildings on the edge of the harbour. Near it was a hulk in which prisoners condemned to the galleys were imprisoned. Some escaped and put out the fuses with their bare hands, while others tried to quench the flames.

Much of the equipment in the Arsenal had already been taken on board, and it is a tribute to probity that it was later auctioned

---

* There is a satirical verse about the Neapolitan soldiers by Murat, who, under Napoleon, became their King. The soldiers wore red or white uniforms. 'Foutez-les en rouge/ Foutez-les en blanc/ Ils foutent toujours le camp.' A genteel translation: 'Whether they're in red/ Whether they're in white/ They'll always take to flight.'

† Few people could swim, then. Even those who joined the navy were not required to do so.

in London and the proceeds used to pay French royalist officers and men serving with the British.

All the troops were taken on board except for 400 Neapolitans who, misinformed about the embarkation point, clustered miserably round the Grosse Tour. One can almost hear their laments, the evocations of their patron, St Gennaro, as they waited with flames illuminating the harbour. Ultimately, they too were collected.

Now the ships were crowded with 7,500 civilians – a quarter of the town's population.

Of the French fleet, nine men of war had been burnt and four were left behind. Eight others assembled with the Allied ships, and one can imagine the gloom of at least the officers as they watched their Arsenal burning, and prepared to sail out with the Allied fleet into a sea which they had once regarded as their own.

At four in the morning, everything seemed ready, and Admiral Hood gave the signal to sail. The ship's lanterns of this vast fleet disappeared into the night, which was calm and resplendent with stars. When the Spanish followed in the rear, dawn had broken. From near Cap Bon on what is still called the 'Chemin de la Batterie Basse', a few harmless shots were fired against this armada of gorgeous galleons. Their white canvas spread to the full as they rode the favourable wind.

The entry of the Republicans into Toulon was marked by the same vengeful massacres which had accompanied other defeats of the royalists. There was a difference, though. Most of those who had helped the Allies had now sailed away, and it could be presumed that those who remained did so because they were loyal to the Republic. The military authorities made this point to the Representatives, Barras and Fréron.

When the first troops penetrated the town, Fréron told Cervoni, their commander, to slaughter all the inhabitants. However, at the official entry the troops were greeted by a cheering crowd, and when Fréron asked Cervoni why he had not carried out his orders, the general replied that the army only obeyed written instructions.

As the occupying troops were marching through, the sound of a military band was heard. Two hundred marines in smart uniforms marched down to join the procession. The officers had all the courtly manners of the old régime: they bowed and removed their hats to the Republicans, used 'vous' instead of the revolutionary 'tu', and

47. Rochejaquelein's Château of Durbelière. (See p. 169) Photograph by Brita Haycraft.

48. Statue of La Rochejaquelein. Photograph by Brita Haycraft.

49. The Château of Clisson. (See p. 188) Images de France.

50. Château of Saumur.
(See p. 171) Editions Greff.

51. Rebel hiding-place
in the woods.
Archives Talladier

52. Signalling windmills:
1. Nothing happening;
2. Assemble; 3. Danger;
4. Danger Over.

1e "en quartier"
(REPOS)

2e "bout au pied"
(RASSEMBLEMENT)

3e "en jambe de chien gauche"
(DANGER PROCHE)

4e "en jambe de chien droite"
(DANGER PASSÉ)

Opposite page:

53. Drownings in the Loire. (See
p. 188) *Bibliothèque Nationale*

54. The bombardment of Lyons
by the Republicans. (See p. 196)
Bibliothèque Nationale

55. Evacuation of Toulon. (See
p. 214) *National Maritime
Museum, Greenwich*

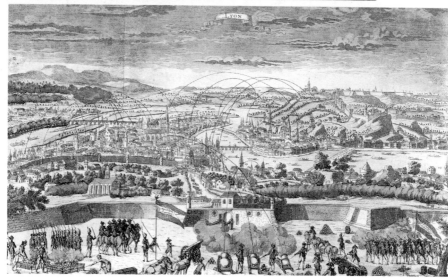

56. Explosion of the powder ship, Toulon 1793.
(See p. 215) Robertson, *National Maritime Museum, Greenwich*

57. Danton's house, destroyed by a bomb in 1940.
Photo Combier, Mâcon

58. Danton on his way to the guillotine.
(See p. 242) Willie fils, *Carnavalet*

59. Corridor in the prison of St Lazare.
Note the casual atmosphere: the boy
with a dog, the man lighting a brazier,
the strollers. Robert, *Carnavalet*

60. Marie-Antoinette going from the Conciergerie
to the tumbril. The courtyard is the same today.
Caisse Nationale des Monuments

61. The courtyard of the Duplay house. The windows of Robespierre's rooms are on the first floor to the left. The sitting- and dining-rooms are now a restaurant. Author's photograph.

62. The Ancien Régime had three hundred brutal executions a year. Here, in 1777, a poisoner is battered before being thrown on the flames. *Bibliothèque Nationale*

63. The guillotine was introduced as a merciful, rapid form of execution. It was the tumbril procession through the streets and the suspense of waiting in a queue which made it so terrible. Demachy, *Carnavalet*

64. Robespierre guillotining the whole of France. *Bibliothèque Nationale*

65. Blind Man's Buff à la Robespierre. *Bibliothèque Nationale*

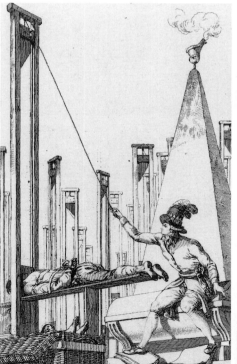

66. A Section Committee. They issued Certificates of Civism, without which one was always suspect during the Terror. *Bibliothèque Nationale*

67. Open-air stalls on the Pont du Change, *Carnavalet*

68. Rousseau's first tomb on the Isle of Poplars in Ermenonville. (See p. 274) Moreau le Jeune.

made the mistake of asking for the general in charge, instead of the Representative. Fréron's reaction was to abuse them, call them traitors, and order their instant execution. And so, with no trial, they were herded off and slaughtered at the wall of La Corderie (which has now been demolished for a motorway). Their bodies lay there for days. Later, it was proved they had kept themselves aloof from Allied operations during the siege.

At three o'clock that afternoon, all men in the town were summoned to the Champ de Mars. This was a broad space lying by the walls to the east of the town, beyond and around the present Avenue Franklin Roosevelt. The men were assembled with their backs to the city wall, and Fréron and Barras ordered cannon to be brought up. However, the army refused to fire, protesting that no one had yet been tried. Furious, the Representatives had to postpone their plan.

This assembly was repeated next day. Fréron and Barras examined each individual, asking for his profession and what he had done in the siege. If the answers indicated that the man was from the 'people', he was spared, but if he was obviously bourgeois, he was executed. Barras himself was noble, known as the 'red viscount', and ferocity was a way of repudiating his class.

As in Lyons, the name of Toulon was changed, this time to 'Port de La Montagne'. The Representatives boasted to the Convention that they were assembling 12,000 masons to demolish the town. How, though, were these masons to be found in small, depleted Toulon? Where were those recruited in neighbouring villages to be lodged? Only sixty were found. Half-heartedly, they managed to demolish four houses. Even their attempts to destroy the home of Admiral Trogoff, the commander of the French royalist fleet, was frustrated, for Trogoff had only rented his house, and the owner objected strenuously.

The last major surge of civil war in France had now been extinguished. Yet although the threats to the new Republic had been triumphantly brushed aside, Terror was still the order of the day. It was to be so for seven months, until the fall of Robespierre. Instead of trying to unite the nation with clemency and concessions, those in power attempted to eliminate all those opposed to the new government. The 'reign of Virtue' was designed to wipe out all those who appeared vicious enough not to believe in it.

IV

Autocracy Through
Vehemence

[20]

DANTON'S ROOTS

'He saw people as people, not as principles on two legs.'
NORMAN HAMPSON

In the turmoil which followed the fall of the Girondins and the destructiveness of civil war, Danton was one of the few leaders who kept a sense of reality, and had a craving for peace and normality. Surrounded by neurotics who fed on excitement, by inexperienced politicians caught on the treadmill of events, and by demagogues who condemned others for fear of losing their heads, Danton was one of the few whose life was rooted in the pleasures of normal living: the wife and family he loved, good wine and good cuisine, the genial companionship of old friends, the delights of all that money can bring, the desire for a country property of his own. It is easy for us who live in more northern climes to forget the pleasures and attractions of *la douce France*, where the sun shines more often, the wine grows nearby, the soil is fertile and for those who are brought up there, the *camaraderie* of neighbours and family creates strong bonds.

Essentially, Danton was a peasant – and not in any pejorative sense. He was strong and courageous enough not to be deflected by fear, or the rationalization of high-sounding principles, or utopian dreams. His simplicity gave him eloquence, the ability to appeal directly to the basic emotions of courage, hope and even humour in his audience. He was shrewd, which gave him his tactical ability. His ruthlessness and common sense, his cunning, the humour which was often mistaken for cynicism, almost certainly derived from his peasant background which so often is misunderstood or ignored by those who live in cities.

To find out more about his roots we decided to visit Arcis-sur-Aube, where Danton was born in 1759, and to which he often returned to find solace and rest from the gruelling conflicts of

221

revolutionary Paris. We arrived there on a day when summer seemed suddenly to have changed to autumn. I had written as usual to the Town Hall to ask if a local expert could help us, but they had not received my letter. After several telephone calls, it was agreed that we would meet the former mayor, M. Piat, who knew a lot about Danton, the following day. We decided, therefore, to explore Arcis beforehand on our own.

Arcis lies on the branches of a crossroads on the main route between Troyes and Châlons, south-east of Paris. Most of it was destroyed in the last war. The houses are therefore undistinguished and recently built. In the centre is a church, much of which was ruined but rebuilt, and nearby a little Place in front of a charming, small eighteenth-century château, with a park behind, which is now the Hôtel de Ville. Down a slope on the road to Châlons is a bridge which, a plaque informed us, had been destroyed in 1940, rebuilt, and then destroyed again in 1944. The bridge spans the shallow river of the Aube, flowing between trees, with mats of weed swaying like tendrils of sodden moss in the current.

In this village, Georges-Jacques Danton was the fifth of seven children of a bourgeois family. His father died when he was only three. In this, Danton resembled Robespierre, whose father abandoned his family when he was seven. Indeed, a thesis could be written on the personal factors which formed Revolutionaries. The most savage were exceptionally small in stature. Some were foreign, and their loyalty was to ideas often not rooted in their adopted country. A proportion were aspiring writers whose mutual jealousy formed enmities which often led to the guillotine. Others were ex-priests with a new fanatical vocation.* In contrast, Danton seems to have been healthy and balanced. His family was made secure by his mother's second marriage and the fact that Arcis was full of his relatives. His feelings for his family and that of his wife were affectionate. Physically, he was large and strong, even corpulent. Vadier, a bitter enemy on the Committee of Public

---

* *Height*: Marat was barely five feet tall, as was Hébert, the journalist who accused Marie-Antoinette of incest with her son.

Foreign origin: Marat had a Sardinian father and a Genevan mother. Rousseau, Necker and Clavière (a Girondin banker) were all from Geneva; Thomas Paine from Thetford, England; Clootz, an anarchist, from Prussia; Chalier from Piedmont.

Aspiring writers: Desmoulins, Mme Roland, Brissot, Fabre d'Eglantine, Hébert, Marat, Robespierre.

Ex-priests: Chaumette, Chabot, Roux, Le Bon and Fouché – all extremists.

Safety, called him 'a fat stuffed turbot'. Unlike Robespierre, he had a healthy appetite for women. 'Virtue is what I do with my wife every night,' he is reported to have told a scandalized Robespierre.

Danton was brought up amidst the rough crudity of those who work on the land, watching and laughing at the coupling of cattle, dirtying his hands with manure, working in the fields, discussing ways of making things grow. According to a schoolfellow, Béon, his lip was scarred and his nose crushed because he was helping himself to milk from a cow's udder when a bull attacked him. Later, a herd of pigs trampled him into the mud, and smallpox ravaged his face still further. As a result, he was ugly. Yet with his powerful voice and shock of hair, these scars gave him character, suggesting force, virility and experience.

In Arcis, we wandered round, trying to evoke Danton amidst the inevitable traffic and small houses. Perhaps appropriately, the only place where one could evoke him was near the river where, in summer, boys still swim, or fish. Or in the surrounding countryside of woods and flat long fields with chalk breaking through the grass.

We decided to go to Troyes for the afternoon. Here, Danton was sent to school with the Oratorians, who had been the main educators of the French bourgeoisie since 1762 when the Jesuits were expelled. We wandered through the narrow streets of beamed medieval houses and asked at the local tourist office for Danton's old school. Bewilderment. 'Danton's old school? The Oratorians?' Phone calls were made and we were finally told that it was almost certainly now a secondary school which, bizarrely, was being used as a temporary market. We walked in the sunlight until we came to a seventeenth-century façade with layers of red brick and white stone. On it, was marked a date, '1621'. There was also a notice which read 'Votre Nouveau Marché' (Your New Market). Inside, the courtyard was covered with transparent plastic and full of vegetable stalls.

This was probably the place where Danton had been a boarder for two years, with an education which included not only the classics but also mathematics, geography and – surprising for that time – English, which he learnt to speak. Indeed, the register of his library in Paris included eight volumes of 'Schakespeare', who was then not well known outside Britain.

From the Oratorians, Danton is reputed to have played truant to see Louis XVI crowned in Reims in 1775 – an ironic venture for one who was to play a major role in the monarch's dethronement, and who voted for Louis's death. This incident, if it really happened, parallels Robespierre's ceremonial Latin address to the new King and his Queen at the college of Louis-le-Grand, in Paris. In Danton's case the journey was long and on foot, while with Robespierre the tribute was smooth and well prepared. In fact, Danton was more successful, as he managed to see the ceremony, while Robespierre stood soaked to the skin, his speech unfinished, as Louis and Marie-Antoinette departed in their coach.

We returned to Arcis to find a small hotel outside the town. Next morning, we presented ourselves to M. Piat, an amiable, white-haired gentleman whose house was full of mementoes: ancient postcards of Danton's house, portraits, photo-copies of a birth-certificate which can still be seen in the Town Hall.

M. Piat was proud of Arcis's greatest son. 'Of course,' he told us, 'there are many who say he was corrupt and unscrupulous. But it all depends on how you look at it. For us, he was a great man. Like all of us here, he loved Arcis. There is reason to believe that he wanted to abandon the cruel politics of the Terror, and settle here on his estate. But he had to leave in order to defend himself, only to be outwitted by Robespierre, and guillotined.'

'Where was his house?'

'We shall go and see the place where it stood.'

We walked through the village and down to the bridge.

'There. It was on the other side of the river, where that villa now is.' We examined a modern house, undistinguished, with large windows. 'Danton's house was here till the German invasion of 1940. When they bombed the bridge, the house burst into flames. It was then owned by a timber merchant. Danton's descendants lived here till 1887.'

'Descendants?'

'Yes. He had two sons. One of them lived here with his house-keeper and kept very much to himself. In the Revolution of 1848, the crowd came to acclaim him, but he shut the door on them. With his housekeeper, he had a daughter who married a M. Menuel and went to Chile. Her grandson, the last of Danton's direct descendants, was born in Santiago in 1901.'

'Are there any descendants in Arcis today?'

'Not now. There was a Mlle Sardin who lived here. She was a

descendant of one of Danton's brothers. But she died recently at the age of 104.'

On one of Piat's postcards from before 1940, the house appears as a long, low building, standing a few metres from the river, with a first floor and attic windows. It looks simple and comfortable, with its shutters and modest front door. Danton's bedroom is supposed to have been on the side. From it, he could look onto the rustling trees of his park, through which a stream flowed to the river.

'One of his contemporaries records seeing him in his night-cap,' added M. Piat ruminatively, evoking domestic informality.

We walked along the road by the garden. 'These stone barns are original,' said Piat. 'And here was the main entrance of the estate.' We stopped in front of two columns with diamond-shaped stone globules on top. Beyond was a ditch choked with vegetation. 'Originally, of course, this was a drive,' said M. Piat.

We retraced our footsteps and walked down the side of the river. 'All this was Danton's estate,' said Piat. 'Eleven hectares. He bought more and more as the Revolution progressed.'

'Where did he get the money?'

'Well, who knows? Even serious historians are uncertain.'

In fact, there is a lot of circumstantial evidence for corruption. Hampson estimates that Danton's expenditure was sixty thousand livres more than his receipts. The French Ambassador in London is said to have named Danton, when he was virtually unknown, as a recipient of English funds. Bernard de Moleville, who was responsible for bribery for the Crown, mentions how wasteful the gift of 30,000 livres to Danton had been. When I talked to the well-known historian François Furet, he said that there was no real doubt about it. The firmest proof, he said, was the money the Spanish had given him to save Louis XVI. He took the cash and voted for the King's death.

However, Danton was not the man to leave papers around. Even most of his speeches are only roughly reported, because he did not prepare them with the meticulousness of a Robespierre. However, given his temperament and the times, it is unlikely that he was a financial virgin. Corruption fits in well with his hedonism and his peasant background. After all, the money was partly spent on land. Even Robespierre was offered money by admirers: in one case by an enthusiastic Englishwoman, whose generosity he refused.

We came to a big field, surrounded by tall trees. 'This is where

Danton played as a boy. Later, he bought this field. Recently, it was acquired by a Société who wanted to build houses on it. So, when I was mayor, I bought it on behalf of the municipality. We use it now for horse races and fêtes in the summer. Danton would have liked that.'

Whatever the circumstances, Danton had certainly done well out of the Revolution. Here was a 'gentleman's estate', acquired in only four years. Apart from the pleasure of ownership, it shows the desire for status which motivated so many revolutionaries. Even Robespierre used the noble particle 'de' in front of his name with no proof of nobility until 1792. Danton styled himself d'Anton, and that priggish proponent of theoretical equality, Mme Roland, spent a long time in various offices in 1784, trying to get her husband ennobled on account of the 'de la Platière' appended to his name. Even Marat applied for a certificate of nobility before the Revolution. *Plus ça change* . . . in the end, much of the motivation which changes society is personal ambition, or vanity – whatever the principles.

We walked back to the village and had a look at the eighteenth-century château. 'It used to belong to the Comte de la Biffe,' said Piat. 'A few years ago, we had a performance of the Revolution on this square, with people dressed as sansculottes, and a cardboard Bastille which was stormed by the children. There was a Robespierre and of course a Danton, who both made speeches. Everyone enjoyed themselves. The Revolution, after all, is a dramatic memory. People still imagine Danton walking in the woods, an open book in his hand, as he was supposed to have done. We bring him into everything. Why, we had a fête in 1982 to celebrate the new supply of gas to Arcis. We lit a special torch in the square and, later, the actor Bernard Bresson performed some of the roles of Danton he had played on television. It was really like lighting a torch of Liberty.'

With his blend of materialism and drama, Danton surely would have approved, as he would the continuing appreciation and tenderness of his fellow villagers.

[21]

DANTON'S DEATH

'Provided they let us speak at length I am sure of routing my accusers, and if the French people is what it ought to be, I shall have to ask it to pardon them.'

DANTON on the first day of his trial.

Danton is probably best known for his death.

In the eighteen months that remained to him between his triumph after the 10th of August 1792 and his execution in the Place de la Révolution, his centre of activity was the Convention, first in the Manège and then after May 1793 in the Tuileries, and in the Jacobin Club in the Rue St Honoré. His home was within walking distance, just over the Pont Neuf and down the Rue Dauphine to his flat in the Cours de Commerce.

Every day, Danton would stride along on his way to the Convention amidst the passers-by, mostly shabbily dressed, with red bonnets on their heads, past stalls with goods laid out on the pavements. As he passed, there were probably nervous glances from those who recognized him, greetings from friends, the sudden questions, almost certainly not about Danton's relations with Robespierre, or the Queen's fate, or any such major questions, but about the price of bread, the effect of conscription on the earnings of a family, or pleas to help a relative get a job.

The political village he walked towards was rather like Westminster, with Assembly, government offices, Jacobin Club and the former palace of the King, all condensed into one area round the Tuileries, and easily crossed on foot.

Until June 1793, Danton was the leading member of the Committee of Public Safety which, with the Committee of General Security, was the executive arm of the Convention. It met on the ground floor of the Tuileries, just next to the Pavillon de Flore, which survived the fire of 1871 but has been reconstructed since.

227

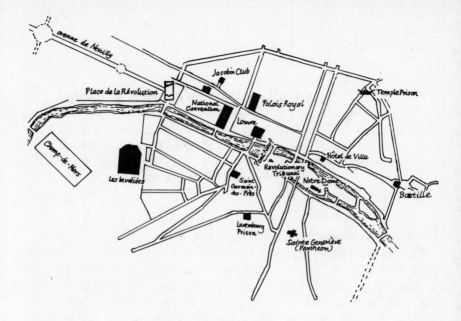

Paris in 1793–4.

This group of fewer than a dozen men – no women – scrutinized reports, reacted to messengers bearing news, argued, while beyond the great windows of what used to be the Apartment of the Queen, the Tuileries gardens stretched out.

One wonders how often these men, who were mostly lawyers, rubbed their eyes in amazement at finding themselves supreme in the palace of a King who, so recently, had been lofty and remote, whom they had been taught to revere as children. When, in winter, the trees were bare, they could probably glimpse the large plaster Statue of Liberty which stood in the Place de la Révolution, just by the guillotine where Louis had been decapitated.

During these months of power, Danton was largely responsible for creating the Revolutionary Tribunal, despite the fact that Vergniaud, a Girondin, described it as 'laying the foundations of an Inquisition a thousand times more terrible than that in Spain'. Although Danton himself was to be its victim, as were many other deputies, he argued that it was a means of preventing the people imposing their own justice, as during the September massacres.

228

'Let us be terrible,' he roared, 'so that we can prevent the people from being terrible.'

Throughout this time, Danton was like a swimmer yielding to a current he could not control. He was not prepared to risk his head and his position as a leader by fighting against major trends. He told a royalist, Lameth, who had come to ask him to save Louis XVI, that the King's execution would serve no useful purpose, yet he would not risk speaking in Louis's defence, and voted for his death. He saw clearly the need for unity with the Girondins, yet their hostility to him provoked him to do nothing to save them. He saw clearly, too, the need to end the Revolution and make peace in Europe. When he was acting virtually as Foreign Minister in the Committee of Public Safety, he negotiated secretly with Britain and Spain, but inevitably to no avail. Despite his tactical ability and clear-sightedness, events were too much for him. He remained a demagogue, unwilling to strike off on a political course that would be unpopular, and preferred hidden manoeuvres. It is this which makes it so difficult to assess him, as so little is known for certain about his intrigues. He covered his tracks, seemingly to avoid commitment. If the wind changed, he could then trim his sails. Thus it is known that he helped plan the assault on the Tuileries, but it is uncertain where he was when the attack was going on. He probably also planned the September massacres, but he did not commit himself openly to them. Again, he was away in newly-conquered Belgium during much of the King's trial. It is possible also that he knew of General Dumouriez's plan to march on Paris in March 1793, but he obscured this when it failed.

Was he one of the few real statesmen at this time of the Revolution, forced by the maelstrom of a France gone mad with fear and frenzy into a situation where he could not achieve what he intended? Was he a loud, blustering, egocentric actor, led by the desire for acclaim into taking up positions which did not represent his feelings? Or was he really only concerned with what served his personal interests of power and money? Probably all of these, but we can only guess.

In July, Danton was weary, and did not challenge his replacement on the Committee of Public Safety by Robespierre. He may well have been disheartened by the way the Revolution seemed to be breaking France apart, and probably he was also influenced by personal motives. His beloved wife, Gabrielle, had died in March 1793. Within three months he had fallen in love with a girl of sixteen, Louise Gély, who came from a conservative, religious family. There is reason to believe that she only agreed to marry him if the ceremony was carried out by a refractory priest. According to the Abbé de Kéreven, who was hiding in the Cordelier district, Danton came to see him secretly, confessed, and the couple were later married by him. If this extraordinary happening is true, it is characteristic of the separation between Danton's private life and his revolutionary principles. Danton after all is sympathetic because he was full-blooded and human, in contrast to Robespierre's frigid singleness of purpose. Here was a man pitted against what was almost a machine. The fact that it was Robespierre who won and had him guillotined has made Danton seem more tolerable, less blood-stained, less ruthless than perhaps he was.

In October, Danton fell ill and asked the Convention for permission to return to Arcis. 'I must retire to the country and breathe my native air,' he wrote.

When he returned in November, it was to lead a campaign with Robespierre against the excesses of the extremists, led by Hébert. On 10 November the Hébertists organized a Fête in Notre-Dame, called the Festival of Reason. Sitting today in the semi-darkness under the Gothic arches, one can picture the wild absurdity of the scene. All religious symbols had been removed, and a Greek temple of cardboard was built in the nave. The mob sang the 'Ça ira', and an actress played the role of the Goddess of Reason, and mounted her throne.

A witness, Mercier, describes it:

The infuriated populace dancing before the sanctuary and howling the Carmagnole. The men wore no breeches; the neck and the busts of the women were bare. In their wild whirling, they imitated those whirlwinds, the forerunners of tempests, that ravage and destroy all that is in their path. In the darkness of the sacristy they indulged in those abominable desires that had been kindled in them during the day.

Already in 1792, Danton had made a speech to the Convention expressing his views on religion, which were not unlike Marx's definition of 'the opium of the people', except that Danton seems tolerantly to have favoured this drug. 'When a man who has nothing sees a rich man gratifying his taste,' he said, 'his consolation becomes the other world. He should be left in this error. The man of the soil regards the Man of Consolation as a saint, because to Him he owed a few happy moments in his youth, his early manhood and old age.'

The increase in the Terror in the winter of 1793–4 also disturbed him. With his friend Desmoulins, he could see no reason for the growing number of executions now that the civil war was over and the enemy on the frontiers had been repulsed. There is the story that, as he and Desmoulins were walking over the Pont Neuf, the Seine was reddened by the sunset and seemed a river of blood, flowing towards them. This, as I have seen myself, is possible even in winter. Danton was seized by horror. 'Take up your pen and plead for clemency!' he cried to Desmoulins. 'I will support you.'

Desmoulins did take up his pen in the first number of his *Vieux Cordelier* in December 1793. His journal had an immediate success, selling out within a few hours. 'Open the prisons!' wrote Desmoulins, 'and release the two hundred thousand suspects that are there!'

Initially, Robespierre supported the *Vieux Cordelier*, as it was also an attack on the Hébertists, whose atheism and anarchistic gatherings he wished to eliminate. However, the third issue purported to be a translation of passages from Tacitus describing the time of Caligula and Nero, and the atmosphere of terror and suspicion under the rule of blood-thirsty despots. A connection with Robespierre and the Committee of Public Safety was not difficult to make.

In the Jacobins, Robespierre counter-attacked. He demanded the burning of the *Vieux Cordelier*, to which Desmoulins replied: '*Brûler ce n'est pas répondre*' (Burning is not answering). These were Rousseau's words when his novel *Emile* was ordered to be burnt by the public executioner, under the old régime. Robespierre was stunned. With his idealization of Rousseau, this was almost blasphemy: Desmoulins's retort identified Robespierre with the oppressor and he himself with Rousseau.

The Committee of Public Safety began undermining Danton and Desmoulins by arresting their close associates, who had been involved in defrauding the French East India Company. In this way

Danton, whose reputation for corruption was still a talking point in Paris, was implicated. Though friends gave warnings, Danton was reluctant to counter-attack. 'Can power be worth the efforts to obtain it that I see about me?' he asked a friend.

In March, the Hébertists were arrested, tried and guillotined. Hébert, who had sought more blood in the last eighteen months than a covey of vampires, who had expressed joy in his *Père Duchesne* at seeing Marie-Antoinette's 'cursed head eventually separated from her tart's neck', proved one of the most cowardly victims of Mère Guillotine. To entertain the crowd, the executioner danced the blade up and down over Hébert's neck before releasing it, while the minuscule anarchist screamed.

Two weeks later, the twenty members of the two Committees were called into the room on the ground floor, next to the Pavillon de Flore. All but two signed the accusation of Danton, Desmoulins and their friends. The document still exists. Then St Just suggested that he read the denunciation in the Convention, and that Danton be arrested in the midst of the deputies. This was thought too risky, and it was decided to arrest him that night. St Just in thwarted rage threw his hat into the fire, while Ruhl, a friend of Danton's who had refused to sign, sent a messenger to warn him.

According to one report, Danton slouched before the fire in his beloved apartment in the Cours de Commerce. 'They will not dare,' he repeated again and again. Nevertheless, he waited up for the police because he did not want to be arrested in bed. When they arrived he offered no resistance, and was taken outside and then up to the Luxembourg, probably by what is now the Rue Condé, or perhaps the Rue Tournon, where Hébert had recently lived in No. 5.

In the Luxembourg Palace, you still have to check into the police office on the left of the entrance, because the building now houses the Senate. As you produce your *pièce d'identité* and entry permit, it is not difficult to transform the situation and imagine your escort presenting your arrest warrant, and your name being taken down with a quill pen by a ragged guard.

Before 1791, the Luxembourg was the residence of Louis XVI's brother, the Comte de Provence. Today, many of the rooms where the prisoners were kept remain. But after the Revolution the boards were taken down from the windows, the filth was cleaned up, the graffiti wiped away, and it became the residence of the Directory, under Barras. Later, Napoleon III gilded it anew, but in a very different style.

When Danton was taken there, the place was virtually a huge house of detention with about seven hundred prisoners, many of them from aristocratic families. They brought in their own furniture, and their meals were served from restaurants, or private houses in the vicinity. Mme Latour, a companion of the Mouchys, one of the noblest families in France, describes a life which still had some of the characteristics of Versailles. At noon, the Mouchys would pay their respects to the Duchess of Orléans, who was also imprisoned there. One can imagine the courtliness and polished dialogue of the old régime, the doffing and bowing, and the use of titles which had been abolished almost three years previously. In the afternoon, the Mouchys sat down to piquet, while the younger prisoners played ball in the gallery where the Rubens had once hung. The corridors were full of passers-by, visitors and hawkers, and coffee was sold in the courtyard. Love was the principal occupation of the young. After all, pregnancy was actually an advantage, because until the baby was born, a woman could not be guillotined.

From what one can gather, Danton and his friends were largely ignored by people absorbed in their own problems and etiquette, and oblivious of the complicated political in-fighting outside. 'Messieurs,' Danton is reported to have said to them, 'I hoped soon to have got you all out of here; but here I am myself, and I don't know how it will end.'

From the Luxembourg, Danton and the other accused were soon taken to the Conciergerie which, with its two pointed medieval towers, still stands by the Seine on the northern bank of the Ile de la Cité. In Wajda's film *Danton*, there is a dramatic scene when the occupants react to Danton's arrival. In the gloom, threatening hands reach through the bars; eyes glare. A prisoner reaches for Danton's hand in apparent friendliness, and then spits on it. The gloating and fierce resentment of those who saw these revolutionaries now flung among them must have resembled the hot breath of lions in a den.

The Conciergerie is part of the enormous Palais de Justice, and still gives an impression of sinister gloom. When you enter the outside courtyard, you are questioned by the police – at least you were during the bomb scares of 1987. You have to push on the

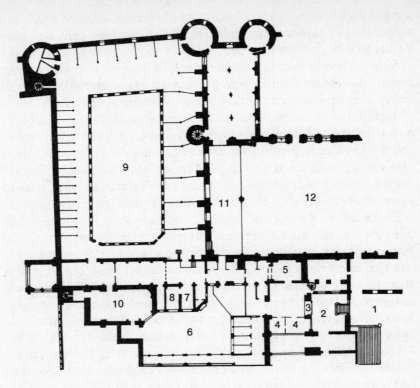

The Conciergerie in 1793–4.
1. Cour de Mai;
2. Small yard;
3. Entry and exit of prisoners;
4. Registration;
5. Room where the hair of the condemned was cut;
6. Women's courtyard;
7. Room of warders guarding the Queen;
8. Queen's cell;
9. Men's courtyard;
10. Chapel;
11. Rue de Paris;
12. Salle des Gens d'Armes.

stiff door to get in. Inside, is one of the most perfect Gothic halls in France, stretching away, arch beyond majestic arch, over bare stone floors with lights on each pillar, shining through the eerie medieval gloom.

In those days, all this part was subdivided by wooden partitions to form innumerable cells. Despite 'Equality' being a key word of the

Revolution, comfort depended on what a prisoner could afford. An inspector of prisons of the time describes one of the cells occupied by those who had little money: 'I know no language to express the feeling of horror which I experienced on seeing in a single room twenty-six men collected, lying on twenty-one straw mattresses, breathing the foulest air, and covered with half-rotten rags.'

Nevertheless, Comte Beugnot, who survived the Conciergerie, describes the way some of the women there changed their dresses three times a day. He writes of delicate meals with the men sitting on one side of the grille which divided the courtyards, and the women on the other. He describes two lovers both condemned at the same time who persuaded the turnkeys to allow them a last night together, draining 'a cup of voluptuousness' before mounting the tumbril. 'I am sure,' he writes, 'that at this time no promenade in Paris offered groups of women dressed with such elegance as the courtyard of the Conciergerie at noon. It resembled a parterre decorated with flowers but surrounded with iron. France is probably the only country and their women the only women capable of showing such an extraordinary contrast, displaying without effort what is most attractive and most voluptuous in the middle of what must be the most repulsive and horrible environment in the world.'

We were shown round this prison by Benoît, from the Ministry of Culture, who was involved in restoring the Conciergerie for the bicentenary of 1989, and by a Curator of the Carnavalet Museum.

The entrance, we were told, was not from the quay as it is now. It was on the other side, through the Cour de Mai on the Boulevard du Palais. The Cour de Mai is also the entrance to the Palais de Justice, and is almost unchanged from before the Revolution when Louis XVI built it. It still has the gold-topped railings, crested by a crown above the bulbous gold disc which is engraved with fleurs de lys. Its solid façade, with the broad, stone staircase leading up to the main entrance, still gives it 'the banality necessary for an official monument', as Le Nôtre wrote about it.

To the right of these steps is an archway with a little courtyard beyond. This now leads to the canteens of the lawyers who work in the Palais, and is one of the most unchanged and memorable places of the Revolution. Through this little courtyard, all those who were to be tried entered the prison. Most came out the same way, with their hair shaved above their necks, to mount the tumbrils which would take them to the guillotine.

235

Here, the mob filled the courtyard until they were forbidden entry in July 1794. The more vocal mounted the steps, jeering and throwing filth at the prisoners below. Now, this part looks strangely modern, with its straight lines of clean stone. Crates with empty bottles stand against the wall, to be collected more innocuously than were those who waited here two hundred years ago.

When you go through the doors into what is now the canteen, lawyers sit and chat, drink Coca-Cola and devour sandwiches. The kitchen is beyond the cash desk, with men in white overalls supervising sizzling pans. 'That is where Marie-Antoinette had her hair cut before leaving for the guillotine,' the cashier told us proudly, waving a hand vaguely towards a micro-wave oven. She was not quite right, as this operation took place beyond the wall which now separates the canteen from the Conciergerie. But Benoît kindly did not contradict her.

To enter the Conciergerie again, you have to go outside, past the ancient clock on the corner and along the quay. 'It's scandalous that the lawyers have blocked the true entrance,' said Benoît, 'but they work here. It is their Palais. Unfortunately, they can do anything they like.'

We passed the gloomy Gothic hall once more, and walked along a broad, bare corridor, which in those days was known as the Rue de Paris. 'This is Marie-Antoinette's cell,' announced Benoît, as we turned right, and then left. 'But it was all changed into a shrine by Louis XVIII after the Revolution.' We looked at the small, bare cell, with coloured glass in the window and a memorial plaque on the wall. 'The window was bigger.'

Benoît indicated the wall with the memorial plaque. 'A screen stood here, and two guards sat behind, day and night.'

It is terrible what Marie-Antoinette suffered. Others certainly went through the same, but none descended so abruptly from such heights of power and splendour. The worst thing must have been her isolation, deprived as she was of those she loved, with only brutality and hatred around her. Gnawing at her continually was the memory of her children, left helpless orphans in the Temple at the mercy of those who had perverted her son, getting him to sign an accusation of incest against her, teaching him obscenities, applauding him for using the crudest revolutionary language.

We stood for a moment, looking at the cell. 'It needs to be illuminated properly,' began the Curator of the Carnavalet Museum.

'No it doesn't!' interrupted Benoît. 'It needs to be torn down. All this sentimental propaganda, put up by the royalists after the Revolution. It needs to be restored to what it was. It's all bogus. The only thing that's original is the tiled floor.'

'Yes, but – ' began the Curator.

'The wall needs to be removed, the two rooms joined as they once were.'

A large key was suddenly produced to open the adjoining door, which swung heavily on its hinges. The dark room where the guards had been was full of dusty chairs, wooden boxes and a vacuum cleaner. 'Here, the guards played piquet all day,' said Benoît. 'It all needs to be re-created.'

'But restoration can also be false,' protested the Curator.

'Maybe. But not if it's accurate. At least it gives an exact idea. Look at what they have done at Versailles with the apartments of the Dauphin. Restored them totally. It's magnificent.'

'Yes, but . . .'

We wandered along the corridor outside. Towards the original entrance, the cell where prisoners had their hair shorn at the back before going out to mount the tumbrils was on the left, with bars separating it from the corridor. A staircase led to an entresol. We climbed up. Various cells looked down on the corridor. At one side, there was a little flat. A WC with chipped china seat stood in a dusty alcove. 'All more recent,' said Benoît.

We returned to the Queen's cell and went through the open space towards the chapel. On our right was another narrow enclosure with no door.

'It's likely that Robespierre spent his last day here, next to where Marie-Antoinette was imprisoned,' said Benoît, 'but no one is absolutely sure. No list of the occupants of different cells survives. People were often here for such a short time, and no official list was kept for fear of rescue attempts.'

We entered the chapel from behind the altar, and I commented that this was strange. 'Of course it is,' said Benoît. 'In 1793, the entrance of the chapel was on the other side, in the corner underneath that balcony with the grille. There was a wall between the chapel and Marie-Antoinette's cell. But Louis XVIII's architect

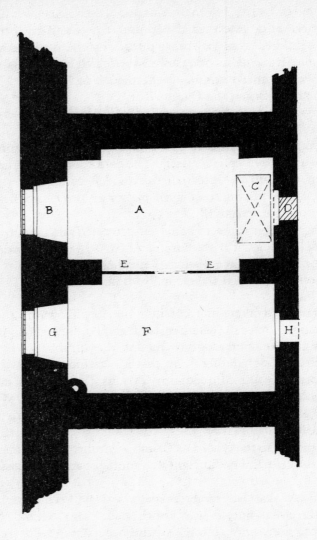

The Queen's cell.
A. Queen's Cell;
B. Barred window;
C. Queen's bed;
D. Walled-up door;
E. Partitions separating Queen's Cell from Guards, with a screen in the middle;
F. Guards' Room;
G. Barred window;
H. Entrance.

connected the two because it gave the Queen a posthumous air of sanctity.'

Otherwise, we were told, the chapel was largely as it had been before the Revolution. It was small because, then, there were few prisoners. We looked at the glass cases round the walls, with relics of the Queen's captivity. There was the note, with the letters marked out with pin pricks, which Marie-Antoinette sent to the Chevalier de Rougeville who had tried to rescue her. There was also a painting of the Queen before the altar as she received Communion, with two guards kneeling by her side. 'Almost certainly an invention,' said Benoît.

Later, Brita and I went to the Musée Grévin, which presents tableaux of the Revolution with wax figures. The one of Marie-Antoinette's cell seemed to confirm Benoît's idea of what it was originally. The window was large, with no stained glass, and the chapel was not connected to the cell. What is now the adjoining store-room was separated by a screen.

The real question is whether the sentimental distortion produced by one period of history should be replaced by the realistic restoration of an earlier epoch. But at least what remains of bare stone, heavy iron doors and black railings, creating an impression of tragedy and gloom, seems genuine.

It was important to the Committee of Public Safety that Danton and his associates be got quickly out of the way, as there was always the possibility of some demonstration or conspiracy in their favour. Their trial began as soon as possible before the Revolutionary Tribunal. This sat in the room once used for the royal 'lit de justice', a ceremony where the King announced his will, which then became law.

In those days, the room was decorated with an oaken, ogival ceiling, hangings on the walls with golden fleurs de lys, a statue of Louis XV, and a lion of justice. When they took possession, the Revolutionary Tribunal eliminated these 'baubles'. On the wall was placed the usual Declaration of the Rights of Man, and the ceiling was made plain and smooth. At the end opposite the present entrance sat the judges, with the Public Prosecutor below them. On their right sat the accused on tiers. Opposite, by the two windows, were the jury. Behind a barrier halfway up the room sat the public.

When we visited it, a court case was going on with a few barristers arguing and secretaries taking notes. The ogival ceiling had been restored, and on the walls was a gold-tinted covering. In the same place, a court was still being held, the past extending in uninterrupted continuity to the present. In this same room, some of the most dramatic trials of the Revolution had taken place. Where now meticulous legal altercations were going on, Marie-Antoinette had been accused of incest with her son. 'I appeal to all the mothers among you,' she implored, turning to the public. Here Charlotte Corday had stood serenely after her assassination of Marat, objecting only to being called 'a murderess'. Here the Girondins had defended themselves brilliantly, and one of them, Valazé, had stabbed himself when the sentence was announced, and had collapsed on the benches. Later, his corpse was guillotined.

Danton's trial was a dramatic farce.

The Committee of Public Safety had deliberately flung in those accused of peculation in the French East India Company, thus associating Danton and the others with the fraud. The first day dealt with this. On the second day, however, Danton spoke for most of the time. He ridiculed all charges, mocked his accusers, and called the members of the Committee of Public Safety as witnesses.

'Will the cowards who have slandered my name dare meet me face to face?' he roared. 'Let them show themselves and I will cover them with their own ignominy . . . Yes, I, Danton, will unmask the dictatorship that is now openly revealing its existence.'*

His great voice is said to have been heard the other side of the river. The public applauded, and the jury, specially chosen for their loyalty to the Republic, nevertheless stirred uneasily. The rumour spread in Paris that Danton was to be acquitted. Fouquier-Tinville and the judges were well aware of their fate if this happened. In panic, they sent an appeal for help to the Committee of Public Safety, and St Just hurried to the Convention to get the supine deputies to pass a law decreeing that 'every accused person who resisted or insulted the National Justice should be forbidden to plead'. As reinforcement, St Just invented a plot by the prisoners in the Luxembourg. 'You have just escaped the gravest danger that has ever threatened Liberty!' he told the Deputies.

* There was no report of Danton's trial. The dialogue cited here is taken from the notes scribbled by a juryman, Topino-Lebrun.

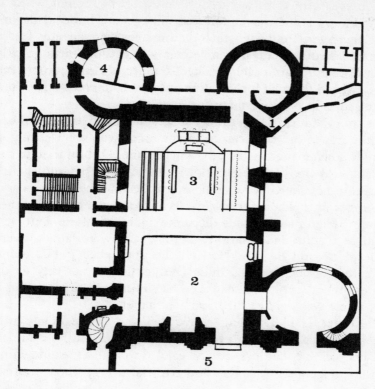

Revolutionary Tribunal in the Palais de Justice.
1. Corridor through which accused were admitted;
2. Spectators' enclosure;
3. Tribunal. There were a table and chairs for the President and judges. The accused were on the benches on the left with the jury opposite them;
4. Judges' offices;
5. Salle des Pas Perdus.

Read out in Court, the new 'law' and details of the 'plot' produced a stupefying silence. 'You are murderers,' cried Danton. 'Look at them. They have hounded us to our deaths.'

The President, Herman, rang his bell, which had sounded so often in vain during the three days of this tumultuous trial. 'The debate will now end,' he announced, after Fouquier-Tinville had cleared up the remaining business.

'End?' shouted Danton. 'How can it end? It hasn't even begun. You haven't read a single document. You have not called a single witness.'

241

The prisoners were not even allowed to be present when the inevitable sentence was announced. They were bundled down to the Conciergerie, outside which the tumbrils were already waiting. To avoid disturbances, it was necessary to execute them quickly.

Rarely has a régime which talked so much of Liberty contrived a more twisted formula for violating Justice. It reminds one of more recent trials in Nazi Germany.

In the Cour de Mai, the prisoners mounted three tumbrils. Danton was in the same cart as Desmoulins, who was weeping like a child, murmuring 'Lucile', his wife's name. Danton tried to comfort him. As they progressed slowly, the mob jeered and shouted. Fearful of not showing Republican zeal, feeling, perhaps, a certain self-importance when hurling insults at those who had ruled them, the crowd had mocked such disparate figures as Marie-Antoinette, Philippe Egalité and Charlotte Corday, and were later to jeer at Robespierre and St Just. Had not Danton called public opinion a whore? At one stage, Camille Desmoulins impulsively tried to address them, shouting that they had been lied to, and that his only crime was to have shed tears of clemency.

'Be quiet,' said Danton. 'Leave that vile rabble.' Only at the end of their career did revolutionaries become fully aware that 'the People' they had praised and cajoled were not the wise, simple citizens, unspoiled by luxury and artificial living, whom Rousseau had depicted.

As they crossed what is now the Pont St Michel, Danton may have looked back towards the Pont Neuf, which led to the Rue Dauphine and the route to his apartment. The tumbrils entered the Rue St Honoré, and were drawn slowly past the Hôtel de Noailles, where once had lived his enemy, La Fayette. Memories must have crowded in during the long, creaking journey: the Jacobin club on his right, its courtyard leading to the church where, in the library above, he had made so many impassioned speeches. Then, on his left, the cluster of buildings leading to the hall of the first National Assembly, which Danton had not belonged to, but where later, in the Convention, he had voted for the death of the King. Then Robespierre's modest house, shuttered now, its solitary lodger hidden within, probably with his copy of Rousseau's *Contrat Social* open on his desk.

'Vile Robespierre!' shouted Danton, in a voice which could well have been heard within. 'You will follow me. Your house will be levelled and the ground where it stands will be sown with salt.'

The death procession was drawing to its end. Perhaps as they turned into the Rue Royale which leads into the Place de la Révolution, and saw the shape of the guillotine, sinister against the gentle spring sky, Danton's thoughts turned to Arcis, which he would never see again: the river, his 'gentleman's estate', the flowers coming out in the flat countryside. Probably he thought of young Louise, his wife, weeping in their apartment. Perhaps he wondered at the futility of it all, at where this tumultuous career had brought him, of how he had fashioned so many of the instruments which had now produced this end.

The Place de la Révolution was full as it only was on special occasions such as the execution of the King and Queen. To imagine it now, you have to sponge away the rushing traffic, and see the crowd stretching from Gabriel's columned buildings to the river, with the ramps at the side of the Tuileries Gardens covered with people, vendors threading their way through, selling lemonade and ginger bread, and excitement welling up in jeers and cries of '*Vive la République!*' as the tumbrils appeared.

The prisoners got down, surrounded by guards, and were separated by Samson, the executioner. 'You will not be able to prevent our heads meeting again in the basket!' quipped Danton. He was last, and waited while the knife descended and rose seventeen times. Now, he alone remained. He mounted the steps. In a last defiant boast, he said: 'You must show my head to the people. It is well worth it.'

The poet Arnault watched, and afterwards wrote the most quoted description of Danton's last moments:

In the dying light of day, the great leader seemed to be rising out of the tomb as much as preparing to descend into it. That great head, even as it was about to fall, appeared to be in the act of dictating laws . . .

[22]

ROBESPIERRE

'Nature has left this tincture in the blood
That all men would be tyrants if they could.'
DANIEL DEFOE, *Kentish Petition.*

In Arras, in Northern France, there was more reserve about Maximilien Robespierre, their most famous son, than we had found with Danton in Arcis. I asked a lady in the Town Hall what local people thought of Robespierre. 'Well,' she said in slight embarrassment, 'I think we feel he was all right in his early years.'

'There is no statue of him?'

'There's a rather stern bust in the Town Hall, and we have changed the name of the street he lived in from Rat Porteurs to Robespierre.' She gave me a hesitant look through her glasses. 'Somehow, he is not commemorated so much.' Her voice trailed away. She was like someone unwilling to discuss the black sheep of the family with strangers.

Apart from his association with the guillotine and the daily decapitation not only of aristocrats but also of people like this lady from the Town Hall, there was his terrifying coldness. Even Eric Hobsbawm, who might have admired his revolutionary dictatorship, called him 'this dandyish, thin-blooded fanatical lawyer with his somewhat excessive sense of private monopoly in virtue'. One of his enemies, the Girondin philosopher Condorcet, described him as 'without an idea in his head or a feeling in his heart'. Certainly he had the suspicious soul of a small provincial, culminating in the end in paranoia – although who can blame him amidst all the threats he created for himself? Even here, at Arras when he was a member of a literary group, he composed a little sententious verse, which exemplifies his wariness of others:

> *Je vois l'épine avec la rose*
> *dans le bouquet que vous m'offrez . . .*

(I see the thorn with the rose in the bouquet you offer me.)

244

Robespierre was certainly not the sort of person whose memory would touch the gentle heart of this lady in the Town Hall. I changed the subject, and we were given a pack of old postcards, showing Arras after the First World War, with the Cathedral battered into ruins, and the Grande and Petite Places with their famous arcades and Dutch-inspired gables, just recognizable amidst the rubble.

'It's all been rebuilt now,' said the lady, glad to get onto a different aspect of Arras's history.

We thanked her and left, anxious to find Robespierre's house.

As in Lyons, I had expected Arras to be an industrial town, smeary and polluted, but it was bright and sunny, with the slow amiability of a provincial town. Descriptions of it when Robespierre practised here as a young lawyer make it sound a little stifling, with its large, respectable bourgeois population, hierarchical aristocratic divisions and clerical predominance, half owned as it was by the enormous Benedictine monastery of St Vaast, whose reconstructed buildings we passed on our way down the hill.

Perhaps it was the very monotony of the town that made Robespierre's father leave his family of two girls and two boys after his wife died when Robespierre was only seven, thus leaving the family with no parental support. For long, this sudden departure was a mystery. Only recently was it discovered that this man, who was also a lawyer, had worked surreptitiously as a French language tutor in Munich, and had died when Robespierre was nineteen.

According to Robespierre's sister Charlotte, the effect on the small boy of being suddenly without a father or mother, and becoming the eldest of the family, was dramatic. From being playful and spontaneous, he became serious and sensible. 'If he joined in our games, it was to take charge of them,' she wrote. The boys were brought up by their maternal grandfather and the girls by their aunts.

We came to a narrow street giving on to the Place du Théâtre. Robespierre's house was sombre, with layers of red brick and grimy white stone, standing in a line of similar houses. It had a first floor and little attic windows in the roof. The date, 1730, was visible under the eaves. By the side of the steps leading to the front door was a dark stain of pee, as if this were the only salute that was now paid it by drunks, or dogs. A sign showed that it was a school of shorthand-typing, normally full of young girls, who perhaps brought it the giggles and high spirits which Robespierre shunned. The door, though, was locked. The school was closed for the holidays, a neighbour told us.

From here, one morning in May 1789, two people came out of the front door. One of them was Charlotte Robespierre, garbed in black. The other was a neatly dressed youngish man, small and thin, with powdered hair, his movements stiff and precise as he controlled his nervous excitement. Brother and sister embraced briefly, and Robespierre walked off over the cobbles, beside the rattling handcart which bore his well-worn trunk. He was on his way to the diligence that would take him to Versailles as one of twelve deputies from Artois, of which Arras was the capital.

He was not to return, except for one short visit two years later. It is extraordinary when one thinks of what was being launched onto the world from this sombre house. The reverberations were also to affect Arras when, in 1793–4, Representative Lebon arrived with his wife to install the guillotine and, like an Oriental despot, to watch from a balcony the executions of 394 people, including the richest men in town, whose houses and wealth he confiscated.

It was as if a deadly virus were setting off to infect the most civilized county in Europe, helping with other germs to rack it with austerity, self-righteousness and blood.

In Versailles, I searched the Rue Duplessis for the Hôtel Renard, a modest hostelry where Robespierre stayed with his three colleagues from Artois. However, although the Rue Duplessis survives, the hotel is now untraceable. He also frequented the Café Amaury on the Avenue de Paris, which has now been absorbed by a bank in whose window you can see a memorial plaque. Here, Mirabeau, Robespierre and other deputies made speeches and discussed their tactics in the National Assembly. These meetings ultimately developed into the Club des Jacobins.

During this period, Robespierre voted and occasionally spoke for humane measures. Ironically, he made a moving speech for the abolition of the death penalty. 'That man means what he says,' remarked Mirabeau.

When the Assembly moved to Paris, Robespierre found lodgings in the Rue Saintonge, a long street which crosses the northern part of the Marais, near the Temple. In the 1950s, the historian Gérard Walter discovered the house empty and waiting for demolition. Two large windows opened on the street. From them, there was a view of the two arches of Porte St Martin and Porte St Denis. The room was large and airy. From it, a narrow corridor led to a small kitchen, with a second room behind.

Here Robespierre set to work. Even in Arras he would rise early, work till eight, and have a brief breakfast, after which a barber would arrive to shave him and powder his hair. He then went to his lawyer's office and, after a light lunch, allowed himself the luxury of a walk before returning to his desk. Evenings he would spend writing reports and preparing for the morrow. When he did mix with others, he was awkward and ill at ease, often sitting alone, thoughtful and dreamy.

So it was in Paris, with the day split between attendance at the Jacobin Club and the Assembly, and then a long walk back to the end of the Rue Saintonge. Like most politicians, Robespierre had little experience of mixing with the common man. Steeped in law and the classics, his ideas were abstract and figurative, emanating from Rousseau's idylls. His speeches were florid with classical imagery and allusions to the early Roman Republic – that austere period which to so many revolutionaries was a model of probity and patriotism.

During his stay in the Rue Saintonge, Robespierre was still a constitutional monarchist, although believing with Rousseau in equality and the goodness of the 'people'. His change of lodging coincided with his adoption of more radical views. The King had returned from Varennes and on 17 July 1791 a crowd signing a petition for the King's dethronement was fired at by troops of the National Guard in the Champ de Mars (see p. 117). On his way home to the Marais, Robespierre was surrounded by an over-enthusiastic crowd who cheered him for speaking against the attempt to patch up the Constitution after the King's return. He was given refuge in the house of a carpenter, Duplay, at what is now 398 Rue St Honoré, where he was persuaded to move in as a lodger. The idea of living with a humble carpenter and his family appealed to him. Also, it must have been convenient, with the Jacobin Club almost next door and the Assembly only a few hundred yards away.

From the end of 1791, Robespierre was no longer a member of

the Assembly. He himself had proposed in a typically self-denying ordnance that those who had belonged to the first Assembly should not be re-elected to the second one, whose first sessions took place in September 1791. Yet he continued to live in Paris and speak at the Jacobins. In the debates about war with Austria, he was among the few who opposed it, as he felt that any failure of French arms would give counter-revolutionaries the opportunity to re-establish the Ancien Régime. There was, indeed, a disastrous failure of French arms, and had it not been for the victory of Valmy his fears would have been justified.

In the new Convention in September 1792 he was elected again, but for Paris rather than Arras. This was significant, as he allied himself closely with the Commune, voted for the King's death, and sat with the extremists on the upper tiers of the Assembly. As such he was a continual target for the Girondins, whose expulsion he supported despite his legalistic attitudes. From now on he abandoned all reservations about sacrificing everything to patriotism and the successful conduct of the war. Elected a member of the Committee of Public Safety in the summer of 1793, he became a part of what was virtually the government executive of France, although he had no official post. Still, though, he was a man of order and precision, opposed to the anti-religious anarchism of extremists like Hébert, intent on proscribing those who did not conform with his narrow idea of 'Virtue', naïve enough to believe that the Catholic religion could be replaced by the deistic concept of the Supreme Being which would save citizens from the evils of atheism and immoral indulgence. His suspicious nature veered towards paranoia in the uncertain chaos of France under the Terror. He was afraid, pessimistic, often ill during this period, and struck out against anyone who appeared to threaten him, or seemed 'impure', even if they were old friends like Desmoulins and Danton.

In the simple house of the Duplays, he must have lived through his own private hell of fear and tortured suspicion. From it, he left to make his speeches in which 'virtue' and 'purity' were key words. From here, he walked out in his blue coat and jonquil trousers to lead the Feast of the Supreme Being, with all its mumbo-jumbo of burning cardboard figures of Atheism and Anarchy, which were intended to replace the festivities of Catholic France. Before his front door passed the tumbrils bearing Danton, Desmoulins, the Girondins and many erstwhile colleagues. Cécile Renault crossed the narrow courtyard: when she was stopped, two knives were found in her basket among the oranges which were Robespierre's favourite fruit. Cronies such as St Just, Couthon and Lebas came to Mme Duplay's 'Thursday At Home'. From here, too, Robespierre set out to that last tumultuous scene in the Convention where he was arrested, and from which he was only to return when he passed by in a tumbril on his way to the guillotine.

Today, Robespierre's original lodgings are still recognizable, now set ironically in a Rue St Honoré which has become one of the most luxurious shopping centres in Paris. Fabergé, the Russian jeweller, sports the golden Easter Eggs which the Tsar of Russia once received every Easter. Furs seem to purr through the plate glass, while kneeling plaster mannequins stare intently at passing men's crotches. Before the Revolution, St Honoré was residential, with noble mansions opening onto it. The Duplays' house was surrounded by the gardens of the Convent of the Conception, where the anarchist Hébert's wife had been a nun, and where Duplay's daughters went to school.

Today, the original entrance of the house where Robespierre lived is partly blocked by a shop, 'Sonar', which sells expensive oriental objects. To get to the inner courtyard, you penetrate a narrow entrance, brushing the metal letter-boxes of present inmates. Within, the layout is much as it was, except that the surrounding buildings are higher, and there is no garden on your right. The original narrow staircase curves round on the left, its walls now covered with pretentious marbled wallpaper. On the first floor, you go into a tourist agency to be confronted by a large room with wall-to-wall carpeting, a reception desk, and a photo-copier in the corner.

Originally, this room was divided into the various small bedrooms of the Duplay children. Robespierre's was at the far end, tiny, looking onto the courtyard. It had the simplicity of the ascetic. A narrow, walnut bed was covered with a quilt of blue damask with white flowers. The shelves on which stood a few books, mainly by Rousseau, were of pine. A small table was often covered with a speech in preparation on closely written sheets, scratched with erasures. Beyond was a small dressing room which led onto a special staircase, built by Duplay, to allow separate access and protection from intruders. This staircase has disappeared, and is now in a country house. The rest of the Duplay family lived in

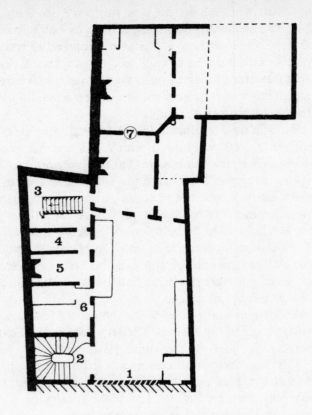

Robespierre's lodging 1791–4.
1. Entry from the Rue St Honoré;
2. Main staircase;
3. Robespierre's private staircase;
4. Robespierre's study;
5. Robespierre's bedroom;
6. Rooms occupied by Duplays;
7. Apartments occupied by Duplays.

the part of the house beyond Robespierre's dressing room, in what are now further offices of the tourist agency.

The original dining room, kitchen and sitting room, at the end of the courtyard, have now become a restaurant, Le Robespierre, where I have often eaten. Their rabbit is excellent. The décor is all red: lamps, tablecloths, wall coverings. Blood or politics?, you ask yourself. As you sit, surrounded by portraits of Robespierre, the restaurant is shaken suddenly by the Métro, passing below. The

250

rumbling is ominous, like the prelude to an earthquake. Perhaps it is a modern echo of Robespierre's feeling of being continually threatened, while France seemed about to crumble all round him. You imagine him leaning on the mantelpiece, paring his nails, or eating his favourite oranges, when a sudden presentiment of destruction makes his fingers tremble, and brings pallor to his greenish cheeks.

A calm blonde lady, Monique Delcroix, has run the Robespierre for twenty-five years. Previously, it was a café for Africans, called the Savernay. When she acquired it, Monique didn't know that it had once been Robespierre's home, she told me. This she discovered only two weeks before the opening. Immediately she sent two thousand telegrams all over France, inviting friends, officials and journalists. The party was a great success and went on till dawn.

'Do you feel Robespierre's presence here?' I asked her.

She shrugged her shoulders. 'No.'

'Do you like him – as a character?'

'I prefer Danton. Robespierre was too cold, too detached. France needed someone strong, tough. The Germans do what they're told, but the French are all individualists – particularly at a time of Revolution.'

'D'you think Robespierre minded the tumbrils passing his door every day?'

'*Bouf*. To him, the condemned were just criminals.'

'He must have had some human warmth. After all, the Duplays liked and admired him.'

'Oh, I think the Duplays felt honoured. It's as though De Gaulle had suddenly descended on a family and lodged with them. They would probably have admired him and done everything for him.'

'And what of Robespierre and love?'

Monique shrugged her shoulders. 'Who knows? The Duplay daughter, Eléonore, was supposed to have been in love with him. But he didn't return her affections. Perhaps he was too absorbed in politics. He was probably just neuter. *Après tout*, people like that seem to exist.'

The Duplays, whatever their motives, must have given Robespierre some of the support he needed. It was not only Eléonore's admiring eyes which fixed themselves on the lodger. M. Duplay was a Jacobin. Madame was furious when Robespierre's sister, Charlotte, persuaded him to move elsewhere with her, and got him back. There was also the reverence of Duplay's young son, called 'our little patriot', and of their nephew, Simon, who lost a leg at Valmy, and was known as 'the Duplay with the wooden leg'.

Robespierre thus found himself in a veritable nest of admiring patriots, whose enthusiasm for the Revolution focused on him. Those of us who are not politicians, or national figures, can only hazard the effect of continual adulation on a person who may well have achieved prominence as compensation for the lack of warmth in childhood. In all the conversations about current events, the Duplays must also have confirmed Robespierre in the weakness which creates autocrats: the belief that he was RIGHT, that it was essential for France to accept his own brand of narrow moralistic regeneration. With this entrenched belief, Robespierre's enemies became 'impure' foes of 'virtue'. 'The only remaining division in the Assembly is that between the virtuous and the wicked,' he said in a speech towards the end.

This attitude found its quintessence in Robespierre, but it was common on both sides of the political divide. Tolerance is a luxury of those who do not feel threatened. The revolutionaries compensated for paranoia and panic with enthusiasm and determination. Events had occurred so rapidly. They could not believe that the ancient power they had overthrown was momentarily so weak that it could be defeated without continual repression. Like De Launay in the Bastille at the beginning of the Revolution, they imagined that even the shadows of trees at night were attackers, lying in wait. Snatched suddenly from dark law offices to the palaces of power, they felt it might well not last. The only way of thwarting those who threatened was to eliminate them and their symbols: not only the religious images in churches, the emblems of royal power, but also the minds and muscle of those who opposed them.

They forgot as Desmoulins wrote in a last number of the *Vieux Cordelier*, that for everyone destroyed at least ten enemies, intent on revenge, were made. Because they assumed office with no tradition of authority behind them, they were officious and aggressive in compensation. Because they had no precedents for Revolution as we have today, they were unaware that slaughter and victimization can never lead to that freedom from oppression which was their original aim.

It is difficult to find a historical figure equivalent to Robespierre. Pol Pot? Stalin? Both have been cited by historians who denounce the Terror. However, neither fits exactly. It is more in the Wars of Religion that a parallel can be found: perhaps Calvin, who was so unyielding in his reign of virtue in Geneva that he had a child executed for striking his father; perhaps Torquemada, whose *autos-da-fé* burnt heretics for the Glory of God — although with Torquemada there were elements of sadism which seem to have been absent in Robespierre.

'The Revolution would end,' said Robespierre to the Convention in his last speech, 'if only all men loved their country and their laws.' Like Calvin, who was also French, he really believed he could establish the Republic of Virtue on Earth.

Often, too, he talked of how he expected to find martyrdom. He seems to have anticipated approaching death when he called his final rambling speech 'My last will and testament'. Indeed, there are theories that he saw himself as a Christ. Already in 1791 he remarked: 'I am called to a stormy destiny. I must follow out its course until I make the ultimate sacrifice for my country.' When a friend, Buonarotti, remarked on his resemblance to Jesus, Robespierre did not demur, and talked of his 'Gethsemane'. Was it just coincidence that he withdrew from public life for forty days, before his via dolorosa to the guillotine?

Robespierre has often been called a dictator, but this can be misleading. Certainly he had none of the necessary apparatus. His power came essentially from his oratorical skill and his ability to manipulate the machinery of government as did Walpole and Newcastle in British eighteenth-century politics. Whereas, in Britain, bribery was used to persuade and lubricate, Robespierre played on the fear of the guillotine.

Robespierre himself never held an office, whether as Minister or Mayor. The Committee of Public Safety, of which he was a member, disagreed on many issues. (We have already seen that it was not unanimous on Danton's death.) Robespierre's eminence derived from having been with the Revolution from the start, and from a reputation for inflexible probity which gave him trust and influence.

Much of his power came from his role as spokesman for the Committee of Public Safety, with an almost hypnotic way of speaking. Those subjected to it describe how he would make a point, and then remove his green spectacles and sweep the upturned faces with cold eyes; or focus on an individual he had denounced, and shrivel him with his gaze. When Danton was arrested, his friend the butcher Legendre protested in the Convention, but Robespierre reduced him to blabbering conformity. In the last scene before Robespierre and his associates were arrested, the success of the conspirators stemmed from their blocking the rostrum so that Robespierre could not speak. It was like covering the Medusa's face so that it would not turn those who looked at it to stone.

23

THE TERROR

'Robespierre tried to remain supreme less through ambition than because of fear.'

MALLET DU PAN, March 1794.

The Terror, which accounted for more and more deaths in the last few months before Robespierre's execution, must be set against the contemporary background of Paris. As Richard Holmes explained in his *Footsteps*, the claustrophobic atmosphere in the city was increased by the walls, twelve foot high, built as a customs barrier in 1785. Its sixty towers were locked every night at curfew time, and during the day, guards checked those going in and out.

Holmes points out that this sense of enclosure is difficult for us to understand, as we live in cities with motorways stretching freely into the countryside. Perhaps, he suggests, the nearest modern equivalent is the enclosed isolation of West Berlin. He quotes Mary Wollstonecraft, the mother of Mary Shelley, who was in Paris at the time:

> The cavalcade of death moves along, shedding mildew over all the beauties of the scene, and blasting every joy. The elegance of the palaces and buildings is revolting when they are viewed as prisons; and the sprightliness of the people disgusting when they are hastening to view the operation of the guillotine, or carelessly passing over the earth stained with blood.

To add to the sense of imprisonment with death, there was the fear of denunciation. As we have seen, Paris was divided into forty-eight sections which each had its own Committee of Surveillance, to which a citizen could be denounced on mere suspicion. From it, a Certificate of Civism had to be obtained, which in many cases depended on a show of revolutionary fervour, or on bribery, or on personal favour. Absurd and tragic incidents have come down to us, like the case of a girl called Germaine Quétier who was guillotined for saying she needed a spinning wheel (*rouet*) which sounded like the word for king (*roi*); or the carpenter's apprentice who swore during a game of cards. On being told sententiously that good patriots never used bad language, he was rash enough to shout 'Fuck good patriots' – for which he, too, went to the scaffold.

Over everything stood the sinister shape of the guillotine. Like that other instrument of capital punishment, the Cross, it came to have symbolic significance. On a repressive expedition to Santo Domingo, it was erected in the bows of the foremost ship, as Columbus, three hundred years earlier, had planted the crucifix. It also created its own flippant and almost affectionate phraseology: 'Mother Guillotine'; 'looking through the little window'; 'the executive power'. During the Terror, it was made into a toy, decapitating small dolls, sometimes filled with reddish perfume.

For the last two hundred years, the guillotine has had a universal fascination. In 1889, at the Paris Exhibition, Thomas Cook organized a charabanc with forty seats to go to a prison and watch an execution. All the seats were taken. Executions in prisons, which the public could attend, continued in France until as late as 1939, coming to an end because the spectators were too tumultuous and sadistic.

Perhaps, apart from its function, the guillotine is remarkable because of its simple shape. One expects the two verticals to end with a piece at right angles, like door frames which one sees every day. And yet the deadliest part, the knife, is slanted, which gives a reflex of surprise and fear: it reminds one of an erect snake with fangs exposed.

Insubstantial, sketched against the sky, it must have appeared a slight if sinister foe. Early victims, before it became well known, must have asked themselves, as, literally, they looked through it, whether this flimsy structure was really powerful enough to end their lives, and, to begin with the mob objected to guillotinings because they were so rapid and undramatic. With hanging or an axe, one man still killed another in the ancient, savage way. With the guillotine, it was impersonal. Its speed bewildered: you scarcely saw the falling blade with the naked eye. One moment, a human being lay prostrate, looking out at buildings and upturned faces. Normal things happened: the sun broke through the clouds; there was a spatter of rain. Then a sudden hiss, like that of a serpent, and the head fell.

Did the victim still see after decapitation? Probably. Almost certainly, thoughts still went through his mind. Experiments made as late as 1956 by two French doctors report that 'death is not instantaneous . . . Every vital element survives decapitation . . . a savage vivisection followed by a premature burial.' You can imagine the bewilderment of Louis XVI, Marie-Antoinette, or guillotined priests, anticipating Heaven. A sudden pain and the sight of the wickerwork basket, coming up towards them. Then, the blurred vision of a sea of faces in the Place de la Révolution, as their heads were held up. The Earth was too much with them.

Guillotining was almost as simple as having an X-ray today. However, of all forms of execution, it was the bloodiest. Red pints surged against the fallen blade, and over the special aprons of the executioner: in the Place de la Révolution, passing herds of cows avoided the actual place. Perhaps part of the fascination was it being so physical, like public sex. Dying too is intimate.

Only the first suggestion for using such an instrument came from Dr Guillotin, and he himself was not decapitated by it, as legend has it, but died in his bed at the age of seventy-six. A similar instrument, called the Maiden, existed in Scotland five centuries before.

Guillotin himself was a meticulous advocate of hygiene and order: one can imagine him being a vociferous anti-smoker today. He recommended the instrument as merciful. With no reason to anticipate mass executions, he was unaware of the macabre ritual of the hair being cut over the neck, the creaking journey on cobbles amidst a howling mob, the agony of forming a queue to wait one's turn, while the machine hissed through the necks of companions above. Most victims died stoically, with haughty indifference. Indeed, if more had screamed and wept, like Mme du Barry, Louis XV's former mistress, spectators would have been more moved to pity, and the Terror might have ended sooner.

It was a Dr Louis who perfected the machine, trying it out on dead corpses of convicts in the Bicêtre prison. Hence its alternative name of 'Louison'. The first one was built by a German harpsichord maker called Schmidt, and decapitated a criminal condemned for robbery with violence. This was in the traditional place of execution, the Place de Grève, in front of the Town Hall, and took place on

25 April 1792, when Louis XVI was still King. Then, after the storming of the Tuileries the following August, the guillotine was transferred to the Place du Carrousel behind the palace, where Napoleon's smaller Arch of Triumph now stands. The Place de la Révolution, now Concorde, was used as a place of execution for the first time to decapitate those who had stolen the Crown jewels in the Garde Meubles, nearby. Later, Louis XVI was guillotined there in January 1793.

As the Terror got under way, there were increasing protests at the miasma of blood and the endless procession of tumbrils through the fashionable Rue St Honoré. For a few days, the guillotine was transferred to the site of the demolished Bastille. However, the workmen of the Faubourg St Antoine would have none of it, and it was moved westward to the extremity of Paris, to what was the Place du Trône Renversé, today the Place de la Nation.

However, the guillotine was not only erected in official places. In November 1793, Bailly, who four years earlier had presided over the Oath of the Tennis Court, and as Mayor of Paris had welcomed Louis XVI after the fall of the Bastille, was guillotined not in the Place de la Révolution but on the Champ de Mars. There was an ancient tradition that a criminal should, if possible, be executed on the site of his crime (see p. 200). Bailly's 'crime' was that, with La Fayette, he had ordered the National Guard to fire on the crowd in the Champ de Mars, where they had come to sign a petition for Louis XVI's suspension after Varennes. In the gloom and mist of a November day, the guillotine was dismantled in the Place de la Révolution, and trundled over the bridge, past the Invalides. The crowd had been fired at by the altar which was dedicated to the Nation. But this was too sacred a place on which to organize an execution, so it was set up between the river and where the Eiffel Tower now stands.

Cold fingers slowly assembled the sinister instrument, while Bailly waited.

'You tremble, old man,' shouted someone in the crowd.

'It is the cold,' replied Bailly.

With the vapour coming off the river, this solitary execution took place, and the guillotine was dismantled once more, and returned to the Place de la Révolution. Revenge had been exacted by the new generation of ruthless revolutionaries on yet another of those moderates who had resisted autocracy in 1789, in hopes of a stable constitutional monarchy.

One of the most moving sites of the Terror is near the Place de la Nation, where the last executions took place, and which still has some of the appearance it then had – the squat, solid gatehouses of the Customs barrier which surrounded Paris, and two tall columns beside it, on which stand the statues of two kings: St Louis and Philippe Auguste.

I arrived there by Métro on a sunny winter day and stood blinking in this enormous Place, with avenues stretching out symmetrically from the round grass lawn in the centre, where stood a typical nineteenth-century group of allegorical sculptures: two lions with a man sprawled over their backs, as they pulled a chariot on which a lady, with a torch and bare breasts, stood precariously on a globe. Behind, a naked girl simpered beside an overturned cornucopia.

The guillotine once stood over to the right as you face this monument, near some trees, in what was then open countryside, planted with vines and dotted with small farmhouses. Here almost half of all the Parisian victims of the Terror were guillotined in only eight weeks, in batches of forty to sixty a day. Here the last group was executed on the very evening after Robespierre's fall. The tumbrils had been stopped by a crowd in the Place de la Bastille, further towards Paris, when rumours of Robespierre's arrest spread. 'Escape!' shouted the crowd, who were tired of blood. However, a detachment of troops passed, led by Hanriot, the commander of the National Guard, who insisted that the law be carried out. So the tumbrils proceeded and the last mass execution of the Terror took place. The batch included the Princesse de Monaco, who had postponed her execution for a day by pretending to be pregnant, so that she could cut her own hair and send it to her children.

However, it is the cemetery of Picpus, nearby, which evokes most directly the horror and the tragedy of this last stage of the Terror.

I walked down a broad avenue bordered by tall, recent blocks of flats, and arrived at the closed gate of 35 Rue de Picpus. Letting myself in by a small door, I entered a large courtyard with a church immediately opposite and the solid building of a convent on the right. On my left was a little pavilion standing against an old wall.

The concierge came out of his small office and accompanied me,

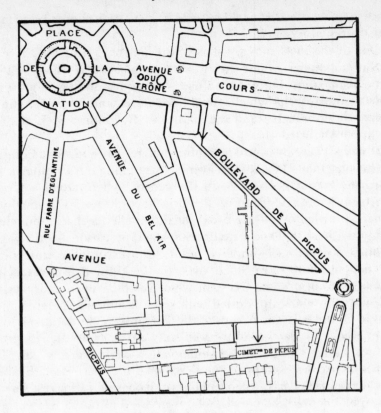

Route to Picpus today.

explaining that this was still a convent and that, in the church, a nun prayed night and day for those executed on the Place de la Nation. He pointed to the remains of the little pavilion, and said it had once been part of a hunting lodge of Louis XIII's. The Château of Versailles had sprung from such an origin.

He unlocked a metal gate and we walked down an avenue of limes, bare of leaves, with knots like old, clenched fists above their trunks. 'It's beautiful in summer,' said the concierge. 'There are roses fringing the grass, and the avenue is lined with leafy trees.' On one side, faded blocks of flats looked down with uncurtained rectangular windows, as if insisting that, despite appearances, this place demanded continual watchfulness.

The concierge pointed to a wall beyond. 'Through an archway that used to be there, the carts bearing the corpses of the executed arrived, every evening. No one knew about this until the relative of a victim followed the grave-diggers.'

We found ourselves in a constricted cemetery, crowded with slabs and little chapels. The names of the most noble families in France were engraved on tombs: Rochefoucauld, Noailles, Montmorency, Rohan, Chateaubriand . . . dukes, marquises, counts and barons. 'Here, the relatives of those guillotined are buried,' said the concierge. Some had been interred as recently as the last war and had died in battle, or in concentration camps. 'Mort pour la France,' informed one of the memorial plaques.

'Also La Fayette,' continued the concierge. 'Many of his wife's relatives were executed.' We looked at a tomb at the end of the cemetery with an American flag beside it. 'Pershing, the American general, came here in 1917. It is here that he is supposed to have said: "La Fayette, here we come!", alluding to the help the Americans were giving France in gratitude for all La Fayette had done in the American War of Independence.'

We stood looking through a little archway onto an enclosure with blowsy cypress trees. The one in the middle was dead. In front of us was a large rectangular patch of gravel. Another lay beside the far wall. 'That is where they buried 1,306 corpses,' said the concierge, with indignation still strong in his voice. 'Every evening, the blood-red carts arrived. The grave-diggers stripped the corpses, removed the valuables and threw the bodies into the ditch. Fires were lit, and thyme, sage and juniper was thrown on the flames to sweeten the stench.'

A plaque on the side of the archway showed the professions of victims. Of the 1,306, only 159 were nobles. There were 131 clerics, whether priests, monks, or nuns. The remainder, over a thousand, were lawyers, soldiers, and people with humble professions.

One of the many myths of the Revolution is that most of those guillotined were noble. It comes perhaps from the contemporary use of 'aristocrat' to denote anyone who was not a good patriot. Of almost fourteen thousand people guillotined throughout France, at this time, only 8.5 per cent were noble, 31 per cent were workers, 28 per cent were peasants, 25 per cent bourgeois. The remaining 6.5 per cent were priests, and another 1 per cent had professions which have not been identified.

Yet, at Picpus, old class divisions remain: only noble names are remembered in the cemetery, except for G. Lenotre, who is buried here as a tribute to all the work he did to uncover the historical facts behind this tragedy.

Robespierre's end and that of the Terror came on the 9th Thermidor, dated by the new revolutionary calendar, or 27 July 1794 by ours.

It was just over five years since the Bastille had been stormed and the King had come to Paris and pinned the new tricolour cockade to his hat in token of surrender. Significant convulsions are rapid, at least in modern times. In four bloody years, the Great War transformed Europe. Lenin's Revolution lasted seven years until his death. Hitler's Reich came to its cataclysmic end after only twelve. The effects last for centuries but the actual searing of bone and tissue is rapid, like a car accident.

The previous day, Robespierre had delivered his last speech in the Jacobin Club, full of references to 'impure men' who would have to be eliminated. He made the mistake of refusing to name them, and as a result, the whole Convention was in dread. The law of 22 Prairial had removed witnesses and defence from the accused. Now, being brought before the Revolutionary Tribunal was in itself equivalent to being condemned to death. During those last few weeks, over fifty deputies slept in different friends' houses each night, for fear of being arrested. Attendance at the Convention had shrunk to two hundred. Who was Robespierre accusing? Which of them would be arrested and guillotined on the morrow?

The day of 9 Thermidor was stifling, part of the extraordinary heat wave which had afflicted Paris for the previous weeks. The sky seemed molten and tremors of distant thunder announced a summer storm. Robespierre walked from the Duplays' house, probably down the Rue St Honoré. Again, he was wearing his best sky-blue coat with jonquil breeches, which he had worn when leading the Feast of the Supreme Being, some weeks earlier.

That morning, he would have turned right from the Rue St Honoré, down the Rue de l'Echelle and across to the main courtyard of the Tuileries, with its enormous Phrygian bonnet on the main tower of the Horloge, and 'LIBERTE' and 'EGALITE' blazoned on the pavilions of Flore and Marsan. As often, political slogans become most prominent when they begin to lose their real meaning.

Robespierre walked through the main door, decorated with eight lions' heads, and into the high arcaded entrance hall, crowded with deputies, messengers and officials, making their way to the grand staircase on the right. Little stalls were set against the pillars, selling pamphlets, newspapers and refreshments. With cheers and greetings on every side, he walked up the stairs and through the Salon de Liberté, to the green curtain over the door of the Convention. As he entered, he was greeted by acclamations from his Jacobin friends in the public galleries.

On that morning, with the hot sun coming through the windows, the President, Collot d'Herbois, rang his bell and the session started. St Just went to the tribune and began his speech in which the accused were to be named. However, he had only said a few words when suddenly objections started. Tallien, a deputy who had been responsible for massacres in Bordeaux, went forward and elbowed St Just aside, and asked that everything should come out into the open. 'I demand that the curtain be torn away!' he shouted. The President, Collot d'Herbois, himself responsible for bloodshed in Lyons, rang his bell to drown St Just's protests. Billaud-Varenne, who had played a role in the September massacres, took Tallien's place. 'They are planning to murder the Convention!' he shouted.

Robespierre tried to speak, but was pushed away and his voice was drowned by the ringing of the bell. After further pandemonium, an insignificant deputy called Louchet proposed Robespierre's arrest. A pathetic drama ensued: Robespierre scuttled from one side of the Convention to the other, sitting down first with the Mountain, who rejected him with reminders of Danton's death, then making for the Centre, who likewise repulsed him, and then going to the Right, where the Girondins had once sat. Finally, he rose to appeal to the galleries, but the fickle populace no longer acclaimed him. 'Arrest him!' they shouted.

Rebuffed by all, Robespierre was finally led away by the gendarmes, along with his brother Augustin, Couthon, St Just and Lebas, a close friend who had married one of the Duplay daughters.

He was taken over the river, and through the old Cordelier district to the Luxembourg, where Danton had first been imprisoned. However, Fleuriot, the Mayor, recently appointed by Robespierre, had heard that his allies had been arrested, and had sent word to the prisons, forbidding them to accept new inmates. So Robespierre found refuge in the Mairie, Fleuriot's official residence. There he dallied. The Convention had declared him and his companions outlaws, and Tallien had accused him of being a new Cromwell, the synonym of a Revolutionary dictator. But Robespierre had none of the experience, or the makings, of a man of action. Fleuriot sent messages urging him to come to the Hôtel de Ville to take command, but only when troops were sent to protect him did he go over the river to join his allies.

Outside, in the Place de Grève, his armed supporters from sixteen of the forty-eight sections were assembled. They stood idly, waiting for orders. As the long evening turned to night, they began to drift away. Thunder sounded in the dusk, and a sudden storm of rain swept down. When it stopped, the glistening Place de Grève was empty.

Inside the now defenceless Town Hall, an endless, uncertain discussion was going on. A significant fact about the Revolution is that at times of assault, the threatened leaders always seem to have vacillated. It started with De Launay at the Bastille and continued with Louis XVI at Versailles and at the attack on the Tuileries. The Girondins, too, trooped out of the Convention like sheep. It is as if any force of revolt in Paris had a magic weapon, as if no Frenchman dared resist 'the Right of Insurrection', and each was cowed by the first gunshot. Or perhaps it was because those who attained power were theoreticians, not men of action. The ex-deputy Malouet was referring to the absence of leadership when he wrote: 'I knew of no such thing in the course of the Revolution until the 18th Brumaire.'*

In the vast rooms of the old Town Hall, lit by candles and oil lamps, Fleuriot tried to persuade Robespierre to sign an appeal to the army and the Sections. 'In whose name shall I sign it?' asked the hesitant Robespierre, legalistic to the last. In a sense, he was right. Who had the legal authority, if not the Convention which had declared him an outlaw? It was a time, though, when only force could triumph. Robespierre, like de Launay, was no soldier.

He had just decided to sign his name when the forces of the Convention burst in, commanded by Barras, another extremist, responsible as we have seen for the massacres at Toulon.

Some say that Robespierre tried to commit suicide, but it is more likely he was shot in the jaw by a young gendarme called Meda. He was taken on a stretcher to the Tuileries and laid on a table in the Committee of Public Safety where the fate of so many others had been decided. Six hours later, he and his colleagues

---

* Date of Napoleon's coup d'état in 1799.

were bundled into the Revolutionary Tribunal at the Palais de Justice. Here their death warrants were signed without a trial, as was customary with outlaws. Robespierre was then carried down on his stretcher, probably to lie in the cell which can still be seen beside the one which Marie-Antoinette occupied in the Conciergerie. Here he waited for four hours while the guillotine was transferred from the Place de la Nation to the Place de la Révolution.

At six in the evening, three tumbrils containing twenty-two people who only yesterday had ruled France rattled over the Pont du Change and up to the Rue St Honoré. People cheered and danced, their joy sharpened by the hatred of those who had lost relatives on the guillotine.

For a moment, the tumbrils stopped in front of the Duplays' house, now locked and shuttered. Someone brought a pail of bull's blood from a butcher's, and threw it at the door. The tumbrils moved on.

Later, in the Place de la Révolution, Samson, the executioner, tore off the bandage round Robespierre's shattered jaw before guillotining him. A sheer cry of agony echoed round the crowded Place, as if all the terror of those who had died there were being expressed in this single howl of pain.

For many, today, the Terror is the period most closely associated with the Revolution. Experimenting casually, I have found that when asked to produce a word suggested by 'French Revolution', many will say 'Guillotine', 'mob', 'aristocrat', or 'Marie-Antoinette' – all associated principally with 1793–4.

Sadly inured as we are to massacres in the two hundred years since the Revolution, the Terror seems a precedent of much that has happened since. The only difference is that we have suppressed executions in public, preferring to confine killing to special camps, or prisons, or stadiums. We are now ashamed of public death, except on film.

Otherwise, the raison d'être behind mass slaughter appears to be the same, with fear and fanaticism at the root. We still attempt to eliminate those who are 'evil' because they do not share our beliefs, and therefore threaten us. Khomeini in Iran, with his grading of enemies in various categories of Satan, is the latest manifestation. Once the Spanish Civil War had started, or Louis XVI had been executed, or Pol Pot had taken Cambodia, or the

Revolutions in China and Iran had unseated their governments, killings of panic and revenge were inevitable. The Terror, though, like the Nazi elimination of the Jews, seems more horrible because it was methodically ruthless, not just part of the flux and impulse of conflict.

However, the Terror must also be put into perspective. In Paris, 2,498 people were guillotined in some eighteen months, which is a tiny number compared to six million Jews, or those wiped out by Stalin or Mao.

Diderot calculated that under Louis XV, three hundred people were executed every year. People were accustomed to public executions in a variety of different, horrible ways, whether breaking on the wheel, the tearing of arms and legs from sockets by horses, wounds filled with boiling sulphur, or witnessing decapitation – perhaps with twenty-three blows of an axe, as happened in one case.

Robespierre, with his cold fanaticism, has long been held mainly responsible for the Terror. But how true is this? When he died, the Terror stopped, so it was natural to impute it to him. The 'crime' of Danton and Desmoulins was to plead for indulgence, and Robespierre had them guillotined, which again implies that Robespierre wanted the Terror to continue.

In fact, Robespierre hardly attended the sessions of the Committee of Public Safety during the last month of the Terror, although he and St Just were in close contact with the Police Bureau which was responsible, among others, for arresting suspects. Whatever the truth, the most significant fact about the denunciation of Robespierre is that those who played the major role were all prominent terrorists, who, on mission all over France, had had a personal hand in massacres more savage than any in Paris in 1794: Collot d'Herbois and Fouché in Lyons, Barras in Toulon, Tallien in Bordeaux, Billaud-Varenne in the September massacres. These men ended the Terror not because they were compassionate but because they themselves were now threatened by it. 'President of Assassins!' shouted Robespierre to the Chair, as he was led out of the Convention. At least, that part of the abuse which flowed from him on that hot morning was accurate.

We will never know the exact truth, but certain it is that these clever, unscrupulous butchers deflected much of the blame for the Terror from themselves onto Robespierre. They defamed him as a monster, creating a picture of this meticulous pedant as one of the great criminals of history. Like the Tudors with Richard III, they had a motive.

A royalist spy, the Duchess of Fleury, who certainly had no reason to defend Robespierre, wrote:

If I do not remember him with bitterness, it is because it seems to me that all the horrors of those who preceded him, surrounded him, betrayed him and struck him down have been heaped on his name . . . his most gushing adherents were the worst assassins, weighing down his memory with the blood of the Terror, which he might well have ended with their heads.

Talking of blame, it is also important not to have the naïve view that all the blood and slaughter was the result of the French national character, any more than Auschwitz and Belsen were a consequence of the German. The refuge of those who shrink from admitting that many human beings have a murderous side, however covered and concealed, is to throw blame on a nationality, forgetting that it is usually historical circumstances which create régimes that bring out the worst or best in a community. Inherently, any nationality is as potentially sadistic, or benevolent, as any other.

Finally, it is important to remember what Robespierre and the Jacobins achieved between July 1793 and July 1794. They found France divided, with rebellion all over the South and in the Vendée, and foreign armies invading from the east and over the Pyrenees. In a year, they saved France from invasion, crushed rebellion, raised and supplied armies. They kept the population fed, and contained inflation. This was done with a determination and ruthlessness of which St Just's instructions when he was a Representative on Mission in Strasbourg are a good example. 'Ten thousand soldiers lack shoes,' he wrote. 'You will take the shoes of all the aristocrats in Strasbourg and deliver them ready for transport to the headquarters by tomorrow, ten am.'

Jean Bon St André, a member of the Committee of Public Safety, compared Revolutionary times with imperial France during the defeats of 1812–13:

[We had] a government of passionate Jacobins in red bonnets, wearing rough woollen cloth, wooden shoes, who lived on simple bread and bad beer and went to sleep on mattresses laid on the floor of their meeting halls when they were too tired to wake and deliberate further. That is the kind of men who saved France. I was one of them, gentlemen, and here in the apartments of the Emperor which I am about to enter, I glory in the fact.

It has the tang of our times. Here could be speaking a Russian Communist of 1917, a defender of Madrid in 1937, a member of the FLN in Algeria in 1959, an ANC member in South Africa today.

The men of 1793–4 were as ready to assassinate, to massacre for causes seen in black and white, as others have been in our day. Rarely did they examine their personal motives, absorbed as they were in ideals whose very fervour, yet vagueness, was their attraction. Unlike the ancient goal of Heaven, their success can be measured in terms of how and whether these ideals were fulfilled, even if no Geiger counters exist to measure their evasive, undefinable aim of universal happiness.

Perhaps much can be explained by the decay of religious belief and the transfer to other causes of the faith and fervour which still seem necessary to many of us.

V

Retrospect

24

ORIGINS AND CONSEQUENCES

'I think it impossible that the great monarchies of Europe last much longer.'

J.-J. ROUSSEAU, *Emile* (1762).

In the evening, we wandered round Ermenonville, a small town some forty minutes' train-ride north of Paris. It was deserted, with everyone apparently watching television. In the emptiness, the old stone houses seemed as they were when Joan of Arc passed this way to fight the English, five hundred and fifty years previously.

On the outskirts, villas stood in their own grassland, surrounded by weeping willows. Beyond was a park, and we walked past some houses to explore it.

'Hey? What do you want?' shouted a man, emerging from his front door. 'This is private property!' His Alsatian dog barked at us.

We decided to postpone our exploration till the morrow.

It is not difficult to imagine the two men in their carriage, a couple of hundred years ago, as they swayed along the broad grassy path which is still visible, gesticulating under the sun-flecked tunnel of branches as they talked.

The first dramatic view which confronted them was the white château with its towers and sloping roofs, through a gap in the trees. When they got down from the carriage, they entered a grotto in a bank. From it, a visitor was encouraged to ascend narrow steps through a rocky shaft. If you go the same way, the sky comes closer and then, suddenly, a lake laps just below your eyes. Before you is a long stretch of quiet water, dimpled with the rings of rising fish. Grass and bushes rise on one side; oak, beech and ash trees stand on the other.

At the far end, a little island almost floats on the water. On it, leafy poplars grow, like the overgrown masts of a ship which has been stranded there for years.

Jean-Jacques Rousseau was entranced. 'For a long time my heart has made me wish to come here,' he said, throwing his arms round his host, the Marquis of Girardin. 'And now my eyes tell me to remain for ever.'

The park and forest was everything Rousseau had idealized, even if, like the first dramatic views of the château and the lake, it had elements of artifice of which, in theory, he disapproved. For Girardin believed in English parks with trees and plants growing naturally, in opposition to the linear French style. Nevertheless, when about to plant a tree he would erect a canvas substitute with painted leaves, in order to see where the best place was. With a pond, he would lay out silver sheets to plan the most tasteful position.

Even now, the park is full of the small, contrived monuments which the French call *fabriques*: a temple of philosophy with each column inscribed with a famous thinker's name; a Bench of Mothers, a Temple of Reverie, a Waterfall of Naiads.

'Girardin believed that everything should be beautiful,' Pierre Barbe, the park administrator, told us. 'Planning was necessary, but then everything should be left to nature. He also built beautiful houses for his peasants, and a dancing green and a range for archery. For he felt that if people grew up with beauty, their souls would flower.'

Rousseau, in any case, was used to contradictions between his own idea of spontaneous nature and reality. He had attacked books, operas and plays as corrupting – while producing a profusion himself. He had written *Emile*, on how to educate the young, when he had given away his five children to a foundling hospital at birth. He had belittled women as vain, empty beings with no soul, while loving and depending on them. He had attacked the rich and the aristocracy as rotten with luxury, while accepting their patronage and help.

Now, in this lovely forest of Ermenonville, in the spring, he wandered through the trees, among the birds and animals, taking botanical notes, 'cleansing' himself.

Girardin, like half France, had an overwhelming admiration for Rousseau, although most of what the 'philosopher' expounded was based on doubtful premises. Thus his belief that primitive man was happier and more virtuous than those who were civilized assumed an unreal Garden of Eden where men and women wandered in blissful solitude, not owning property, meeting casually to mate like cats, and then separating with no responsibility for the father to bring up children. 'One longs to get down on all fours,' mocked Voltaire in a letter.

In politics, Rousseau had simplified and resolved everything by inventing what he called 'The General Will'. This was the collective impulse and decision of the whole community, which was always right. Those who went against it were put to death. In practice, Rousseau gave little indication of how the General Will could be assessed, or applied.

Rousseau's real appeal was the direct and indirect criticism of his contemporary world. Cities, the web of luxury and artifice, the Church, were all evil and corrupt. As with the French Revolution, which he affected profoundly, Rousseau's achievement was to sweep up people on a wave of enthusiasm for simplicity, purity and love of mankind. 'No author has inflamed his readers like him,' wrote the Abbé de Véri in an obituary.

Rousseau was helped in this by the music and spontaneity of his prose, which was new to French literature. This expressed his greatest asset: his imagination. In his frank *Confessions*, he related how, when he masturbated in adolescence, he did so only by evoking the erotic forms of women he desired, so that his imagination became more pleasurable than reality.

Inevitably, he was persecuted. De Beaumont, the Archbishop of Paris, published a denunciation of his works, and at one stage he was threatened with arrest in three different states: France, Berne, and his home town of Geneva. This added to his aura as an author harassed for his idealism.

In Ermenonville, today, one can almost hear the conversations held with Girardin. Apart from discussions on Voltaire's recent death, there must have been the expression of enthusiasm for new ideas, the optimism, the sentimentality of people living in a beautiful environment far from the hustling centres of power. It was a 'rose' period before an upheaval which would shatter the society they lived in. It is reminiscent of Thomas More and his friends before the Reformation, or the Bloomsbury group, or Rupert Brooke, in large country houses before the First World War.

Rousseau's idyll at Ermenonville was not to last, however. On 2

July 1778, only six weeks after his arrival, he went out for his usual walk at five in the morning. When he returned for his café au lait, he complained of a chill in the spine, and a searing headache. At eleven, he had a fit of apoplexy and died.

Next day, the sculptor Houdon came to make a death mask, and the following evening Rousseau was buried by the light of flaming torches in the island of poplars at the end of the lake.

One can almost see the procession, with no priest, and the reflection of the burning brands in the water as the coffin was carried over the little bridge which then connected the island to the bank.

Later, a stone tomb, which is still there, was constructed. On one side, is engraved: 'Here rests the Man of Nature and Truth.' Today it is said to contain only one of Rousseau's bones, which was stolen from the Pantheon in Paris, to which his body was transferred in 1794.

Robespierre visited Ermenonville, glimpsing the 'philosopher' on one of his early morning walks. 'I saw you in your last days,' he wrote, rhapsodically, 'and for me this memory is a source of pride and joy; I gazed upon your majestic features and I saw there evidence of the dark despair to which man's injustice had condemned you.' Already, Robespierre was beginning to identify with the 'Man of Nature'. He was perhaps the first politician who tried to apply Rousseau's ideas in practice.

Expression of the 'General Will' became the sacred right of insurrection, however few and unrepresentative were the 'People' involved. Rousseau's 'Supreme Being' and State Church replaced God and Papal authority. The guillotine punished those who defied the 'General Will'. A republic replaced the monarchy.

Rousseau's ideas were inevitably distorted by the majority who could not read: Marie-Antoinette's supposed suggestion that the starving poor should eat cakes derived from an anecdote in Rousseau's *Confessions* about a foreign princess who had lived many centuries before.

Rousseau and his contemporary *'philosophes'* created an ideal world which stirred fervour, particularly among the young. For it is significant how young the revolutionaries were: Danton, Robespierre and La Fayette were only just thirty in 1789; St Just was twenty-two. Among them, Mirabeau seems old, at forty. Fashion had reflected the previous century's domination by the old ever since Louis XIV had introduced long black wigs because he was going bald. Later, powdered hair ensured that everyone had white hair, and that therefore the old were not conspicuous. The Revolution of the young swept all this away, as it did the elaborate women's dresses and towering hair styles, replacing them with longish undressed hair, the striped trousers of the Sansculotte, black hats, and simpler dresses.

It was also a Revolution of young men, in the sense that women played no major role. Some tried to guide events through their husbands, like Mme Roland and Marie-Antoinette. Charlotte Corday assassinated Marat, but had no great effect, except that repression became more extreme. Apart from the women who stormed Versailles in October 1789, and the legendary tricoteuses before the guillotine, it was men who took the Bastille, who were deputies in the national assemblies, who ruled the country through the Terror. Like so much else, feminism was born, but poor Olympe de Gouges, who created her own Declaration of the Rights of Women, was never successful, and ended on the scaffold; while Théroigne de Méricourt with her pistol, the feather in her hat, her fervent speeches in the Jacobins, went mad after being stripped naked and flogged by her fellow women in the Tuileries Gardens.

It was a Revolution with all the fervour, ruthlessness and idealism of the young. But need it ever have happened? Certainly, with the forthcoming Industrial Revolution, with the extraordinary lassitude of the Old Régime, some political change was inevitable. However, perhaps it was part of this young man's revolution that no mature leader arose to control circumstances. There was no one like Lenin in Russia until Napoleon ten years later 'found the Crown in the gutter and picked it up with his sword.' The eruptions came too fast in the beginning. Mistaken, impulsive decisions on both sides, like the Civil Constitution of the Clergy or the absurd flight to Varennes, or the Declaration of War in April 1792, threw everything out of control. As Louis XVI said, plaintively, in a conversation with Fersen in February 1792: 'But no one has ever found himself in such a difficult situation.' It was too much even for Danton.

Certainly, the conflagration cost France dear. It ruined commerce, eliminated some of the finest churches and monuments, cost two million lives in the wars that continued till 1815, set back industrial development, and produced a long-term split in the country which in one form or another subsists until today. As a result, France lost the struggle for predominance with Britain, its great rival, which gained immensely from the Revolution, not only in the exhaustion of its opponent but also in the warnings of the effects of repressing change too severely. Above all, the Revolution sapped France's confidence with further turmoil throughout the nineteenth century, and broke the thread of all that France had been proud of in the Ancien Régime.

In a sense, it was all indulgence. Young people with their minds formed by Rousseau's imaginary world experimented with ideas which brought bloodshed and civil war, fought with purist rage for things they felt were right, created the Romantic hero in contrast to rational symmetry of thought.

It is difficult to judge it, because it is us. One cannot help being stirred by the exhortations, the belief in justice and equality, the hope of fraternity, the drama of that extraordinary time, even if there are so many things to deplore: the bloodshed, the naïvety, the birth of aggressive nationalism, the neurotics such as Marat and Hébert, thrown up into power, and tyranny disguised as liberty.

Rousseau himself would probably have been horrified to see the application of his ideas – as was the Abbé Raynal, an aged *philosophe* who survived to see the Revolution. The Marquis of Girardin was shocked at how his simple peasants rewarded his attempts to beautify their homes. In 1793, they invaded his estate and defaced his '*fabriques*', symbols of balance and harmony. He and his family were imprisoned and only released because he had been Rousseau's friend.

Some years later, Napoleon visited Ermenonville when he was First Consul. He is reported to have said to the aged marquis that it might have been better for the repose of France if Rousseau had never existed, as he had paved the way for the French Revolution.

'It seems to me, Citizen Consul,' replied his host, 'that you are the last person to complain about the French Revolution.'

'Well,' said Napoleon, 'the future will show whether it would not have been better for the peace of the world if neither I nor Rousseau had existed.'

If Rousseau generated many of the ideas of the Revolution, it was Napoleon's armies which disseminated them and carried them all over Europe.

And the future of which Napoleon spoke? Perhaps the worst

heritage has been aggressive nationalism, which only now is moderated a little. It tormented the nineteenth century and culminated in the two great wars of our time. Perhaps the best has been the sense of man as an individual, rather than as a fixed element in hierarchy.

But the 'peace of the world' has been most affected by the restlessness for new ideas, born in the Revolution, fermenting and exploding, and then forming and re-forming like bits of coloured glass in a kaleidoscope, shaken, and shaken, and shaken again.

BIBLIOGRAPHY

Barry, Joseph, *Versailles*, Gollancz, 1972.

de Beer, Sir Gavin, *Jean-Jacques Rousseau*, Thames & Hudson, 1972.

Bertaud, H. Jean-Paul, *La Vie Quotidienne de France aux Temps de la Révolution (1789–95)*, Hachette, 1983.

Blanc, Olivier, *Dernières Lettres*, Laffont, 1984.

Bluche, Frédéric, *Septembre 1792, Logique d'un Massacre*, Laffont, 1986.

Bordonove, *La Guerre de Vendée*, Julliard, 1964.

Bougourd, A.H., *Saint-Pair-sur-la-Mer et Granville-La-Victoire*, Goache, 1912.

Brookner, Anita, *Jacques-Louis David*, Chatto & Windus, 1980.

Buckman, Peter, *Lafayette*, Paddington Press, 1977.

Carlyle, Thomas, *The French Revolution*, Chapman & Hall, 1888.

Carr, John Lawrence, *Robespierre, the Force of Circumstances*, History Book Club, 1972.

Castelot, André, *Louis XVII*, Fayard, 1960.

Chabot, Françoise de, *Henri de Rochejaquelein et la Guerre de la Vendée*, Salmon, 1890.

Champdor, Albert, *Lyon pendant la Révolution*, Albert Guillot, 1983.

Chanteret, Pierre, *Lettres à mon Cousin*, Editions d'Art et d'Histoire Lyonnaises, 1985.

Charlety, Sébastien, *Histoire de Lyon*, Editions J.C.B., 1972.

Chiappet, Jean François, *La Vendée en Armes*, Perrin, 1982.

Christophe, Paul, *Les Prêtres dans la Révolution*, Editions Ouvrières, 1986.

Cobb, Richard, *The People's Armies*, Yale University Press, 1987.

Cobb, Richard, *Reactions to the French Revolution*, Oxford University Press, 1972.

Cobb, Richard, *A Second Identity*, Oxford University Press, 1969.

Cobb, Richard, *Terreur et Subsistances*, Librairie Clavreuil, 1965.

Cobban, Alfred, *Aspects of the French Revolution*, Paladin, 1971.

Cobban, Alfred, *A History of Modern France, Volume 1, 1715–1799*, Penguin Press, 1974.

Colignon, Maurice, *La Haute-Ville de Granville, Revue du département de la Manche*, Tome 18, 1976.

Cronin, Vincent, *Louis & Antoinette*, Collins, 1974.

Eynard, Georges, *Joseph Chalier, Bourreau ou Martyr*, Editions Lyonnaises d'Art et d'Histoire, 1987.

Feuga, Paul, *L'Hôtel de Ville de Lyon, 1789–95*, Editions Lyonnaises d'Art et d'Histoire, 1985.

Ford, Franklin L., *Europe 1780–1830*, Longman, 1970.

Friedlaender, Walter, *David to Delacroix*, Bailey Bros & Swinfen, 1968.

Furet & Richet, *French Revolution*, Weidenfeld & Nicholson, 1970.

Gallo, Max, *Lettre Ouverte à Maximilien Robespierre sur les Nouveaux Muscadins*, Albin Michel, 1986.

Gauthéot, *Suppliciés de la Terreur*, Perrin, 1926.

Gilchrist and Murray, *The Press in the French Revolution*, Cheshire Ginn, 1971.

Godechot, Jacques, *La Contre-Révolution*, Presses Universitaires, 1961.

Godechot, Jacques, *France and the Atlantic Revolution of the Eighteenth Century, 1770–1799*, Collier Macmillan, 1965.

Godechot, Jacques, *La Prise de la Bastille*, Gallimard, 1965.

Greer, Donald, *The Incidence of the Terror throughout the French Revolution*, Harvard University Press, 1935.

Guéry, Louis, *Jacques Cathelineau*, Artaud frères, 1983.

Hampson, Norman, *Danton*, Duckworth, 1978.

Hampson, Norman, *The First European Revolution, 1776–1815*, Thames & Hudson, 1969.

Hampson, Norman, *Life and Opinions of Maximilien Robespierre*, Duckworth, 1974.

Hampson, Norman, *A Social History of the French Revolution*, Routledge & Kegan Paul, 1963.

Hampson, Norman, *Will and Circumstance*, Duckworth, 1983.

Haslip, Joan, *Marie Antoinette*, Weidenfeld & Nicholson, 1987.

Herold, J. Christopher, *Mistress of an Age, The Life of Mme de Staël*, Hamish Hamilton, 1959.

Hibbert, Christopher, *The French Revolution*, Allen Lane, 1980.

Hilairet, Jacques, *Connaissance du Vieux Paris*, Métro Editions Internationales, 1956.

Hobsbawm, E.J., *The Age of Revolution*, Mentor Books, 1962.

Howarth. T.E.B., *Citizen-King*, White Lion Publishers, 1961.

Huguet, Jean, *Un Coeur d'Etoffe Rouge*, Laffont, 1985.

Huisman & Jallut, *Marie-Antoinette*, Edita Lausanne, 1970.

Hutt, Maurice, *Chouannerie and Counter-Revolution*, Cambridge University Press, 1983.

Bibliography

Johnson, Douglas, *France 1789–1815, Revolution and Counter-Revolution*, Fontana Press, 1985.

Kershaw, Alister, *A History of the Guillotine*, Calder, 1958.

Lallier, Alfred, *Les Noyades de Nantes*, Libraros, 1879.

Lefebvre, Georges, *La Grande Peur de 1789*, Armand Collin, 1932.

Legg, Wickham, *Selected Documents Illustrative of the History of the French Revolution*, vol.1., Oxford, 1905.

Leigh, R.A., *Correspondance Complète de Jean-Jacques Rousseau*, Voltaire Foundation and Taylor Institute, Oxford.

Lenotre, G., *Le Drame de Varennes*, Perrin, 1913.

Lenotre, G., *Le Jardin de Picpus*, Perrin, 1955.

Lenotre, G., *Les Massacres de Septembre*, Perrin, 1907.

Lenotre, G., *Les Noyades de Nantes*, Perrin, 1912.

Lenotre, G., *Paris in the Revolution*, Hutchinson, 1925.

Le Roi, J.A., *Récit des Journées des 5 et 6 octobre, 1789, à Versailles*, Aubert, 1867.

Lidove, Marcel, *Les Vendéens de 93*, Du Seuil, 1971.

Loomis, Stanley, *The Fatal Friendship*, Davis Poynter, 1972.

Loomis, Stanley, *Paris in the Terror*, Penguin Books, 1970.

Manceron, Claude, *La Révolution qui Lève*, Laffont, 1972.

Manceron, Claude, *Le Sang de la Bastille*, Laffont, 1987.

Manceron, Claude, *Les Vingt Ans du Roi, 1774–78*, Laffont, 1972.

Marguery-Melin, Bruno, *La Destruction de l'Abbaye de Cluny, 1789–1823*, Centre des Etudes Clunésiennes, 1985.

Markham, Felix, *Napoleon*, Weidenfeld & Nicholson, 1963.

Martin, Jean-Clément, *La Vendée et la France*, Seuil, 1987.

Mathieu, René, *Ermenonville*, Touring Club de France.

Maurice, Marguerite, *Cluny sous la Révolution (1789–99)*, Bassy-Offset, 1987.

Maurin-Carcopino, Paul, *Bonaparte au Siège de Toulon*, Serge Candela, 1969.

Michelet, Jules, *Episodes de la Révolution Française*, Alpina, 1959.

Mitchell, Harvey, 'The Vendée and Counter-Revolution: a Review Essay', *French Historical Studies*, vol. V, no. 4, Fall 1968.

Morton, J.B., *Camille Desmoulins*, Werner Laurie, 1953.

Moustiers, Pierre, *Un Aristocrate à la Lanterne*, Gallimard, 1986.

Ozouf, Mona, *Fêtes Révolutionnaires, 1789–99*, Gallimard, 1976.

Petitfrère, Claude, *La Vendée et les Vendéens*, Gallimard/Julliard, 1981.

Roberts, J.M., *The French Revolution*, Oxford University Press, 1978.

Ross, Michael, *The Banners of the King*, Seeley Services, 1975.

Rostou, du, Loic, *Histoire extérieure et Maritime des Guerres de la Vendée*, Le Cercle d'Or, 1987.

Rudé, George, *Paris and London in the 18th Century*, Collins, 1970.

Rudé, George, *Revolutionary Europe, 1783–1815*, Fontana, 1964.

Scott, William, *Terror and Repression in Marseilles*, Macmillan, 1973.

Secher, Reynaud, *La Génocide Franco-Française: La Vendée Vengée*, Presses Universitaires de France, 1986.

Sedillot, *Le Coût de la Révolution Française*, Perrin, 1987.

Soboul, Albert, *La France à la Veille de la Révolution*, Société d'Edition d'Enseignement Supérieur, 1966.

Vieillefosse, Pierre, 'Le Siège de 1793' (Manuscript).

Vigée Le Brun, *Memoirs, 1755–89*, John Hamilton.

Walter, Gérard, *La Révolution Française vue par ses Journaux*, Payot, 1948.

Willcocks, M.P., *Madame Roland*, Hutchinson, 1936.

Williams, Merryn (ed.), *Revolutions, 1775–83*, Penguin Books, 1971.

Revue du Souvenir Vendéen, no. 159, June–July 1987.

Royal Memoirs of the Revolution, John Murray, 1823.

Guide Historique et Touristique de la Vendée Militaire, Les Editions du Choletais.

Guides Verts of Poitou, Vendée, Charentes, Châteaux de la Loire, Bourgogne, Environs de Paris, Vallée du Rhône, Normandie, Bretagne.

Guide de la Révolution Française, Levèque & Belot, Pierre Horay, 1986.

Guide Bleu: Paris, Hachette, 1968.

Official Handbooks:

La Chancellerie à travers les Siècles.

Le Palais Royal.

La Place Vendôme.

L'Hôtel de Ville de Paris, François Morand, Editions Morand.

Le Sénat.

INDEX

Abbaye prison, Paris, 135
Achard (agent of Robespierre), 202
Agniau, M. L', 165
Agoult, Comte d', 102
Algeria, 81–2
Amis de la Vendée Militaire, 167
Angers, 173, 187
Anjou, Duke of, 150, 151
Antraigues, Comte d', 92
Arcis-sur-Aube, 221–3, 224–6
Argonne forest, 107
aristocracy, see nobility
Arras, 244–6
Artois, Comte d', 29, 60, 85, 93, 192
Assembly, see National Assembly;
    Legislative Assembly
August Decrees, 69, 71
'Austrian Committee', 126
Avignon, 92
Avrillé, 188

Bailly, Jean Sylvain, 9, 28–9, 30,
    61, 117, 122, 258–9
Barbe, Pierre, 272
Barère, Bertrand, 174
Barjeon, Dr, 208
Barnave, Antoine, 115
Barras, Vicomte de, 216–17, 264,
    266
Bastille, 45, 46–58, 59
Beauce, 95
Beauharnais, Joséphine de, 138
Beaurepaire, Colonel, 140

Bernis, Cardinal, 92
Beugnot, Comte, 235
Beysser, General, 174
Billaud-Varenne, Jean Nicolas, 263,
    266
Bois-Chevalier, Château de, 185
Bombelles, Marquis de, quoted, 40,
    112
Bonaparte, see Napoleon Bonaparte
Bonchamps, Marquis de, 168, 175,
    176–7
Bondy, 102
Bouillé, Marquis de, 106, 113
Boulainvilliers, Henri de, 15
Brissot, Jacques, 94, 95–6, 125,
    222n.
Britain, support for royalists from,
    182, 205, 206, 207–16
Brittany, guerrillas in (Chouans),
    178
Brogan, Denis, 95
Brunswick, Duke of, 126, 140, 141,
    143

Café Amaury, Versailles, 246
Café de Foy, Paris, 38
Café du Parnasse, Paris, 118–19
Café Procope, Paris, 120
cahiers de doléance, 5
Calonne, Charles Alexandre de, 15
Carcy, Madame, 23–4
Carlyle, Thomas, quoted, 6, 18, 110
Carmes, Paris, 136, 137–9

Carrier, Jean Baptiste, 188–9
Carteaux, General Jean-François, 207–8
Cathelineau, Jacques, 168, 174, 175
censorship, abolition of, 88
Certificate of Civism, 255–6
Chabot, François, 222n.
Chaintrix, 104
Chalier, Marie Joseph, 192–3, 196, 222n.
Châlons, 105
Champ de Mars, Paris, 32, 89
Chanzeaux, 163, 186–7
Chapelle Expiatoire, Paris, 150–1
Charette de la Contrie, François Athanase, 169, 174, 184–5
Charpentier, Gabrielle, 118
Chartres, 93–7
Chartres, Duke of, *see* Orléans, Duke of
Chateaubriand, Vicomte de, quoted, 11
châteaux, destruction of, 62–4
Chaumette, Pierre Gaspard, 222n.
Cheviré, 189–90
Choiseul, Duke of, 105–6, 111
Cholet, 163, 174–5
Chouans, 178
Church, *see* clergy
civil war, 158; *see also* Lyons; Toulon; Vendée
Claude, René, 100, 101–2, 102–4, 108–12, 113–15, 142
Clavière, Étienne, 222n.
clergy, Church
    in States-General, 4–5, 6–7, 27–8, 29–30, 31–2, 92
    bishops, 15
    tithes abolished, 64
    possessions confiscated by Assembly (1789), 86, 92
    Civil Constitution, 90, 91, 92–3, 94–5, 98, 167

attitudes to Revolution, 91–2
destruction of churches, 95–8
    see also monasteries
Clermont, 107
Clisson, 188
Clootz, Anacharsis, 222n.
Cluny, 92, 97–8
Collot d'Herbois, Jean Marie, 201, 202, 204, 263, 266
Committee of General Security, 227
Committee of Public Safety, 227–8, 229, 231–2, 248, 253
Committee of Surveillance, 255–6
Commune, Paris, 131, 136, 154, 155
Commune (1871), 61, 77
Conciergerie, Paris, 233–9
Condorcet, Marquis de, 158, 244
Constitution, 29, 34, 117
Conti, Prince de, 145
Convention
    decrees execution of Louis XVI, 148, 149
    expels Girondins, 156–8
    and Vendée, 174, 188
    defied by Lyons etc., 195, 197–8
    mentioned, 227, 248
Corday, Charlotte, 158
Cordeliers, Club des, 117, 121–2, 123
Cormatin, château of, 63
Cottereau, Jean, 178
counter-revolution, possibility of, 32–3, 34, 58, 85, 93, 116, 148, 192
Couthon, Georges, 197–8, 201, 204, 263
Craufurd, Quentin, 102
Crown, *see* monarchy

Damas, Colonel, 107
Dampierre, Comte de, 115

Danton, Georges-Jacques, 118–20, 122–3, 130–1, 155, 195–6, 221, 227–33, 274
early life, 221–4
estate at Arcis-sur-Aube, 224–6
trial and execution, 239, 240–243
Dauphin, 7, 74–5, 100, 101, 115, 145, 147, 148
De Gaulle, Charles, 4, 165
De Launay, Bernard, 48, 51–6 *passim*, 61
Dean, Sir John, quoted, 76–7
Defoe, Daniel, quoted, 244
Delcroix, Monique, 251
Denechau, M., 171
Desmoulins, Camille, 38, 118, 120, 123, 222n., 231, 232, 242, 252
quoted, 41
Deux Brézé, Marquis de, 30
District Assemblies, *see* Sections
Dorset, Duke of, quoted, 59
Drouet, Jean-Baptiste, 106–7, 108, 109–10, 114
Du Barry, Madame, 3
Dumouriez, General Charles François, 140, 141, 142, 143, 156
Duplay family, 247, 249–50, 251–2
Dupont de Nemours, Pierre Samuel, quoted, 117

Ecole Militaire, Paris, 32
Edinburgh, Duke of, 187n.
Elbée, Maurice d', 168–9, 175
Elisabeth, Madame (sister of Louis XVI), 100, 147
English Speaking Union, 187n.
Entrammes, 180
Epinay, Roussel de l', quoted, 121–122
Ermenonville, 271–2

Fabre d'Eglantine, 222n.
Fédérés, 136
Ferrières, Marquis de, quoted, 31, 65
Fersen, Axel, 100, 102
feudal rights, abolition of, 64–6
Feuga, Paul, 198–201
Feuillants, 123
Fleuriot, Edouard, 263–4
Fleury, Duchess of, 267
Fort Mulgrave, Toulon, 209, 210, 212–14
Fouché, Joseph, 201, 222n., 266
France, the French, 3–4
French Guards, 42, 53–4, 75
Fréron, Louis-Marie, 216–17
Furet, François, 92, 225

Garde Meuble, Paris, 43–4
Girardin, Marquis of, 272, 276
Girondins, 118, 125, 126, 154–6, 157–8, 195
Gouges, Olympe de, 275
Grande Peur, La, 62–4
Granville, 181–2
Grasse, M., 164–5
Guillaume, Captain, 43–4
Guillotin, Dr Joseph Ignace, 9–10, 28, 69, 257
guillotine, 256–9, 261, 266

Hanriot, François, 157, 259
Haussmann, Baron Georges Eugène, 36
Hébert, Jacques (expert on the Tuileries), 82–8, 156–8
Hébert, Jacques René (revolutionary journalist), 82, 116, 118, 198, 222n., 230, 232
Hobsbawm, Eric, quoted, 244
Hôtel Britannique, Paris, 118
Hôtel de Ville (Town Hall), Paris, 43, 61
Huguet, Jean, 166

Invalides, Paris, 44–5
Isherwood, Christopher, quoted, 19

Jacobins, 117, 123–5, 154–6, 227,
246, 267–8
at Lyons, 192–3, 195
at Toulon, 206
Jefferson, Thomas, quoted, 61
Joly, Roger, 93, 94–7
jury system, 88

Kellerman, François Christophe,
140, 142
king, *see* monarchy
Kléber, Jean Baptiste, 174
Knights Templar, 144

la Chabottière, Château de, 185
La Fayette, Marquis de, 10, 71, 76,
88, 89, 99, 101, 113, 117, 122,
123, 274
his tomb, 261
Laclos, Pierre Ambroise François
Choderlos, 40
Lamballe, Princesse de, 139
Lambert, Dominique, 167–70,
186–8
Lameth, Alexandre, 229
Laval, 186
Le Bon, Joseph, 222n.
Le Chapelier, Isaac René Guy, 65
Le Mans, 183
Le Petit Luc, 186
Lebas, Joseph, 263
LeCadre, Madame, 184
Legé, 185
Legislative Assembly, 117, 248
Lenotre, G., quoted, 46
Léonard (hairdresser), 106, 115
Leopold II, Emperor of Austria,
117, 125
Les Aubiers, 170
Lescure, Marquis de, 175, 180

Loménie de Brienne, Étienne
Charles, 15
Louis XIV, King, 5, 11, 15, 16,
17–18, 34, 44, 95
Louis XV, King, 3, 13, 16, 17–18,
32, 34
Louis XVI, King, 16–19, 275
summons States-General, 4
and opening procession of States-
General, 5–6, 7
appearance, personality, 5, 6, 17,
18
ceremonious existence, 15–16
wedding, 16, 105
coronation, 23
relations with States-General, 27–
32
plans counter-revolution?, 32–3,
34, 58, 116, 148
wins acclaim from Assembly, and
in Paris, 59–61
abolition of feudal rights, 64–6
brought to Paris from Versailles,
66, 67–78
a prisoner in the Tuileries, 83–6
at Festival of 14 July 1790, 89
signs Civil Constitution of the
Clergy, 92
letter to King of Spain, 98
prevented from leaving Paris, 98–
99
flight to Varennes, 100–116
signs Constitution, 117
and the war, 125, 126
in the Temple, after attack on
Tuileries, 127–9, 147–8
rule suspended, 130
trial and execution, 148–50, 152–
153, 229
Louis XVIII, King, 189n., 212
Louis, Dr Antoine, 257
Louis-Marie Montford, St, 166–7
Louis-Philippe, King, 74, 131

Louveciennes, 3
Lubersac, Bishop, 94
Luckner, General Nicolas, 140
Luxembourg Palace, Paris, 232–3
Lyons, 32, 34, 192–204

Malesherbes, Chrétien Guillaume de Lamoignon de, 60, 149
Malouet, Baron Pierre Victor, quoted, 81, 264
Manège, 86
Marat, Jean Paul, 118, 120, 123, 156, 157–8, 222n., 226
    quoted, 130, 131
Marie-Antoinette, Queen
    and opening procession of States-General, 6, 7–9
    unpopular, 7–9, 17
    wedding, children, 16, 105
    taken to Paris from Versailles, 71–8
    flight to Varennes, 100–116 *passim*
    in the Temple, 147–8
    execution, 158
    cell in the Conciergerie, 236–9
    mentioned, 67–8, 145, 274
Marie Leszczynska, Queen, 9
Marie-Thérèse (daughter of Louis XVI), 74–5, 100, 101, 110–11, 114, 147
Marilyn and Raoul, 131–9
Maurice, Mlle, 62–3
Maury, Abbé, 92
Melito, Miot de, quoted, 9
Menus Plaisirs du Roy, 23, 24, 26–7, 33
Méricourt, Théroigne de, 275
Ministry of Justice, Paris, 130
Mirabeau, Comte de, 9, 30, 60, 85–6, 99, 246
Moira, Lord, 182
Moleville, Bernard de, 225

Monaco, Princesse de, 259
monarchy, kingship, the Crown
    before the Revolution, 14, 15–16
    weakness of, 18, 115–16
    Orleanist view, 40
    sovereignty challenged, 65–6
    end of, 153
    recent hopes of restoration, 150–1, 187
monasteries, monks, 36, 86, 92, 97, 121, 124
Mounier, Jean Joseph, 69, 71
Mulotins, Les, 166–7

Nancy, Bishop of, 9
Nantes, 173–4, 188–9
Napoleon Bonaparte, 26, 32, 39, 128, 144, 163, 189, 198, 264n., 276
    his tomb, 44
    on the Vendée, 171–2, 176
    at Toulon, 207, 208, 209, 210–11, 213
National Assembly
    States-General declared to be, 28–31, 34
    addressed by Louis XVI, 60
    feudal rights abolished by, 64–6
    women of Paris and, 69
    at Tuileries, 82–3, 86–8
    its achievement, 88–9
    not anti-clerical, 91
    arrests royal family, 113–16
    Louis XVI takes refuge with, 127–8
    delegates excluded from Legislative Assembly, 248
National Guard, 59, 71, 88, 99, 114, 127, 168, 194–5
Necker, Jacques, 15, 31, 32, 41, 222n.
nobility, aristocracy, 14–15

in States-General, 4–5, 6, 27–8, 29–30, 31–2

emigration, 60

feudal rights abolished, 64–6

Noirmoutier, 175

Notre-Dame, Versailles, 5

Oratorians, 223

Orléans, Duke of, formerly Duke of Chartres, later 'Philippe Egalité', 7, 34, 38, 39–40, 68, 149

Paine, Thomas, 222*n.*

Palais de Justice, Paris, 233, 235

Palais, Royal, Paris, 37–9, 40–1

Paris, 34–7
  ferment in (1789), 31, 32, 34, 41–5, 60–1, 66; *see also* Palais Royal; Bastille
  royal family brought to, from Versailles, 66, 68, 77–8, 83–6
  Assembly moves to, 82
  Festival of 1790, 89–90
  royal family prevented from leaving, 98–9
  royal family's escape from, 100–101
  royal family brought back to, 115
  revolutionary government of clubs and sections in, 117–25
  attack on the Tuileries, royal family taken to the Temple, 126, 127–9, 144–8
  September massacres, 131–9
  revolutionary confusion in, 154–8, 227–43, 247–54
  walls of, 255
  the Terror, 255–65, 266
  guillotine in, 258–9
  see also Chapelle Expiatoire

peasant risings, 62–4; *see also* Chouans; Vendée

'People', the, 91, 122, 242

Père Duchesne, Le, 82

Pétion de Villeneuve, Jérôme, 115, 158

Philip IV, King, 144

Philippe Egalité, *see* Orléans, Duke of

Piat, M., 222, 224–6

Picpus, cemetery of, Paris, 259–62

Pierregat, Madame, 188–9

Pin-en-Mauges, 168

Pius VI, Pope, 92–3

Place de la Concorde (Place Louis, Place de la Révolution), 41–2, 258

Place de la Nation (Place du Trône), 43, 258, 259

press freedom, censorship, 30, 88

Provence, Comte de, 60, 74, 100

Prussia, war with, 126, 131, 140–3

Raymonde, Dr, 164–5

Reason, Festival of, 230

Representatives on Mission, 188

Revolution, French, 275–7
  beginnings of, 4, 37–8, 39–41
  inevitable?, 25–6

Revolutionary Tribunal, 228–9, 239–40

Rights of Man, Declaration of, 65

Robespierre, Augustin, 263

Robespierre, Charlotte, 246, 251–2

Robespierre, Maximilien, 244–54
  opposed to war, 125, 248
  replaces Danton on Committee of Public Safety, 229
  opposes Hébertists, 230, 231
  cell in the Conciergerie, 237
  overthrow and execution, 262–5
  blamed for the Terror, 266–7
  and Rousseau, 274
  quoted, 144, 155, 253
  mentioned, 9, 118, 222*n.*, 223, 224, 225, 226, 242–3, 274

Rochejaquelein, Madame de, quoted, 180–1, 181, 183–4
Rochejaquelein, Henri de, 169–70, 171, 177, 186
Roland, Madame, 118, 155, 222n., 266
quoted, 154
Rouget de Lisle, Claude Joseph, 126
Rousseau, Jean-Jacques, 101, 222n., 231, 272–4
Roux, Jacques, 222n.
Royal Allemand, 42, 43
royal family
taken from Versailles to Paris, 74–8
in the Tuileries, 85
prevented from leaving Paris, 98–99
flight to Varennes, 100–116
in the Temple after attack on the Tuileries, 127–9, 144, 147–8
Rue de Rivoli, Paris, 86
Rue St Honoré, Paris, 124, 247, 249
Rue Saintonge, Paris, 246–7

St André, Jean Bon, quoted, 267–8
St-Florent-le-Vieil, 167–70, 175–7
St Germain des Prés, Paris, 135
St Just, Louis Antoine Léon de, 148, 203, 232, 240, 263, 267, 274
St-Laurent-sur-Sèvre, 165, 166–7
Ste Menehould, 106–7
Salle des Machines, 156
Sansculottes, 154, 155
Sauce, M., 109–11, 114–15
Saumur, 171
Savenay, 183–4
Secher, Reynald, 165, 186
Sections (formerly District Assemblies), Paris, 117, 122, 123, 155, 255
Senozan, château of, 63–4

September massacres, 131–9, 229
Sombreuil, M. de, 44
Souvenir Vendéen, Le, 164–6
Staël, Madame de, quoted, 75
States-General, 4–5
opening procession, 5–10
site of, at Versailles, 21–4, 26–8, 33
sessions of, 28–32
mentioned, 92
Stofflet, Jean Nicolas, 168, 171, 185, 186, 187
Strasbourg, 62
Supreme Being, Feast of the, 248

Talleyrand-Perigord, Charles Maurice, Prince de, 9, 89, 90
Tallien, Jean Lambert, 263, 266
Talmont, Prince de, 174, 185–6
Temple, Paris, 129, 144–7
tennis court, Versailles, 28–9
Terror, 231, 255–68
Third Estate, Commoners, 4–5, 6, 7, 9, 27–30, 31–2
Torfou, 174
Toulon, 197, 205–17
Tournon, Antoine, quoted, 3
Tourzel, Pauline de, 90, 100, 101, 102, 104
Town Hall, Paris, *see* Hôtel de Ville
tricolour, 61
Troyes, 223
Tuileries, Paris, 77–8, 82–4, 86, 156–7
royal family's escape from, 100–101
attack on, 126, 127–8, 136, 229
Turreau, General, 186, 189

Vadier, Marc Guillaume, 222–3
Valmy, 141–3
Varennes, 108–15
Vendée, 158, 161–91

Vergniaud, Pierre Victurnien, 128, 228

Versailles, 3–4, 11–16, 17, 18–19, 67–8
 States-General procession, 4, 5–10
 Cathedral, 9
 recent restoration, 19–20
 site of States-General, 21–4, 26–8, 33
 a radical town in 1789, 25
 tennis court, 28–9
 Louis XIV makes it his capital, 34
 troops summoned to protect, 66
 royal family's departure from, 68–77

Vezins, forest of, 187

Vieillefosse, M., 209–12

Vieux Cordelier, 231

Viguès, Jean-Louis, 49–50, 57–58

wars, French Revolutionary, 125–6, 131, 140–3, 205–16, 248

Westermann, François Joseph, 174, 184

Wollstonecraft, Mary, quoted, 148, 255

Wordsworth, William, 90

Young, Arthur, 18, 31, 41, 62